Living Landscapes

Living Landscapes

MEDITATIONS ON THE FIVE ELEMENTS IN HINDU, BUDDHIST, AND JAIN YOGAS

CHRISTOPHER KEY CHAPPLE

Foreword by
John Grim and Mary Evelyn Tucker

SUNY PRESS

Cover art permissions obtained for the use of the John Singer Sargent painting, *The Hermit*, on the cover and the use of the line drawings created by Gabriela Ayala-Cañizares.

Published by State University of New York Press, Albany

For information, contact State University of New York Press, Albany, NY
www.sunypress.edu

Library of Congress Cataloging-in-Publication Data

Names: Chapple, Christopher Key, 1954– author.
Title: Living landscapes : meditations on the five elements in Hindu, Buddhist, and Jain yogas / Christopher Key Chapple.
Description: Albany : State University of New York, 2020. | Includes bibliographical references and index.
Identifiers: LCCN 2019049140 (print) | LCCN 2019049141 (ebook) | ISBN 9781438477930 (hardcover : alk. paper) | ISBN 9781438477947 (pbk. : alk. paper) | ISBN 9781438477954 (ebook)
Subjects: LCSH: India—Religion. | Yoga. | Nature—Religious aspects.
Classification: LCC BL2003 .C55 2020 (print) | LCC BL2003 (ebook) | DDC 294—dc23
LC record available at https://lccn.loc.gov/2019049140
LC ebook record available at https://lccn.loc.gov/2019049141

10 9 8 7 6 5 4 3 2 1

to

Thomas Berry (1914–2009)

Contents

Illustrations ix

Acknowledgments xi

Foreword xv
John Grim and Mary Evelyn Tucker

Introduction: Yoga and Landscapes xix

1. The Inner World as Precondition for Experience 1

2. Earth: Loving the Land 23

3. Water: Life-giver and Purifier 71

4. Fire: Locus of Desire 87

5. Air: Wind and Breath 109

6. Animal Stories from the Upaniṣads, the Jātaka Tales, the Pañcatantra, Jaina Narratives, and the *Yogavāsiṣṭha* 125

7. The Yoga of Space 151

Appendix: Constructing the Maṇḍala through Yoga Sādhana 187

Illustrations

1. Goddess in dance and every element is within her body. An arm made of wood, shoulders are mountains, the hair is the night sky and rising sun. Her belly is an ocean wave, one leg is flowers and the trunk of a tree. One leg has wheat growing up her thigh and the trunk of tree with mushrooms. LAM is seen above her body. Title: "Earth" / Artist: Gabriela Ayala-Cañizares / Owner: Individual 22

2. Goddess leaping with a moon on her head and most of her body is made of ocean waves. Her legs are sea shells. VAM is seen above her body. Title: "Water" / Artist: Gabriela Ayala-Cañizares / Owner: Individual 70

3. Goddess walking toward the viewer with fire in her hands. Her body is made of crystals and the light reflects off of them. RAM is seen to the left of her body. Title: "Fire" / Artist: Gabriela Ayala-Cañizares / Owner: Individual 86

4. Goddess in flight; she has the body of a hummingbird and you can see her lungs. Her hair blows behind her and you can see YAM above her body. Title: "Air" / Artist: Gabriela Ayala-Cañizares / Owner: Individual 108

5. Goddess sitting peacefully looking to the left. Her body is made of plants and a bird's nest sits in her hair. She is one with the elephant, tiger, eagle, wolf, bear, swan, frog, and rabbit. Title: "As One" / Artist: Gabriela Ayala-Cañizares / Owner: Individual 124

6. Goddess leaping into the air. The outline of her body is made entirely of dots, showing her in form in space. Title: "Space" / Artist: Gabriela Ayala-Cañizares / Owner: Individual 150

7. Thirty-seven figures demonstrating a sequence of yoga postures. Title: "Untitled" / Artist: Gabriela Ayala-Cañizares / Owner: Individual 186

Acknowledgments

Several people helped in the preparation of this book, including Griffin Guez, Jodi Shaw, Wijnanda Jacobi, Natale Ferreira, Amparo Denney, Nadia Pandolfo, Christopher Patrick Miller, Viresh Hughes, Ben Zenk, Daniel Levine, Kija Manhare, Erika Burkhalter, Alexandra Berger, Ulhas Bala, Ralph Craig III, Ana Funes Maderey, Joseph Cadiff, and Jensen Martin, who all participated in the Tuesday afternoon Sanskrit translation seminar that has convened at Loyola Marymount University for more than two decades. Arindam Chakrabarti pointed out the elemental chapters of the *Yogavāsiṣṭha* during a seminar he convened at the University of Hawaii in 1997, the translation of which occupied the Tuesday group for more than two years.

Francis Clooney sparked the field research project of visiting the five elemental temples in South India when he brought them to my attention nearly thirty years ago. Karthik Dhandapani facilitated an amazing journey for Chris Miller and me to visit each of these temples in 2013, which helped Chris with his MA thesis on Yoga and the Environment and lends field experience to the current work.

Trudy Goodman, during the early years of InsightLA, offered for me to substitute at her weekly sitting group when she taught elsewhere. This provided an opportunity to share the elemental concentration practices in the context of Buddhist Vipassana. Jack Kornfield provided helpful resources included in this study that explain the modern Buddhist diffidence toward this practice and also highlight its historic importance.

The Green Yoga Association, founded by Laura Cornell, convened hundreds of Yoga teachers with an interest in Yoga and ecology from 2004–2013. These teachers learned about Yoga's foundational meditations upon the elements. My Yoga Teacher Training students on Sunday mornings at the Hill Street Center, including Jasmine Lieb, Edward Moondance, Lisa Leeman,

Chris Miller, Devon Fitzgerald, Teri Roseman, Mehdi Mansouri, Charlotte Holtzerman, and Ruth Goodman practiced the elemental meditations over the course of several months in the early 2010s.

In the appendix to the book one finds a Yoga routine that reflects the theme of the book. This practice developed over five decades of daily practice of meditation, *prāṇāyāma,* and *āsana.* Though the individual Yoga teachers who helped build this sādhana are too numerous to mention, a few were key to the unfolding journey of bodily awareness and purification: Padmini Higgins, Gurāṇi Añjali Inti, John Doukas, Carol Rossi, Lisa Walford, Denise Kaufman, Jasmine Lieb, Beth Sternlieb, and Larry Payne.

The faculty, deans, and other administrators at Loyola Marymount University have been consistently supportive of this work, which has been shared with community members through LMU Extension's Center for Religion and Spirituality, as well as with our undergraduate students from all majors and colleges, and our graduate students in bioethics, education, theology, and Yoga studies. University support, combined with an endowment provided by Navin and Pratima Doshi, have allowed many trips to India and various international and national conferences where these ideas have been tested and explored with others. YogaGlo, an online learning platform founded by Derik Mills, has been amazingly supportive of this work in every way, and many of these practices can be found in the YogaGlo online video archive. A Fulbright Nehru Fellowship has supported the time required here in India for the final editing process.

I want to extend deep gratitude to my wife Maureen and our children Dylan and Emma for their unflagging support and patience. Gabriela Ayala-Cañizares created the beautiful line drawings that accompany each chapter. Her talents became abundantly obvious as she shared her vision of Mother Earth with us during the graduate seminar on Yoga Philosophy and later created a stabilizing Yoga sequence as part of her final Yoga studies MA thesis project, which she now teaches to elder Bhutanese refugees living in the greater Seattle area. Meghan Brown of Art Resource diligently obtained permission from the Metropolitan Museum of Art for use of the cover art, *The Hermit* (1908) by John Singer Sargent. Profound appreciation goes to Nicolás Arias-Gutiérrez and Alexandra Jones who completed the final copy editing and the indexing of the book.

Finally, I want to share my final conversation over the telephone with Thomas Berry, to whom this book is dedicated. A group of several dozen scholars had gathered at Pendle Hill, the Quaker retreat and education center adjacent to the campus of Swarthmore College, in November 2005. The purpose of our meeting was to inaugurate the International Society for the Study of

Religion, Nature, and Culture, founded by Bron Taylor of the University of Florida. John Grim and Mary Evelyn Tucker, who graciously wrote the Foreword of this book, had founded the Berry-inspired Forum on Religion and Ecology at Harvard University's Center for World Religions in 1997, which is now located in the School of Forestry at Yale University. While at Pendle Hill, they beckoned me to the phone to speak with Thomas Berry. Thomas, who directed the history of religions doctoral program at Fordham University for many years, was a self-proclaimed geologian. He had studied Thomas Aquinas in the Passionist monastery in the 1920s and '30s, had learned about and experienced Confucianism and Daoism alongside Theodore deBary in China in the 1940s, turned his attention to Buddhism, Hinduism, and the study of Sanskrit in the 1950s and 1960s, and to the study of North American indigenous traditions in the 1970s. Having chaired the American Teilhard Association for many years, he immersed himself in the study of cosmology in the 1980s, and eventually published the award-winning book, *The Dream of the Earth* and, with Brian Swimme, *The Universe Story*.

From the first day we met, Thomas inspired me with his curiosity, his openness, his insight, and his penetrative gaze. I took all his graduate seminars at Fordham, and he served on my dissertation committee. As the conversation opened, he asked, "Tell me, where does your work take you these days?" As if possessed with a visionary spirit, the following response spilled out of me like a penitent at confession: "Well, Thomas, it concerns me deeply that everyone seems to think that Yogis hate the world and want to redeem themselves out of materiality. My own practice and experience have proven quite the reverse! The current project seeks to reveal Yoga and Sāṃkhya as gateways to a renewed sense of intimacy." In his inimitable, low-key manner, he offered the simple affirmation of "Very good!" And now, ten years after his passing, this work has come into manifestation.

Hauz Khas Village, New Delhi, October 5, 2019

Foreword

John Grim and Mary Evelyn Tucker

In this marvelous journey through living landscapes of rich biodiversity, elemental forces, and cosmic powers, Chapple guides the reader into an ecological interiority that is both ancient and modern. He illustrates how South Asian texts and traditions have rich teachings regarding the ways humans have aligned themselves with the cosmos and the Earth through elaborate systems of micro-macro relations. The correlative correspondences of the elements with the human body are evident throughout these texts and in the meditative practices of our times. Something new arises through this process reflecting upon emergent dynamics that is deeply related to that which has preceded, yet strikingly different. Drawing on traditional yogic practices of meditating on the five elements of earth, water, fire, air, and space, Chapple connects classical texts with the seasonal flow of day-to-day activities. As he observes: "In India meditation on the elements provides the cultural code for daily life. It acknowledges human embeddedness in nature. It also evokes an underlying grammar for ritual." The author also reveals a contemporary connection to ecological spiritual practices as indicated in the dedication of this book, in his personal stories, and in referring to India's wondrous understanding of the generative cosmos pouring forth from a dynamic, unfolding universe.

Chapple describes how the cosmos becomes manifest in these traditions. He draws on the term *cosmicization,* used by the historian of religions Mircea Eliade to indicate that the human is not only part of the Earthly elements, but of the whole cosmos. This is significant as it illustrates the ways in which the human body is identified with the whole universe and both are thus affirmed.

Chapple writes: "The 'metaphor' of the cosmic person in Hinduism, the *dharma-kāya* in Buddhism, and the *loka-kāya* in Jainism within the experiential meditative traditions of Yoga and Tantra become more than metaphors. The body itself, rather than being an impediment to liberation, becomes its very vehicle." There is no escaping the world, but rather the sole task of affirming the world.

As K. L. Seshagiri Rao observed in commenting upon the *Bhagavad Gītā* (7:45): "Primordial nature is eightfold: the five elements plus mind, intelligence, and ego-sense, which constitute the lower nature of the Divine. The higher nature of the Divine relates to living beings, which uphold the world. Life has a higher value than things or property. There is not a thing in the world that is apart from the Divine."[1] This exploration of the elements in the contexts of awareness, intelligence, and interiority is ancient in India and, as Chapple so admirably lays out, is treated in many of the oldest and most insightful texts of Hinduism, Buddhism, and Jainism.

This powerful meditative pathway is explored capably and intelligently by Chapple as he weaves numerous stories, deftly handles texts, and shares insights into yogic practices. In exploring the continuity of interiority from the elemental world that spirals toward the human, Chapple effectively lays out a roadmap of yogic practices within the Hindu, Buddhist, and Jain traditions that reveal the interconnectedness between the human and the world. Building on a lifetime of scholarship and practice, Chapple brings an erudition that impressively honors his teacher, Thomas Berry. Berry observed that: "The Universe is not a collection of objects, but a communion of subjects." This book offers a wealth of reflection on that "communion of subjects" from the standpoint of texts, traditions, and practices of South Asia.

In this way, Chapple brings into realization what Thomas Berry, his seminal mentor in ecological spirituality, described as the "Great Work." Berry wrote years ago: "In India, the Great Work was to lead human thought into spiritual experiences of time and eternity and their mutual presence to each other with a unique subtlety of expression. . . . The Great Work before us, the task of moving modern industrial civilization from its present devastating influence on Earth to a more benign mode of presence, is not a role that we have chosen. It is a role given to us, beyond any consultation with ourselves. We did not choose. We were chosen by some power beyond ourselves for this historical task."[2] Chapple presents a seminal exploration of classical Yoga texts in relation to the Great Work that confronts us today.

This joy-filled study is an eco-affirmation of life through practices such as Yoga and meditation that have emerged in new ways, yet stand in the lineages of past sages and teachers. Even as we know these insights to be in direct touch with the resilience of the collective past of the Earth community, we shiver at the loss of life in this current Sixth Extinction Period. Yet, we also know in our hearts that what calls us is stunningly charged with the freshness of budding life. As Chapple observes, this sense of the Divine-within always calls anew the need to cultivate human awareness of our living world.

John Grim and Mary Evelyn Tucker
Forum on Religion and Ecology, Yale University

Introduction

Yoga and Landscapes

This book explores the practice of Yoga in regard to a systematic technique of performing concentration on the five elements. It examines some ideas that also concerned the pre-Socratic philosophers of Greece. Just as Thales mused about water and Heraclitus extolled the power of fire, Indian thinkers, theologians, and liturgists reflected on how the elements interweave with one another and within the human body to create the raw material for the experience of life. In a real and metaphorical sense, according to Indian thought, we live in landscapes and landscapes live in us.

For more than 3,500 years, India has identified earth, water, fire, air, and space as the foundational building blocks of external reality. Starting with literary praise of these elements in the Vedas, by the time of the Buddha, the Upaniṣads, and early Jainism, this acknowledgment had grown into a systematic reflection. This book examines both the descriptions of the elements and the very technical training tools that emerged so that human beings might develop regard and consideration for them. Hindus, Buddhists, and Jain Yogis explore the human-earth relationship each in their own way. For Hindus, nature emerges as a theme in the Vedas, the Upaniṣads, the Yoga literature, the epics, and the Purāṇas. The Yogis develop a mental discipline of sustained interiorization, known as *pañca mahābhūta dhāraṇā* (concentration on the five great elements) and as *bhūta śuddhi* (purification of the elements). The Buddha himself also taught a sequential meditation on the five elements. The Jains developed their own unique reflections on nature, finding life in particles of earth, water, fire, and air. They also developed their own form of sequential elemental meditations.

Indian culture recognizes the elements and the senses in myriad ways, encoding them into the rhythms and rituals of daily life. Rituals begin with the kindling of a small flame, the lighting of incense, the sprinkling of water, the preparation of offerings of flowers and food. Such practices acknowledge human embeddedness in and indebtedness to nature. They also express an underlying grammar for ritual writ large. Personal rituals and large public rituals incorporate the honoring of earth, water, fire, air, and space.

The book begins with an exploration of the celebration of the five elements in Indian literature chronologically, starting with Vedic texts and extending into Buddhist, Jain, and later Hindu literature. It also includes an exploration of select descriptions of contemporary field encounters with element-based rituals in India and in North America. In addition to a systematic look at how the fundamentals of physical constituents help enfold the human person into a sense of connectedness with inner and outer landscape, this book also explores some aspects of other beings in this landscape, animals that are other than human. Animals reflect possibilities of human consciousness, speaking to human connectivity with an unknowable past. Hindu, Buddhist, and Jain literature abounds with animal fables and instructive past life animal narratives. Concern for animals throughout Indian history can be seen in Aśokan proclamations requiring the protection and feeding of animals, cow shelters, and in current animal welfare activism. Various campaigns seek to save the tiger, the elephant, the Himalayan antelope, and even the feral urban dog. Humans and animals live in a web of interconnectedness. This book seeks to provide some appreciation for what is possible in both the inner and outer realms of the living landscape, within the elements of human and animal physiology as expressed through and within the wider world.

Yoga as explored in this book goes far beyond the familiar physical practices of poses and breathing exercises. The word *yoga* originally referred to the yoking of horses to a chariot, and a plow to oxen. It eventually gained association with yoking the mind and exerting control over the outflow of the senses. By time of the middle Upaniṣads the word *Yoga* came to refer to specific spiritual disciplines and eventually became a catchall phrase in Hindu, Buddhist, and Jain literature for religious practice. Yoga as a path of spirituality appears in the *Mahābhārata*, the *Bhagavad Gītā*, the Yoga Upaniṣads, the texts of Mahāyāna Buddhism, handbooks for the practice of Jainism, and, by the middle of the current millennium, in manuals for Haṭha Yoga.

The emergence of Yoga as a cultural phenomenon within America and Europe can be traced to the lecture tours of Swami Vivekananda in the 1890s. This was preceded in New England with the Transcendentalist fascination with the *Bhagavad Gītā* as well as with the notion that the yogi somehow dwells outside societal confines. As has been well documented by historians of modern

Yoga, Paramahansa Yogananda was among the first of many immigrants from India who introduced and adapted Yoga-focused practice for Western consumption. During the 1960s, counterculture poets and philosophers expanded the reach of Yoga and meditation among the young people seeking alternative lifestyles. Many Yoga-focused communities took root in the 1970s, such as Yogaville (Swami Satchidananda), the Himalayan Institute (Swami Rama), various Yoga Vedanta Centers (Swami Vishnudevananda), the Sri Chinmoy meditation network, the International Society for Krishna Consciousness (A. C. Bhaktivedanta Swami Prabhupāda), and several others. After a lull during the 1980s, partly due to various scandals that plagued some organizations, a resurgence of interest occurred in the 1990s with the emergence of younger, female teachers, most notably Swami Chidvilasananda (a disciple of Swami Muktananda) and Mātā Amṛtānandamayī Devī (Ammachi).

At the same time, a new physicality was injected into the practice of Yoga. Disciples in the lineage of Krishnamacharya opened studios worldwide dedicated to the perfection of Yoga Āsana. These included Yoga Works, established in Santa Monica, California, by Chuck Miller and the late Maty Ezraty and now franchised worldwide, the B. K. S. Iyengar network of studios, and the Hot Yoga popularized by Bikram Choudhury. More than 35 million Americans are now estimated to practice Yoga regularly.[1]

Along with this increase in popularity, scholarly interest in the study of Yoga flourished. Mircea Eliade (1907–1986) published the first comprehensive study in the West of Yoga traditions based on his doctoral dissertation at the University of Paris (1933), which was later adapted and translated into English as the book *Yoga, Immortality, and Freedom* (1958). This book surveys the far reach of Yoga. It documents the intersection of Yoga with various religious and philosophical traditions, including Buddhism and Jainism. Students of Eliade at the University of Chicago conducted research for decades that advanced knowledge of Yoga, theoretical and applied.

Several Yoga worlds now run in parallel. One world of Yoga promulgates physical practice in studios, meditation centers, and increasingly in clinics, schools, colleges, universities, and even churches and synagogues throughout North America. Various professional organizations have emerged to manage aspects of this public Yoga, including Yoga Alliance and the International Association of Yoga Therapists.

Another world of Yoga can be found in more religious or devotional settings, including the many Hindu and Jaina centers that have been built by members of the Indian immigrant community since the 1980s, as well as the Vedanta centers that date from the nineteenth century, and the meditation centers that were built in the early twentieth century, primarily by Paramahansa Yogananda.

Academic study comprises a third world of Yoga discourse. In India, fifty-four colleges and universities have received authorization to offer a Diploma as well as Bachelor, Master, and Doctoral Degrees in Yoga.[2] Graduate degree programs in Yoga are offered at the School of Oriental and African Studies in London, the Ca' Foscari University, Venice in Italy, and Loyola Marymount University in Los Angeles. Scholars have both celebrated and critiqued the Yoga movement. In earlier publications, I have surveyed various modern studies and many translations of the *Yoga Sūtra*,[3] including the analysis of modern Yoga in India by Joseph Alter which explores scientific studies of Yoga in India and suggests that Yoga evades politicization;[4] the discussions by Sjoman taken up later by Mark Singleton that attest to hybrid influences at the Mysore Palace that combine European body culture with Yoga practices;[5] and Elizabeth De Michelis's assessment of Yoga as a form of public esotericism that brings "solace, physical, psychological or spiritual in a world where solace and reassurance are sometimes elusive."[6] I have also edited a book on the relationship between Yoga discourse and the post-modern issue of ecology.[7]

More recent scholarly analyses have pointed to the multivalency of Yoga throughout history. David Gordon White's edited volume *Yoga in Practice* presents original texts of Yoga from the various schools of Hinduism as well as Buddhism, Jainism, Islam, and Sikhism. Geoffrey Samuel's *Origins of Yoga and Tantra* similarly examines classical sources in regard to Yoga, as does the volume *Roots of Yoga* co-edited and co-translated by Mark Singleton and James Mallinson.[8] Each of these works continues a tradition established by scholars of the nineteenth century seeking to find textual affirmation of Yoga theory and practice.

Alongside these decidedly Indological studies, several theoretical critiques of Yoga have examined modern Yoga and its expression in India and throughout the globe. Andrea Jain has analyzed the commercialization of Yoga suggesting that the "selling" of Yoga often results in compromises in regard to its original intent, but that sincere expressions of Yoga can be found in India as well as abroad.[9] Farah Godrej explores the paradoxical quest for authenticity within modern Yoga, pointing out that in some ways its contemporary practice serves to reinforce "neoliberal subjectivity" while it other ways it provides a counter-narrative to conformity, a way of resisting cultural hegemony in any form.[10] Christopher Miller has published a study of the annual Yoga Day movement initiated by the Government of India in 2015 and ratified by the United Nations. Yoga Day envisions a Yoga that will create more productive workers.

This is perhaps somewhat at odds with the original intent of Yoga, which in its meditative forms is used more as a respite from the world than as a tool to improve GDP. Miller notes that "Modi's domestic brand of therapeutic yoga does in fact serve as an instrument of biopower as it primarily focuses on the production of an efficient, healthy, docile, and stress-free labor force."[11] Many of these studies suggest that a subverting of Yoga has taken place. As the title of Andrea Jain's book asserts, what was once subversive and countercultural, both in India and throughout the world, has been transformed into a mainstream commodity.

The methodology employed in this study of Yoga in relationship to elemental concentrations does not fit into a strictly Indological category, though it includes textual analysis and translation. Nor does this book offer a sociological descriptive approach or analysis of the practice of Yoga, though it does describe Yoga practices and many field experiences. Rather, in keeping with my own disciplinary training and prior research projects, this book is a work of constructive theology. It seeks to explore how various Yoga texts and practices and social realities regard the intersection between the human being and nature as expressed through the five elements and animals.

One task of the theologian is to find and offer inspiration to help redress or even redeem the all-too-obvious difficulties that surround and sometimes overwhelm the human condition. The impetus for writing this book came from a concern for what has now been named "nature deficit disorder." As noted by Richard Louv, a deep disconnect from nature has imperiled a sense of well-being for many persons.[12] This was not the case in my own life, which from childhood has been deeply rooted in a sense of nature connection. A sustained connection with the natural world has provided solace in times of trouble and a strong foundation for a happy life. For this I am abidingly grateful. This research has been undertaken to honor my teachers and family who have consistently valued and fostered a close relationship with the natural world.

Some may find this work to be fanciful or even incorrect, protesting that Yoga and meditation and the religions of India are designed to release a person from nature, not to embrace nature. However, as scholar George James, a student of environmental activist Sunderlal Bahuguna, has noted, the world to be negated is "not the world of nature" but "the world of . . . politicians [and] technicians,"[13] those who seek to instrumentalize and abuse nature rather than understanding or appreciating nature. James's book-length study of the Chipko and related environmental movements in India can paraphrased as follows: "Nature is not the problem; human industrialization and the manipulation of nature are the problem."[14]

This book examines Yoga literature from multiple religions on the topic of the elements and animals. From this literature, a sense can be gleaned not of a disdain for the elements in Hinduism, Buddhism, and Jainism, but a concern to develop intimacy, to perform rituals that reinforce a connection with the most foundational aspects of reality.

It is not the intent of this book to create a Romantic vision of the Indian subcontinent. The environmental problems of India are immense. New Delhi, the capital of India, suffers from the worst air quality in the world. Garbage lines the highways and byways of India. Untreated industrial and human waste foul India's rivers. The deleterious effects of overpopulation can be seen as cities fail to cope with basic housing needs and villagers by the millions move to the cities.[15] However, it would be oversimplistic to blame the religions of India for its current predicament. Ecological degradation in India can be more readily traced to the aftereffects of European colonization and the slowness of governments and individuals to respond to the throwaway ethos of globalized consumerist economies.

Writing this book has become an occasion to reflect back on a five decade career as a theologian. The task of the theologian, in addition to knowing history and languages and philosophy, requires that we observe and interpret culture. We also participate in a feedback loop of our own experience as the ground for our hermeneutical endeavors. In my twenties, a time of uncertainty and growth, my research focused on the issue of human agency and will, resulting in the book *Karma and Creativity*. Ethics, personal and global, as well as child-rearing, occupied my thoughts and concerns during my thirties, during which I published *Nonviolence to Animals, Earth, and Self in Asian Traditions*. Comparative religious thought and grappling with philosophical pluralism guided the work of my forties and the appearance of *Reconciling Yogas: Haribhadra's Collection of Views on Yoga with a New Translation of Haribhadra's Yogadṛṣṭisamuccaya*. The fifties presented an opportunity to honor my teachers and professors, many of whom passed in the early years of the new millennium, through an-in depth study into the philosophy and practice of Yoga, the mainstay and wellspring for my own well-being; hence the publication of *Yoga and the Luminous: Patañjali's Spiritual Path to Freedom*. And now, in my sixties, reflections on the ritual and liturgical aspects of religious practice have brought forward the current work.

This book places Yoga ethics within a global context. Yoga, as we have seen, means connection. Despite colonialist insistence that Yoga implies hatred for the world,[16] the evidence from the texts and from the material presence of temples and ongoing practices within daily life tells a different story. Yoga, regardless of tradition, seeks to honor the five great elements. It also encourages discovering kinship with animals. Though far more suggestive than comprehensive, this book seeks to provide some appreciation for what is possible through Yoga in both the inner and outer realms of the living landscape.

1

The Inner World as Precondition for Experience

We live in landscapes and landscapes live in us. The exterior landscape helps shape our inner orientation. The first segments of the *Bṛhadāraṇyaka Upaniṣad* and the *Ācārāṅga Sūtra* as well as the story of the Buddha's enlightenment under the Bodhi Tree all emphasize the need for a person to know location and directionality.[1] Do we face north? South? East? West? The exterior landscape grounds and orients the human. Furthermore, the interior landscape predisposes the human in relation to that external context. If unhappy, the world becomes a frightening place. To know the source of our predispositions, predilections, and prejudices allows us to move purposefully from the inside out.

This book explores the human-earth relationship through the prism of a mental discipline of sustained interiorization, known as *Pañca Mahābhūta Dhāraṇā* and as *Bhūta Śuddhi,* concentration on the five great elements, and purification of and through the elements. In India, meditation on the elements provides the cultural code for daily life. It acknowledges human embeddedness in nature. It also evokes an underlying grammar for ritual. Each ritual in traditions arising from India in some way includes aspects of earth, water, fire, air, and space. Daily life in India often entails kindling the cooking flame before dawn, sprinkling a business with water before it opens, touching the earth in gratitude for her support. The book includes an exploration of the celebration of the five elements in Indian literature, as well as descriptions of contemporary field encounters with this elemental grammar in India and in North America.

The book also turns to the other-than-human presence within living landscapes, following literary and contemporary contours. Animals reflect possibilities of human consciousness, speaking to our connectivity with an unknowable past, whether called to presence through animal fables, instructive past life animal narratives, or the world of current eco-activism such as contemporary efforts to save the tiger, the elephant, the Himalayan antelope, or even the feral urban dog. We live in a web of interconnectedness. We live in a landscape defined by the absence or presence of animals.

This book seeks to provide some appreciation for what is possible in both the inner and outer realms of the living landscape. The interior life as experienced by the practice of Yoga meditation can be enriched by periods of reflection on how the human body connects with the world of the elements through the senses and the mind. The mind can be seen as laden with memories and emotions, with tendencies toward and away from the afflictions of hatred, greed, and delusion according to the Buddhists; ignorance, egotism, attraction, and repulsion according to the Hindus; and violence, anger, greed, fear, and cynicism as taught by Jainism. By focusing on the elements of nature, one can redirect one's thoughts, intentions, and actions through a Yogic process called *pratipakṣa bhāvanaṃ* and be restored to a place of equilibrium, elevated into a happier state of being.

The role of nature in Indian literature and traditions can be linked with one of the great sentences from the Upaniṣads: thou art that, *tat tvam asi*. By correlating the natural world with the human body, a motif that first appears in the *Ṛg Veda* more than three thousand years ago, Indic culture operates from a place of intimacy with the environment. Techniques of self-reflection and meditation, developed in multiple traditions over millennia, comprise a treasure trove of resources that find enduring application. This book highlights a sampling of this literature from India that affirms the core insight of eco-critic David Gatta: nature makes a difference.[2]

The Vedas, the Upaniṣads, and the early texts of Jainism and Buddhism give attention to the five elements. The Vedas honor earth, water, fire, and air with names of Goddesses and Gods, including Pṛthivī, goddess of the earth; Āptya or Varuṅa, god of waters; Agni, the god of fire and the most mentioned deity in the *Ṛg Veda*; and Vāyu, the god of wind. The *Aitareya*, *Maitri*, *Kauṣītaki*, and *Śvetāśvatara* Upaniṣads discuss the five elements. Classical Sāṃkhya, one of the six classical Hindu philosophical schools or *Darśanas*, delineates five great elements or *mahābhūtas* as part of its twenty-five-fold analysis of the components of reality (*tattvas*). In later traditions, these become threaded with the construction of ritual space as well as with internal meditations. For instance, the seventeenth-century *Gheraṇḍa Saṃhitā* (verses 68–81) associates each element with a color, a root syllable, and a location in the body, echoing material from the much earlier *Yogatattva Upaniṣad*, which has been dated anywhere from 150 to 1200 CE.[3] Vedic rituals and post-Vedic *pūjās*, including

Tantric ceremonies, generally begin with a brief or extended meditation known as *bhūta śuddhi* through which one purifies the body by recognition of the presence of each element and its connection with the senses.

Correlationalism and Cosmicization

The emergence of meditation techniques in the Upaniṣads, the texts of Theravāda Buddhism, and medieval Jainism indicate a core underlying belief structure that espouses progressive ideas of correlationism and cosmicization. These ideas, which become the frame for meditative practice, can be traced to the ritual practices of the *Puruṣa Sūkta* and the first cantos of the *Bṛhadāraṇyaka Upaniṣad*. Although both Buddhism and Jainism criticize the violence inherent in the performance of animal sacrifice described in the Vedic literature, these traditions nonetheless develop forms of meditation that reflect the Vedic paradigm of seeing similarities between the inner operations of the human body and the outer connection with greater forces. This philosophy makes a correlation between microcosm and macrocosm.

Joel Brereton has written on this aspect of Indian thought, where homologies are made between different sets of categories, such as the feet of the body corresponding to the worker caste, and the head corresponding to the priests.[4] Correlationalism lies at the core of religious practice in Indian traditions, leading to a highly valued experience of cosmicization, a term coined by Mircea Eliade. This state indicates a high level of meditative achievement leading to or inseparable from *samādhi*. This book will focus on the foundational practice that expresses the grammar of correlationism leading to cosmicization: concentration on the five great elements, the *mahābhūtas* of earth, water, fire, air, and space, as found within the Hindu, Buddhist and Jaina Yoga meditation practices. As we will see, for the Buddhists, this practice leads to a focusing of the mind resulting in an "erasure" of self. For the Jainas, it leads to meditation on the pure state of the soul (*jīva*) made possible by burning away the fetters of karma. For Hindus, it enables a joining of the individual consciousness with the universal.

The *Ṛg Veda* (ca. 1500 BCE) names the various elements through divinized categories. This short hymn gives a sense of Vedic rhetoric, simultaneously celebratory and plaintive:

> Yes! (It is) just so: you bear the pressure of the mountains, O Earth,
> As you bring the ground to life with your greatness,
> O gently sloping one.

Praises sound in response to you, oscillating lady, through the nights,
as you fling the swelling moisture forward
like a horse neighing for a prize, Silvery One!
You who, steadfast yourself, keep fast the trees all across the earth
by your strength when
the lightning bolts of the dark clouds
and the rains from heaven rain for you.[5]

Pṛthivī, or the goddess of the earth, also earns her own text, the *Pṛthivī Sūkta*, a section of the later *Atharva Veda*. Water (*āpaḥ* or *jalaḥ*) finds frequent mention in the *Ṛg Veda*, and comes to be associated with water goddesses known as Apsaras as well as with the god of flow, Varuṇa. Agni or fire is the most frequently invoked god in the *Ṛg Veda*. Vāyu or wind also receives divine status in the *Ṛg Veda*. The fifth element, Ākāśa, is associated with the sky and the deity Dyaus, the Indian version of Zeus.

The earliest surviving text of Jainism, the *Ācārāṅga Sūtra* (ca. 350 BCE) categorizes individual life forms or *jīvas* according to categories that include elemental beings. The Jaina doctrine of plural souls, echoed also in the Sāṃkhya tradition, claims the existence of innumerable individual centers of awareness in clods of dirt, in stones, in drops of dew, in flames of fire, and gusts of wind. Each unique life form is to be protected through the practice of nonviolence. In order to enhance sensitivity to the reality and existence of these life forms, Jaina postulants perform successive meditations on each elemental state. Mahāvīra, the twenty-fourth and most recent great teacher or Tīrthaṅkara of Jainism, tells his monks and nuns to inspect carefully each of the elemental realms. For instance, in this section of the *Ācārāṅga Sūtra*, Mahāvīra proclaims, "There are beings living in water, many lives; of a truth, to the monks water has been declared to be living matter. See!"[6]

Sāṃkhya, particularly in Īśvarakṛṣṇa's *Sāṃkhya Kārikā* (ca. 450 CE), sets forth a twenty-five-fold grid that correlates the gross elements with the subtle elements, showing their link with mental and emotional states. When the active, material form (Prakṛti) comes in proximity of the witness consciousness (Puruṣa), she begins a dance that vibrates in a particular way depending upon the conditions (*saṃskāras*) that predispose her emotions (*bhāva*) to imagine and then make real the material world. The twenty-five *tattvas* include consciousness and activity as mentioned above, a repository for all past impressions called the Buddhi, the sense of ego or Ahaṃkāra, and the mind or Manas. From the creative impulse, rooted in desire (*kāma*), emotions, ego, and mind push out into the sense organs of ear, skin, eyes, tongue, and nose, and welcome sense data from the five subtle connections to the earth through hearing, touching, seeing, tasting, and smelling, which connect with space, air, and form made visible through light, water, and earth respectively. Given this combination of emotions, thoughts, and sensory experiences, the body then takes action through the organs of elimination and reproduction, as well as grasping, moving about, and talking. Harnessing this process through active attention to the great elements allows for a deeper understanding of both the external world and the machinations of the subtle body that predetermine one's impulses and consequent actions.

The instructions set forth in the *Visuddhimagga* (fourth century), the *Jñānārṇava* (tenth century), the *Yogavāsiṣṭha* (eleventh century) and the *Gheraṇḍa Saṃhitā* (seventeenth century), spell out step by step the process of the *mahābhūta dhāraṇās,* the progressive concentration on the great elements. This study provides a comparative analysis of these texts and how they provide specific instruction for engaging the elements as a gateway to meditative experience.

Microphase and Macrophase

From the time of the *Ṛg Veda* forward, Indian philosophy has posited an intimate relationship between the microphase and macrophase. According to the *Puruṣa Sūkta*, the eyes of a person reflect the sun and the moon; the breath correlates to the wind; human feet stand on the earth itself. In the Sāṃkhya and the Tantra philosophical schools, the five great elements (*mahābhūtas*) stand in reciprocity with five subtle elements (*tanmātras*), experienced through the great gods of perception (*buddhīndriya*). Specifically, the earth (*pṛthivī*) reveals itself through the sense of smell (*gandha*) linked to the human nose (*nasa*). Water (*jal/ap*) reveals itself through taste (*rasa*) found in the mouth (*mukha*). Fire (*agni/tejas*) reveals form (*rūpa*) experienced through the eyes (*akṣa*). Wind (*vāyu*) unveils touch (*sparśa*) known through the human organ of the skin (*tvak*). Space (*ākāśa*) contains all sound (*śabda*), which is perceived through the ears (*karṇa*).[7] The outer world only emerges when the sense organs are directed by the mind to identify them as such. The particulars of physical reality obtain fruition only on contingency. Without the basic orientation and directionality and intentionality of the mind, no world can take shape. The world and consciousness exist in reciprocity.

This perspective contrasts with the articulations of some leading thinkers of Western thought, philosophers who at first acquaintance might seem like a good fit with some of the ideas of classical India but whose underlying presuppositions prevent them from becoming useful interlocutors. Consider a few statements by Ludwig Wittgenstein. In his *Philosophical Investigations* he closes off the possibility of taking a concern with the so-called non-sentient world. Wittgenstein writes: "Could one imagine a stone's having consciousness? And if anyone can do so—why should that not merely prove that such an image-mongery is of no interest to us?"[8] "And can one say of the stone that it has a soul and *that* is what has the pain? What has a soul, or pain, to do with the stone? Only of what behaves like a human being can one say that it *has* pains."[9] Further stressing what to him is the absurdity of a sensuous stone, he writes: "Look at a stone and imagine it having sensations. —One says to oneself: How could one so much as get the idea of ascribing a *sensation* to a *thing*? One might as well ascribe it to a number."[10] Throughout this discussion of thinking, consciousness, and feeling, Wittgenstein clearly distinguishes between the animate, which is capable of moving, which he considers to be sensate if not rational, and the inanimate or "smooth," to which he allows human emotion to be imputed or imparted and does not accept any notion of self-consciousness on the part of these realities. This attitude stands in stark contrast with Jainism, which sees life in soil, waters, flames, and even in the wind.

The philosopher Ed Casey examines the history of Western philosophy of place in his *The Fate of Place: A Philosophical History*.[11] He quotes Collingwood as stating: "The world is a world of dead matter, infinite in extent and permeated by movement throughout, but utterly devoid of ultimate qualitative differences and moved by uniform and purely quantitative forces."[12] One could also quote Aristotle and Aquinas whose anthropocentric and androcentric views tend to denigrate or even fail to consider the relevance of other beings such as women, animals, plants, and elemental forces.

In contrast, Indian philosophical traditions abound with homologies: making correspondences and observing correlations between outer and inner realities. These include feet and earth, eyes and the moon and sun, the breath and the wind. As noted by Brereton, "[B]ecause the parts of the world are equivalent to the parts of a person, humans include everything within themselves."[13] Brian K. Smith provides an exhaustive survey of all these homologies, itemizing them as found in more than seventy Sanskrit texts. He draws the conclusion that Brahmin priests who composed this literature classified the universe in such a way that advantaged themselves. Smith concludes that by explaining the cosmic order and linking its sustenance to their own ritual activities, they effectively gained prestige and wealth: "The Veda is the Brahmin's account of the world; it was written in part to establish and promote Brahmin interests."[14] This book takes a different approach to many of the same texts. As indicated in the preface, the impetus behind this exploration comes from a direct experience of learning and applying practices that arise from the homological view.

The five elements are not seen as abstractions or metaphors but literally compose the reality of the world and of one's own body. The *Mokṣadharmaparvan*, one of the books of the *Mahābhārata* epic, summarizes the relationship between body and cosmos first articulated in the *Ṛg Veda* and the *Bṛhadāraṇyaka Upaniṣad*:

> The Lord, the sustainer of all beings, revealed the sky.
> From space came water and, from water, fire and the winds.
> From the mixture of the essence of fire and wind arose the earth.
> Mountains are his bones, earth his flesh, the ocean his blood.
> The sky is his abdomen, air his breath, fire his heat, rivers his nerves.
> The sun and moon, which are called Agni and Soma, are the eyes of Brahman.
> The upper part of the sky is his head.
> The earth is his feet and the directions are his hands.[15]

This vision of the relationship between the body, divinity, and the order of things becomes both descriptive and prescriptive in terms of the human relationship with nature in India. The world cannot be separated from the human body nor can the human body be separated from the world.

In the traditional Hindu view, the world exists as an extension of the body and mind; the body and mind reflect and contain the world. In describing the women of the Garwhal region of the Himalayas, Carol Lee Flinders notes that they "enjoy a connection with trees, rivers, mountains, livestock, and plants that is simultaneously their connection with divinity, and that connection is seen as absolutely reciprocal."[16] From the texts above, we can understand this continuity as an expression of what Vandana Shiva calls "embedded in nature" and Vijaya Nagarajan refers to as "embedded ecology." This notion of intimacy with the natural world, culturally supported by an anthropocosmic vision of the earth, instantiates a person in immediate and intimate contact with one's surroundings. Just as the Hymn of the Person (*Puruṣa Sūkta*) in the *Ṛg Veda* identifies human physiology with the cosmos, correlating the feet with the earth and the head with the sky, so also a vision of deep ecology in the context of Hindu faith will seek to integrate and include its understanding of the human as inseparable from and reflective of nature.

Perhaps the most-quoted passage that provides support for the emergence of a philosophy of American love for nature can be found in Emerson's essay *Nature*, published in 1836:

Standing on the bare ground,
My head bathed by the blithe air,
And uplifted into infinite space—
All mean egotism vanishes.
I become a transparent eye-ball.
I am nothing. I see all.
The currents of the Universal Being circulate through me.
I am part or particle of God.[17]

The Asian traditions such as Yoga that influenced Emerson and Thoreau, like the Quaker traditions of their peers, emphasize interiority and the immanence of God. In this view, the realm of spiritual experience does not reside in outward worship but in states of meditation and contemplation of the natural order.

One of the earliest detailed accounts of the relationship between the microphase aspect of the body and the system of ascending energies that blossoms in the later Tantra can be found in the *Markaṇḍeya Purāṇa* (ca. 450 CE). This text makes correlations between the senses, the elements, and the *cakras,* outlining an ascendant interiority similar to that found in Emerson's famous poem. Just as Emerson ascends to a state of sublime contemplation while in a most natural state, so also the *Markaṇḍeya Purāṇa* describes an inward journey that culminates in a state of rapture. Beginning with the earth and increasing in subtlety through water, fire, air, and space, this text suggests that one enter into full understanding of one's thoughts and soul, correlating an energy center or *cakra* to each of these seven steps.

The Yogi of the *Markaṇḍeya Purāṇa* as described in chapter forty, begins with the *mūla cakra* at the base of the spine and disappears at the seventh stage into supreme bliss:

16. Thinking about the highest Brahman,
having inclined the mind toward that goal,
the Yogi is always yoked by Yoga,
abstemious in regard to food
and in control of the senses.
17. One should hold seven subtle concentrations
in the head, starting with the earth.
The Yogi should hold to the earth
and enter its subtle quality.
18. [The Yogi] thinks on its expansive nature
and moves beyond its fragrance.

Likewise in regard to the subtle flavor in water
and the form [revealed by] fire.
19. This concentration extends similarly
to the touch of the wind.
In the subtle activity of the sky,
one moves beyond sound.

These verses specify the relationship between the five elements and the five senses. The earth links with fragrance, water with flavor, from the illumination of fire and light one perceives forms, wind allows touch, and one connects with sound through space.

20. Thus one enters all of the elements
of the mind through the mind.
Carrying this mental concentration,
the subtle mind is born.

The "sixth sense" is the mind, the organizer of all data, which allows various sensory input to be interpreted and processed.

21. The one who knows Yoga,
having associated the intellect (*buddhi*)
with those states of illumination (*sattva*)
free of karmic residue
renounces all that has been obtained
with an unsurpassed, super subtle intellect.

Above the mind, one moves into meditative states, "states of illumination free of karmic residue." Loosely following the pattern outlined in the *Bhagavad Gītā* III:42[18] one moves beyond the senses, the mind, the "intellect" (*buddhi*), to the highest:

22. The knower of Yoga rises above these seven subtleties.
O Alarka, worldly existence is not known for that person
with this even minded wisdom.
With these seven concentrations,
one possesses a subtle self.
23. This person would stride with accomplishment
beyond the seen and the unseen,

beyond that which has been renounced,
and that which has not yet been renounced.

Having mastered the seven preliminaries, one can move beyond all things, entering a state of freedom.

24. O King, even the one who experiences pleasure in the elements,
having obtained even-mindedness in the midst of attachment,
destroys [attachment].
25. Therefore, having known the various subtle attachments,
the embodied one who renounces,
would attain the next step.

Attaining the state of transcendence does not negate the presence of the senses and their contact with the elements. It does not negate the mind nor the intellect (*buddhi*) that determines the predilections within the mind. This state of transcendence allows one to renounce attachment yet remain even-minded.

26. O Parthiva, the one who gathers all seven subtleties and quells all these elements
[earth/smell, water/taste, fire/sight, wind/touch, space/hearing, manas, buddhi,
correlating to the seven cakras] frees the knower of true existence.
27. The one who re-attaches to the senses perishes;
and returns again to the human realm, O King,
separated from Brahman.
28. Having gone beyond [or mastered]
these seven concentrations,
the Yogi attains whatever is desired.
O Nareśvara, the Yogi becomes absorbed
into any of the subtle elements.

Mastery over the senses, mind, and intellect allows one to attain what one seeks to attain without being brought down into the realm of attachment.

29. The Yogi becomes absorbed into gods, demons,
celestial beings, serpents, and protective spirits,
without becoming attached in any way.

> 30–31. The Yogi obtains these eight powerful qualities,
> becoming minute, light, great, accomplished,
> powerful, lordly, magical, and self possessed
> leading to Nirvāṇa.[19]

This list of accomplishments also appears in the *Yoga Sūtra* and other texts, though the Yoga system will claim that these powers are not a precondition for freedom and can become an impediment.

The *Markaṇḍeya Purāṇa* provides an early account of what later develops in the subtle body theories of Tantra. At the base of the body, one finds earth, associated with the Mūla Cakra at the very base of the spine in the area of the anus, and water, associated with the Svādhiṣṭhāna Cakra in the realm of the genitals, named Liṅgam for men and Yoni for women. In the central part of the body, one finds the heat and fire of digestion in the abdomen, referred to as Nābhi (cognate with the word navel) or Maṇipūra, the city of jewels, indicating the internal organs. Above the belly, one finds the operations of the respiratory system, the lungs and heart, which connect with the element of air. Names for the heart *cakra* include Hṛdaya and Anāhata. The realm of space starts in what is later designated as the Viśuddha Cakra located in the throat and extends up into the head, the realm of discernment and eventually transcendence, associated with the Ājñā and Sahasrāra Cakras, respectively.[20]

In Hindu and Tibetan Buddhist narratives, the spiritual life unfolds as the adept moves the energy coiled at the bottom of the spine up through the realms of power and love into the realms of nonattachment and insight, culminating in freedom. The knots (*grantha*) of karma and *saṃskāra* and *vāsanā* impede an individual, keeping the energy in the lower realms. Through practices (*sādhana*) found in various forms of Hindu, Buddhist, and Jaina Yoga, one purifies the gross body which in turn purges the subtle body of its habitual impulses. With this release of tightly held patterns, one is able to ascend to the realm of the heart, gain discernment, and move toward freedom, a vertical rise from the lower realms of anus, genitals, and stomach to heart, throat, and forehead. Eventually, one achieves a sense of bliss and freedom beyond even the confines of the human skull.

The Hindu and Buddhist practices of Yoga often follow this path of ascent: earth, water, fire, air, space, insight, and freedom, correlating with Mūla, Svādhiṣṭhāna, Nābhi, Hṛdaya, Viśuddha, Ājñā, and Sahasrāra. The Jaina practice of Śukla Piṇḍastha meditation, explained in chapter six, follows a different course. Acknowledging the density of karma and associating it with the earthy, vegetative mass of a lotus, one invokes fire to incinerate the stuff of karma, air to serve as a bellows to beckon the monsoon, water to wash away any lingering impurities, allowing one to move into a space wherein one sees oneself as the self of a fully liberated being.

Meditative Mastery

Hinduism, while revering the five elements and venerating many gods and goddesses, places ultimate importance on the attainment of spiritual liberation (*mokṣa*). The path toward liberation requires a skillful reciprocity between spirit and materiality. Yogic practice *(sādhana)* cultivates an awareness of and intimacy with the realm of manifestation and materiality (*prakṛti*). Just as the *Bṛhadāraṇyaka Upaniṣad* proclaims a relationship between the body and the universe, so also the Yoga system urges one to gain mastery over how the body stands in relationship to the cosmos. The *Yoga Sūtras* of Patañjali state, "From concentration on the significance and connection of the subtle [body] and the essence of gross manifestation, there is mastery over the elements."[21] This statement acknowledges a linkage between the realm of bodily sensation and the experience of the physical world. By concentrating on this relationship, one gains an intimacy with the elements that results in an understanding of one's embeddedness with one's environment.

The yogic accomplishment of mastery over the elements (*bhūta-jaya*) entails a detailed training that focuses on the elements over a period of several months. In this regimen, one begins with concentration on the earth, moving toward an appreciation of the special relationship between the sense of smell residing in the subtle body (*sūkṣma śarīra*) and the earth (*pṛthivī*). Moving up in subtlety, the practitioner then concentrates on the link between subtle taste (*rasa*) and water (*āp*); between visible form (*rūpa*) and light and heat (*tejas*); between touch (*sparśa*) and the wind (*vāyu*); and between sound (*śabda*) and space (*ākāśa*). Beginning with earth, the most gross aspect of manifestation, one progresses to the lightest. This insight into the relationship between the senses and the elements leads to an ability to acknowledge and withhold the outflow of the senses (*prapañca*). Through this mastery, one gains freedom from compulsive attachment; this lightness (*sattva*) ultimately leads to liberation (*mokṣa*).

On the one hand, it might be argued that this process could lead to an introspective but objectivizing distance from nature. On the other hand, it could also be stated that this meditative practice can result in a greater rapport with nature, an entry into a purified, immediate state of perception freed from residues of past attachment. In the words of David Abram, "The recuperation of the incarnate, sensorial dimension of experience brings with it a recuperation of the living landscape in which we are corporeally embedded. As we return to our senses, we gradually discover our sensory perceptions to be simply our part of a vast, interpenetrating webwork."[22] By entering fully into a reflection on the workings of the senses through the practices of yogic meditation, a person can gain an intimacy with the foundational presence of objects that transcends their specificity, leading to a state of unity with the natural world.

One example of the enactment of this state can be found in Preston's description of the priest Kumar Panda as he performs Durgā Pūjā. During this ritual, Panda concentrates on the elements, seeing them within his body, which fills with divine power or *śakti.* He becomes possessed by the goddess herself. Kumar Panda describes his inner vision during meditation: "After performing meditation and the ritual for two or three hours, lightning flashes before my eyes. . . . I become the goddess. She who is Ma (Mother) is me. . . . Water and the coldness of water, fire and the burning capacity of fire, the sun and the rays of the sun; there is no difference between all these things, just as there is no difference between myself and the goddess."[23] This journey through the relationship between the body and the elements to the point of unity with the goddess bring the meditator to a point of visionary immersion, which may be seen as a form of profound and deep ecological awareness arising from connection and felt correlation.

Within the context of celebrating the special relationship between the human person and nature, each region of India has developed an extensive ritual cycle. These festivals often coincide with times of harvest or renewal. For instance, the Pongal festival in South India takes place each January to acknowledge the rice harvest. Many Hindu rituals include reverence for sacred traditional plants such as the Tulsi tree; many explicitly invoke the elements as mentioned above and many celebrate the earth goddess or Bhū Devi. Vijaya Nagarajan has extensively described how the practice of the Kolam morning ritual establishes in Tamil women a sense of connectedness with their environment.[24] Madhu Khanna writes about how rituals practiced in the urban context maintain significant agricultural and hence ecological meanings. Ritual acknowledges and invokes one's position in the order of things and connects the worshipper directly with fecundity cycles.[25] Eliza Kent, who studied both village and urban attitudes toward sacred groves in Tamil Nadu, has written that "there is a profoundly ecological ethos embedded in the religious cosmology that their (the villagers) beliefs and rituals articulate, which rests on an awareness of being ensconced in a dense network of relationship with a wide range of beings such that if one affects one element, one affects all others."[26]

The Body in Hinduism, Buddhism, and Jainism

sarvaṁ dehaṁ cinmayaṁ hi jagad vā paribhāvayet
yugapan nirvikalpena manasā paramodayaḥ

When an aspirant contemplates, with mind unwavering and free,
the whole body and the entire universe simultaneously as of the nature of consciousness, that person experiences Supreme Awakening.

—*Vijñāna-bhairava*, 63[27]

The Hindu, Buddhist, and Jaina traditions hold similar yet divergent interpretations of the body. We first will examine the notion of "cosmic body," wherein the human body is seen as a metaphor for the totality of existence. We will then investigate some of the explicitly physical descriptions of the body as found in the philosophical literature of each religion; medical and erotic descriptions of the body, though innately interesting, will not be considered in detail. The subtle body will be discussed as composed of karmic accretions in each system, followed by a brief summary of the anatomy of the *cakras* and *nāḍīs*.

In the religions that have originated in greater India (Hinduism, Buddhism, and Jainism), three terms are used to designate body: *kāya, śarīra,* and *deha*. All three terms can be used interchangeably, though the first (*kāya*) tends to be used more metaphorically and expansively, particularly in the Buddhist tradition, where the term *kāya* also refers to "body" or "corpus" in a larger sense. The later Mahāyāna traditions refer to the teaching, transformation, and enjoyment bodies (*kāya*) of the Buddha, each of which assumes cosmic proportions. Other cosmic body allusions abound in South Asian traditions. In the *Puruṣa Sūkta* of the *Ṛg Veda*, the body parts of the cosmic person are identified with the various realms of the universe: head with sky, feet with the earth, etc. This cosmicization is also seen in the *Bṛhadāraṇyaka Upaniṣad*, where first the parts of a horse and then the parts of an anthropomorphized deity are similarly interpreted (I.1–2). In the eleventh chapter of the *Bhagavad Gītā*, the body (*deha*) of Krishna assumes mammoth proportions, literally swallowing and chewing up entire armies. And in the Jaina tradition, the entire cosmos takes on a the form of a quasi-human being, with the upper heavenly realms, including the state of *kaivalyam,* at the "head," and the lower, hellish realms at the base or "foot."[28] The later tantric or tantric-influenced aspects of all three religions explicitly enfold the body-as-cosmos metaphor into both their presuppositions and their intentionality. But before completing our discussion of the cosmic body in Indian religions, let us first examine the interpretations of the gross body (*sthūla śarīra*) and the subtle body (*sūkṣma śarīra*).

The physical or gross body (*sthūla śarīra*) comprises an assemblage of the earth, water, fire, and air elements, connected with the organs of action and the sense organs. The Buddhist Abhidharma tradition, the Hindu Sāṃkhya and Vedānta systems, and the Jaina explication of karma all provide details regarding the structure of the physical body. In the *Abhidharmakośa*, a Buddhist text, the twelve *gotras* (six internal senses and their respective six external objects) or eighteen *āyatanas* (a similar listing that also includes six respective consciousnesses) account for the body's constitution.[29] The *Taittirīya Upaniṣad* speaks of a five-layered person, a self that is covered by sheaths (*kośas*) made of food, breath, mind, intellect, and bliss.[30] In the *Sāṃkhya Kārikā*, the five gross elements (*mahābhūtas*) compose the physical body, said to be "born of mother and father."[31] This body is comprised of the five action organs (*karmendriyas*), and the five sense organs (*buddhīndriyas*), the five subtle elements, the ego, the mind, and the intellect. As we will see below, no body can operate without the presence of a variously construed driving karmic force. In the Jaina Karmagrantha texts, the *Nāma-karmans*, subdivided into ninety-three *uttara prakṛtis,* account for all possible bodily forms that *jīvas* can assume in the four states of existence (celestial, human, animal, infernal).[32]

In all three philosophical traditions of body, relatively little emphasis is placed on the physical composition of the body. Rather, the discussion focuses on the body in its role as vehicle for consciousness. Although the Jaina Karmagrantha texts discuss bone joints and posture, this information is clearly secondary in importance to the modality of being-in-the-world that one assumes. These traditions emphasize the body as subject rather than object. In the erotic traditions of India, particularly the *Kāma Sūtra*, the human body is grouped into such objective categories as elephant-woman, stallion-man, etc. However, although sex can be sanctified for householders as a part of one's *dharma,* it is generally associated with remaining within the clutches of *saṃsāra* and hence antithetical to the highest goals generally associated with religion. One exception is the Tantric tradition, which will be considered below.

Both like and unlike the dualistic Platonic tradition of a soul independent of but trapped in the body, the religious traditions of India talk about a driving essential component of identity that guides and motivates the body of each person. The term most universally applied for this entity is *jīva,* used by both the Hindus and Jainas; the Buddhists used the term *pudgala* in a similar fashion. In all instances, the bodily "organizational bundle" consists of karmic constituents, memory residues from past experiences that determine present and future action. These karmas also determine personality as well as body type. This subtle body composed of karmas and their residues (*sūksma-śarīra,* as referred to in the Hindu tradition) determines both the physical structure and psychic dispositions of the body.

In the Sāṃkhya tradition, the subtle body is the repository for the effects of past action (*saṃskāras*). It is considered to be constant while that "born of mother and father" is perishable. In other words, this special form of body transmigrates following the death of its temporary physical location in a body. Both the quality of its life and the nature of its future embodiment are governed by the modes or *bhāvas* assumed by its accumulated karmic residues. According to one listing in Sāṃkhya, these *bhāvas* take eight forms, dyadically arranged (virtue, vice; knowledge, ignorance; strength, weakness; detachment, attachment); according to another account, they take fifty forms (five ignorances, twenty-eight incapacities, nine complacencies, and eight perfections).[33] The goal of the Sāṃkhya system, akin to that of the Vedānta and Jñāna Yoga, is to establish oneself in knowledge or *jñāna bhāva* so that liberation (*mokṣa* or *kaivalyam*) may be obtained. Though one continues to suffer due to a continued relationship with the physical body (SK 52, 55, 67), upon final separation from the body (*prāpte śarīrabhede*, SK 68), one is not again subjected to rebirth but dwells eternally in pure consciousness (*puruṣa*). In this system, the body exists because of its relationship with karmic forces; yet the goal of the system is ultimately to transcend those drives that cause embodiment. In Sāṃkhya, the mechanics of the gross or physical body are succinctly described, while the subtle body, the *sūkṣma śarīra*, the driving force behind the apparent body, is described in great detail.

In the Abhidharma schools of Buddhism, the bodily constituents mentioned above are prompted into operation by the persistence of desire. This desire or thirst (*tṛṣṇa*) causes a host of mental processes to arise (*caitta-dharmas*). In both the early and later schools of Buddhism, the physical body is to be regarded with great distrust. In order to reverse the pathology of physical attraction, which distracts the practicing Buddhist from his or her meditation, the tradition advised bringing forth an opposite thought when attraction arises. Perhaps the most graphic example of this practice is "concentration on foulness," popularly referred to as the Buddhist graveyard meditation, and discussed at great length in Buddhaghosa's *Visuddhimagga*. Designed to help monks overcome the influences of bodily lust, this meditation involves reflection on the following aspects of a human corpse in the process of decay: "the bloated, the livid, the festering, the cut up, the gnawed, the scattered, the hacked and scattered, the bleeding, the worm infested, [and] the skeleton."[34] By witnessing or visualizing these aspects of the ultimate putrefaction of all human corporality, one will most likely retreat from pursuing what might have been initially regarded with desire. Buddhaghosa writes: "A living body is just as foul as a dead one, only the characteristic of foulness is not as evident in a living one, being hidden by adventitious embellishments."[35] At a later date, Vasubandhu elaborates on how to meditate on the body in such a way as to reduce and eventually eliminate bodily attraction, advising one to conjure images of a blue corpse, a body partly eaten by insects, an immobile corpse, and finally a skeleton:

> The Yogi who wishes to practice meditation upon the unattractive begins by fixing his mind upon some member of his body such as the toe of his foot or the middle of his forehead or any area desired. He should imagine that the flesh in that area rots and falls away and gradually continue the practice until the entire body is regarded as a skeleton. . . . [H]e should apply the same process to a second person and continue until he has conceived of the temple and compound, the town, the outlying regions and finally the limitless ocean as being filled with skeletons.[36]

The idea of body here is further elaborated on in the later Mahāyāna tradition:

> . . . the body is a mass of filth and putridity. It exudes such malodorous and impure substances as sweat, pus, bile, phlegm, urine, saliva, and excrements through its nine apertures. It is indeed a rotten carcass, and it is infested by eighty thousand worms.[37]

Without doubt, these images of the body helped gird Buddhist monks for a life of solitude!

In Buddhism, as in the Sāṃkhya system, the body cannot be separated from the karmic forces that underlie its very being, also referred to as *saṃskāras*. Forty-six such mental *dharmas* are categorized in the Sarvāstivādin Abhidharma school, producing multiple embodiments. These range from impurities such as ignorance, carelessness, heaviness, lack of faith, sloth, and addiction to pleasure, to vicious traits such as anger, deceit, envy, jealousy, violence, vanity, etc. Neutral mind states such as memory and absent-mindedness are also listed, as well as ten aspects of goodness, including faith, strength, equanimity, self-respect, decorum, lack of cupidity, lack of hatred, nonviolence, nimbleness of mind, and acquiring and preserving good qualities. Each of these modalities are expressed through the body due to the accumulated action that one has accrued through countless rounds of rebirth. Though as in all schools of Buddhism, the substantialist language of self is not used, this array of *dharmas* accounts for the arising of self and body identity, albeit subject to eventual decay and dispersal. Past actions mandate a person's present constitution; though no self is said to continue, the bundle of karma wanders from one embodiment to the next since beginningless time, until one seeks to extinguish the desires that lie at the root of this process.

Despite its insistence on the nonexistence of an abiding self, the Buddhist tradition offers the most comprehensive account of the rebirth of the individual. The *Tibetan Book of the Dead* gives detailed instructions for the dying person, as he or she leaves the body, to proceed with care through the various post-life states (*bardo*) in search of enlightenment or at least embodiment in a better situation.[38]

Although in the early Buddhist schools the state of *nirvāṇa* as attained by Śakyamuni Buddha seemingly did not allow for the continuation of any bodily form, either gross or subtle, later schools of Buddhism ascribed a logos-style docetism to the "body of the Buddha," saying that the Buddha continues through his teachings. The Mahāyāna school eschews the notion of forever escaping any form of embodiment in favor of the Bodhisattva Vow to purposely return birth after birth in bodily form in order to help save other sentient beings. In the *Bodhicaryāvatāra* of Śāntideva, this also involves a commitment to sacrifice one's own body for the sake of helping to relieve the suffering of others:

> I have devoted this body to the welfare of all creatures.
> They may revile me all the time or bespatter me with mud;
> they may play with my body and mock me and make sport of me;
> yea, they may even slay me. I have given my body to them:
> why should I think of all that?[39]

In another, often cited Buddhist tale, a hungry tigress gives up her own flesh to prevent her cubs from starving. These examples illustrate the importance of giving to others in the Buddhist tradition, and provide a unique perspective on the body as a vehicle to help others in their quest for salvation.

The notion of subtle body is perhaps most fully developed in the Jaina tradition. In Jainism, the various driving forces that guide one's path in embodied form are found in several fundamental species (*mūla-prakṛti*) of karma: five karmas that obscure knowledge, four karmas that obscure insight, five that cause different forms of sleep, two that cause feelings of pain and pleasure, three that pervert religious views, twenty-five that disrupt proper conduct (sixteen that cause passion, six modes though not passionate are nonetheless disruptive such as inappropriate joking, and three forms of sexual desire, including homosexuality), four karmas that determine the nature of one's birth, ninety-three *nāma-karmas* that describe bodily forms in celestial, human, animal, infernal realms (mentioned above), two that determine family status, and five that inhibit the *jīva*. Hence, the total number of possible karmic factors that determine one's experiential body is 148.

Of particular interest in Jainism is the use of color or *leśya*, presumably seen in aura form, in association with the discussion of karma:

> The hostile, pitiless, cruel, barbarous, impious man, who has a
> bad tongue and who takes pleasure in torturing other beings,
> has a black *leśya*.
> The fraudulent, corruptible, inconstant, hypocritical,
> voluptuous man has a dark *leśya* (dark blue, *nīla*).
> The thoughtless one, who in all his actions does not weigh the
> evil and the wrathful, has a grey one.
> The prudent man who stops the influx of new karman,
> the liberal, honorable one, who has a friendly mind toward
> religion, has a fiery [red] *leśya*.
> The compassionate, bountiful, steady, intelligent one
> has a lotus-pink *leśya*.
> The pious man who performs good deeds, is passionless
> and impartial, has a white *leśya*.[40]

Bodies of all four realms (animals, humans, gods, and demons) are said to demonstrate *leśya*. The so-called animal realm includes the elements, plants, and geographical and meteorological entities such as stones, dew, etc.; the pan-animism of Jainism considers all these entities to be suffused with *jīva*. However, all of these sorts of beings, whose bodies are said to possess only the sense of touch, exhibit the three darkest forms of *leśya*. Likewise, those whose bodies carry two senses (touch and taste), including worms and leeches; those who have three senses (adding smell), including bugs and ants; those who have four senses (adding sight), including bees and flies) are said to have black, dark, or grey *leśya*, as are the five-sense animals such as aquatic, terrestial, and air-borne animals that do not possess reason. Those born of the womb, including "cattle, goats, sheep, elephants, lions, tigers," and humans, are said to exhibit all six forms of *leśya*, and hence are capable of purposive ethical action. Likewise, all six *leśya* are attributed to the gods and goddesses, while hell-beings carry the three darker colors.[41]

In the Jaina tradition, corporality extends both below and above its accepted definitions in other systems of thought. Due to the doctrine of reembodiment following death, each life force has the potential to evolve into a higher (or lower) state; each human being has achieved its status only after innumerable births as a piece of dirt, a drop of rain, a blade of grass, a lowly insect, and both invertebrate and vertebrate animals. In a real, biological sense, Jainism asserts that we are identical with all life forms.[42] Consequently, Jainism advocates treating all beings, including the earth and water itself, as not different from one's own being. It teaches that one can slowly release the essentially pure *jīva* from its bodily attachments through practices of nonviolence, delivering one into an eternal state of energy, consciousness, and bliss.

Thus far, we have investigated several models of body arising from South Asian traditions: various notions of cosmic body, definitions of the physical body linked to the gross elements and the senses, and several "takes" on the subtle body: one that says it is powered by consciousness (Sāṃkhya), one that considers it to arise from desire but to be linked to no abiding self or soul (Buddhism), and one that posits subtle bodies linked to a soul that suffuse all of the manifest world, exhibit certain colors, and ultimately must be shed in order for highest religious freedom to be attained (Jainism).

The Yoga tradition introduces another, more positive view of body that in later tantric thought complements and complexifies the various notions of body that we have already considered. Yoga is perhaps best known for its series of postures known as *āsanas* through which one stretches the body to its limits and imitates a host of animals, as well as its numerous breathing exercises (*prāṇāyāma*).[43] Yoga also includes its own interpretation of the subtle body. In this unique view of the body, ascending centers of energy are found, each of which is associated with a particular power. The earliest mention of these *cakras* or "wheels" of consciousness and *nāḍīs,* the "rivers" through which this energy flows, is found in the *Yoga Sūtra* of Patañjali, a text that probably dates from the first century of the common era. A brief description of these is given in the third section of the text, the Vibhūti pāda, which deals with various powers that a practitioner of yoga can cultivate:

> 29. [From concentration] on the central (navel) *cakra*,
> knowledge of the ordering of the body.
> 30. On the hollow of the throat, cessation of hunger and thirst.
> 31. On the tortoise *nāḍī*, stability.
> 32. On the light in the head, vision of perfected ones.[44]

When these centers are awakened, one then becomes open to an experience described by Mircea Eliade as "cosmicization." Eliade writes that through the awakening of this *kuṇḍalinī* power, "Not only does the disciple identify himself with the cosmos; he also rediscovers the genesis and destruction of the universe in his own body."[46] As Sanjukta Gupta has noted, the human body itself becomes identified with the powers of the universe.[47] The Hindu goddess tradition is particularly associated with this religious insight. Katherine Harper writes that

> [t]he body as the *imago mundo* has a sevenfold order that found its internal expression in the seven chakras of the body. Each of the seven chakras was envisioned or symbolized by a goddess (more specifically a Śakti) residing in a lotus. . . . When the consciousness had traversed the seven-fold path of the chakras, *mokṣa* was achieved.[48]

The "metaphor" of the cosmic person in Hinduism, the *dharma-kāya* in Buddhism, and the *loka-kāya* in Jainism within the experiential meditative traditions of Yoga and Tantra become more than metaphors. The body itself, rather than being an impediment to liberation, becomes its very vehicle. By understanding the operations of first the gross and then the subtle body, and by plumbing the depths and heights of its various energy flows, the practitioner of *sādhana* enters into a mode of embodiment that both embraces and transcends the mundane.

The chapters that follow take in turn the elements, one by one, inseparable from the body, examined through the prisms of text, ritual, and temple. The body provides the context for experience and for liberation. Beginning with earth, the following chapters will explore the concentrations on the elements that allow the body to arrive at states of self-understanding and transcendence.

LAM

2

Earth

Loving the Land

The land, the earth, the soil all evoke thoughts and images of rootedness. This most dense and present of elements carries connotations of geography, of smell, of agriculture and manufacture. Diana Eck has described the earth of India as a sacred, peninsular expanse extending from the Himalayas to the tip of Kanya Kumara and from the Khyber Pass to the Assamese jungle. Through narratives about Hindu pilgrimage and myth, she weaves a living, interlinked literary and ritual history. She writes that "landscape constitutes its own kind of primary text, a topographical text,"[1] noting that just as Simon Schama has observed that "landscape is a work of the mind," so also, India's "forest and wilderness are richly figured with cultural meanings."[2]

Landscape intersects with the human body in specific ways. David Abram urges one to pay attention to "dark, stygian smells . . . the aromatic dank of the soil . . . the faintly fermented fragrance [of scat] prying open your nostrils . . . and a host of other whiffs sometimes merged and sometimes distinct."[3] James McHugh, in his study of India's olfactory history and culture, links earth and fragrance, noting that "odor and earth mutually define each other."[4]

Thomas Berry, a cultural historian with deep interest in the well-being of the earth, writing about his childhood, tells of crossing a creek to reach a meadow: "It was an early afternoon in late May when I first wandered down the incline, crossed the creek, and looked out over the scene. The field was covered with white lilies rising above the thick grass."[5] This experience caused him to reflect, even at a young age, on the possibility of wonder and to enter the gateway to what he calls "the understanding, the power, the aesthetic grandeur, and the emotional fulfillment needed to heal the Earth for a viable future."[6] This childhood insight spurred by an encounter of a meadow perhaps informed Berry's reading of immanence in Hindu scriptures: "The god in fire, in water, the god who has entered into all this universe, the god in plants, in trees, to that god, praise and adoration."[7] Douglas Christie makes note of this formative stage of human development:

> The simple awareness of the goodness and beauty of the living world seems to lodge itself in the mind most deeply in childhood—in that time of innocence and purity before a mature consciousness of the self emerges, a consciousness that inevitably brings with it an awareness of one's own divided self and of the profound ambiguity and brokenness of existence. I do not think it is a coincidence that reflections on paradise so often arise from memories of this cherished, mysterious place. Here, in memory at least, one lives in the wild world fully and unambiguously, with feelings of tenderness and regard for other living beings whose rightness and truth are unquestioned.[8]

This book provides a tool kit drawn from India's rich traditions of Yoga and meditation for recovering a sense of wonder, a process through which to engage in inquiry into the mysteries of the natural world. Attention to the five great elements of Earth, Water, Fire, Air, and Space provides a space of creative play, a way to reconfigure and recover a childlike relationship with the most primary constituents of reality, manifested as the world and inseparable from the body.

The method in this and the following chapters will follow these contours. First, the chapter will begin with a brief, perhaps poetic evocation drawing from personal experience, in the tradition of narrative theology, followed with a short description of pilgrimage to temples dedicated to the elements in Tamil Nadu and Andhra Pradesh and, for the concluding section, animal shelters and hospitals in Karnataka and Delhi. Then, each chapter will explore representative references to the element from the earliest strata of Vedic literature. These will include the *Ṛg Veda*, the *Atharva Veda*, and occasionally a reference to the Upaniṣads. Then attention will be turned to the *Visuddhimagga*, introducing Buddhist approaches to the elements in meditative context. We will then visit Jain literature, including the *Ācārāṅga Sūtra* and the *Tattvārtha Sūtra* for their explication of cosmology, and the Tantric correlations found in Jainism, particularly the linkages between color, mantra, geometry, and element in Śubhacandra's *Jñānārṇava* and Hemacandra's *Yogaśāstra*. Tantra across traditions takes particular importance in the chapter on space. We return to the Hindu context in an attempt to enter the phenomenological practicalities of elemental meditations informed by Sāṃkhya, exploring the elemental meditations (*mahābhūta dhāraṇās*) in the *Yogavāsiṣṭha* and the *Gheraṇḍa Saṃhitā*, bringing the opening reflections at the start of the chapter into philosophical and textual context.

Pṛthivī Dhāraṇā

My connection with the earth began in Western New York, near Buffalo and Rochester. About six months after my first birthday my mother brought me to the window in our sunroom and showed me a purple crocus thrusting color up through the snow. She explained that spring was on its way. Some seven years later, my father, who had trained in forestry and had lived in his youth for a time with the Ojibway peoples on Bruce Peninsula in Ontario, brought me deep into the old growth forest beyond the fields and orchards that surrounded our house and showed me a hive of wild bees, their honey oozing amber liquid high over our heads, creating a moment of magic. As a family we gathered wild strawberries, picked apples, pears, peaches, cherries, and enjoyed the harvest of an abundant kitchen garden. We moved from the old lakebed plain south of Lake Ontario to the Genesee Valley when I was eleven. Dairy farms and sweeping vistas replaced orchards and flat fields. The bus ride to high school in Avon, New York, was forty-five minutes, winding through hills and forests and fields illuminated by the rising sun. New lands to explore on Mulligan Farm revealed hidden ponds, more old growth forest, waterfalls, and bubbling streams and springs. With newfound friends came long hikes on the railroad bed, camp outs on the cliffs above Conesus Outlet, as it flowed from the westernmost Finger Lake to the Genesee River, and, eventually, with Maureen, who became my wife, discovery of the Upper Falls and Lower Falls in the city of Rochester. Nature framed and defined my youth.

Moving from the western rural area of New York to the Long Island suburbs of New York City at the age of eighteen proved emotionally challenging. The houses were so close together, the fields and orchards were few and far between, the traffic was heavy, the people somewhat gruff. The education offered at Yoga Anand Ashram and Stony Brook University prompted the move and, thankfully, Yoga training soon turned our class's collective attention to the earth. The Monday night Yoga class was assigned, one month at a time, to focus on the great elements of earth, water, fire, air, and space. This practice complemented our weekly focus on different combinations of precepts and observances and daily practice of *āsana* and *prāṇāyāma*.[9] Our instructions were specific: take a plate, dig up some soil, bring it inside, and sit for twenty minutes in the early morning and twenty minutes before dinner, gazing upon the earth.

Palfrey Street, where I lived in a rented room, dead-ended at a truck farm. The soil was a mix of loam and sand, quite different from the rich dark earth of Orleans County. Gazing upon its texture and color conjured thoughts and memories, images of the fields back home and the sandy beaches of Long Island's South Shore and the rocky beaches surrounding Stony Brook Harbor. It proved quite pleasant, a respite from studies and the daily anxieties that confront any teenaged college student far from home. While walking along the field and through the forest preserve to hop on the bus to central campus, the rows of onions and the dense second growth oaks glistened with new meaning. The Stony Brook campus itself yielded new treasures, with patches of meadow and groves softening the macadam walkways and brutalist buildings. Forgiveness arose for the built and built-up environment once it dawned that the concrete and the bricks were made of earth. The highway often traveled to Amityville similarly took on a mood of the familiar: the cars were made of steel, made of earth, as were the hulking presence of Pilgrim State Hospital, the concrete pavement of Sagtikos Parkway, and the stately pines lining Southern State Parkway as we traversed Belmont Park. Later, when commuting to Fordham University, this perspective of earth-connection softened the harshness of the Long Island Expressway and the emptied, sometimes burning tenements in the South Bronx.

The Earth Temple in South India

Some forty years later, this experience of and direct encounter with the five elements took on a new dimension with pilgrimage to the five great elemental temples that, strategically, rise impressively within the landscape of southeast India. Three of us participated in a whirlwind pilgrimage and road trip: myself, Christopher Miller, and Karthik Dhandapani, whose father also joined us when possible. Karthik, who grew up in Pondicherry and now works as an engineer in Los Angeles, was happy to revisit these holy sites and to share his connections at each place. Chris Miller was conducting research for his MA thesis on environment in India. For me, this was a magnificent opportunity to finally visit these important places, first described to me decades earlier by comparative theologian Frank Clooney, then at Boston College and now at Harvard.

Each temple is actually a complex of buildings spread over as many as twenty-five acres. They include four towers or Gopurams facing each of the four directions, evoking the first teaching given by the bull to Satyakāma in the *Chāndogya Upaniṣad*: know your orientation in space. Three of the five temples have been constructed on the exact same longitudinal axis. The temples for earth, air, and space all align at 79 degrees and 41 minutes east. Each temple includes nine gates, representing the nine orifices of the body. Each is sited in a manner that evokes the element being honored, as will be described. Each temple narrates some aspect of the relationship between Śiva, lord of death and the dance, and Pārvatī, the goddess of manifestation.

These temples date back to the Pallava Dynasty (ca. third to ninth century). They were most likely transformed from timber to stone during the Chola Dynasty (ca. ninth to thirteenth century), came under the protection of the Vijayanagar Empire (1336–1646), and endured through various periods of French and British occupation until India's independence in 1947. State government ministries that oversee Hindu temples administer them today with input from the Archaeological Survey of India.

Ekambaranatham or Ekambeśvarm Temple, in Kanchipuram, just west of Chennai, honors the Earth, Pṛthivī. It stands on an expansive plain, not surrounded by mountains nor near any obvious river. In this temple, as well as in the fire and wind temples, the images of Śiva and Pārvatī are placed back to back, with the deities facing opposite directions. We walked the outer perimeter of 1,008 columns before reaching the inner sanctum. We paid homage to the *lingam* that symbolizes Śiva and then circled around to take *darśan* of the image of Pārvatī. The marker for Śiva symbolizes the meditative state of the pure witness. The image of Pārvatī evokes the dance of materiality within the world. Their complementarity and mutuality ensure the ongoing manifestation of the universe. Their symmetrical positioning, back to back, signals their full union and coproduction of the world.

At the far side of the temple stands a mango tree, estimated to have first been planted 1,500 years ago, marking the site where Pārvatī once protected an earthen Śiva *liṅgam* from a flood. The mango tree evokes the best of India: abundance, sweetness, and a sense of comfort, both in the deliciousness of its fruit and in the calming presence of the tree itself. Mango groves calm the eye with their soft shape and deep green hue. Their shade brings coolness. Just as with conversations remembered from my childhood about different varieties of apples, so also in India most people have strong opinions about which mango is best in texture or sweetness. And just as the apple figures prominently in the story of Eve and the pomegranate in the story of Persephone, so also it seems appropriate that the mango plays an important part of the Pārvatī narrative. From the fruits of the earth we are born and sustained.

The association of the goddess with Kanchipuram can be found on the other side of town as well, at the famous Sapta Matṛkā archaeological site that depicts Śiva, Ganeśa, and all seven forms of the mother goddess, some who are fierce and others benign.[10] We feasted on chikkus while in Kanchipuram, a delicious earthy fruit that, while indescribable, nonetheless seems to gather into one the best of an apple, a super ripe pomegranate, a kiwi, and a date.

Hinduism: The *Atharva Veda*

India's Vedas are the ancient bedrock for her moral, spiritual, philosophical, and artistic self-understanding. A Veda is a sacred text of five to fifty or so verses gathered into one of four collections that include hundreds of hymns each. The earliest of these was the *Ṛg Veda*, initially composed around 1500 BCE. Its verses, filled with praise of various gods, goddesses, and cosmic forces, are repeated and quoted throughout the the *Sāma Veda*, a collection of most efficacious chants. Subsequent texts include the *Yajur Veda*, which provides ritual instructions, and the *Atharva Veda*, our primary focus, which includes proto-science and medicine as well as a full segment on the earth (Pṛthivī) and land (Bhūmi). These texts have been transmitted orally for thousands of years through a rigorous memorization process that begins in a priest's early boyhood. To hear a section of one of the Vedas chanted today is to hear a link extending back many generations.

The *Atharva Veda* is the first Indic text to mention iron, leading some scholars to place its inception at no later than the twelfth to tenth century BCE to correspond with India's Iron Age, although it could be a more recent text. Nineteenth-century Western scholars posit that it was first placed into written form around 200 BCE, nearly three hundred years after the technology of writing was introduced to India. The written tradition was considered inferior to its precisely memorized oral recitation, a practice that continues into the present.[11] All Vedas were recited privately and only in the company of other Brahmins until the rise of the Brahmo Samaj, a nineteenth-century Bengali movement that sought to make the Vedas more accessible. The Vedas were first translated by Jesuits into Latin, by Goethe into German, and through the work of Max Mueller and others into English. They helped inspire the New England Transcendentalist movement, and the early Theosophists, who in turn inspired Mahatma Gandhi.

The *Atharva Veda* was translated into English a number of times at the end of the nineteenth century by the premier scholars of the day, beginning with William Dwight Whitney in 1855–56, Ralph T. Griffith in 1895–96, and Maurice Bloomfield in 1897. The Orientalist biases of the period classified the text as lower than the other Vedas. It was described as filled with magical formulas and as something both simplistic and superstitious that catered to the "common" people in comparison to the more lofty philosophical ideas found in the *Ṛg Veda*. In 1965, Abinash Chandra Bose published *Hymns from the Vedas* in part to reintroduce these texts to Western readers as something more than historical poetry, as part of India's vital, living tradition both theologically and ethically. He included translations of various hymns from all four texts and a full translation of the Earth Verses, the *Pṛthivī Sūkta*.

The *Pṛthivī Sūkta* is poetic, mystical, and practical. It contains hymns devoted to medicinal plants, to interhuman relationships, and to Mother Earth. It celebrates the *dharma* of nature. *Dharma* connotes a range of meanings, including law, righteousness, and ethics. In short, all human activities that seek to hold the world together are dharma. By seeking a deep connection with nature, one finds an emotional foundation for taking correct action to protect the earth.

The earliest of India's texts, the *Ṛg Veda,* composed more than 3,500 years ago, celebrates Agni as the god of heat and light, Indra as the deity of the thunderstorm who releases the waters of each year's monsoons, and Soma, the creator of a special herbal elixir. The *Ṛg Veda* also extols Dyaus, the Lord of the heavens (referred to by the Greeks later as Zeus), and Pṛthivī, the goddess of the earth. The *Atharva Veda* proclaims that all works and endeavors rely upon the earth, and that medicines arise from the earth. It praises Mother Earth in various ways, stating that "on her body food is grown everywhere and on her the farmer toils . . . the earth is home to cows, horses and birds . . . sacred are your hills, snowy mountains and deep forests. . . . You are the world for us and we are your children."[12] Without the beneficence of the earth, all would perish.

The section that follows presents verses from the *Pṛthivī Sūkta* on the earth, with commentary relating to how this text might be seen in relation to select examples of contemporary environmentalism in India. In subsequent chapters, passages from this same text will be shared in relation to the other elements.[13]

Truth, strength, artistry, ferocity, dedication, fervor, effulgence,
and sacrifice are the attributes among human beings that
sustain the Earth.
Drawing upon Mother Earth's feminine power,

> these attributes have been and continue to be all that will be with us.
> May the world Mother provide us with a wide and limitless domain for our livelihood.

This opening verse applauds the feminine powers of creativity and all that is associated with the creative process. Beginning with the quality of truth, the author extols the benefits that accrue in a person that respects and sustains the earth. Such action gives one strength, a strong aesthetic sense, and a tenacity of purpose. The notion of dedicating oneself to a noble, selfless cause generates a warmth and glow. Sacrifice, in this context, does not entail giving up, but of taking on greater responsibility for the greater good.

As we observe environmentalists who are active in protecting the world, they often display these qualities. M. C. Mehta, founder and director of EcoAshram near Rishikesh in northern India, has dedicated years of his life and professional efforts to several noble causes. Aware of the deleterious effects of air pollution on the Taj Mahal, he successfully sued to create a reduced emissions area around the great monument. For several years now, only electrical vehicles are allowed within about a half mile of the Taj. Several polluting factories have been relocated at a greater distance and thankfully the disintegration of the marble has been significantly reduced. Mehta's persistence prevailed.

Another instance of Mehta's success can be found in the streets of Delhi. By the mid-1990s, the air quality in India's capital had become so degraded that many people took to wearing masks for simple tasks around town. The cause of this pollution was a huge fleet of unregulated vehicles that relied upon a very dirty mix of gasoline and kerosene. After seventeen years since the initial suit was filed with India's Supreme Court, a new law went into effect on April 1, 2001. All public transport vehicles, including motorized rickshaws, taxis, and buses converted to compressed natural gas (CNG) for their fuel. Around the same time, the government enacted stricter emissions standards for private vehicles, which had been proliferating dramatically. However, in the intervening years, the proliferation of private vehicles in Delhi has brought progress in the clean air movement to a stalemate. New Delhi suffers from the worst air pollution in the world. There is still work to be done!

The text continues with praise for the many forms and gifts of the earth:

> The Earth is adorned with many hills, plains and slopes.
> She bears plants with medicinal properties.

May no person oppress her;
and may she spread prosperity for us all around.

The Earth expresses herself in various terrains, from flat to rolling to steep. To contemplate the contours of earth indicates an intimacy. Each reader or listener to this text can visualize her home environment, whether the Doon Valley nestled beneath the Himalayas, or the Genesee Valley shaped by post–Ice Age glacial retreat or the heights of the Sierras or Alps.

Knowing the healing secrets of plants can be seen as a gift from the Earth to her human denizens. Even today, researchers are learning of cures arising from remote forest lands such as the jungles of Madagascar, where the Rosy Periwinkle yielded a remarkable cure for childhood leukemia. Just a few years ago, a diagnosis of leukemia presaged the death of a child. Now, thanks to a willingness to investigate the forests of the world's fourth-largest island, recovery is almost certain. Scientists associated with the Institute for the Conservation of Tropical Environments at Stony Brook University are working with village healers in Madagascar to learn of other remedies, including a potential medicine to treat specific forms of sarcoma.

To the Earth belong all the four directions of space.
On her body, food is grown everywhere and on her the farmer toils.
She sustains all kinds of living-beings.
May the Land replenish us in plenty with cattle and food.

In traditional cultures, the four directions take on particular significance. In India, the East not only indicates the place of the rising sun, it also brings people to the shores of the Bay of Bengal, which receives the sacred waters of the Ganges River. The South of India, with its abundant monsoons, expanses of rice paddies, and groves of coconuts, carries stories of such great importance, including the story of Rāvaṇa who captured Sītā and took her to Sri Lanka, of Hanuman who spied on Rāvaṇa and helped raise an army of monkeys to assist in her rescue, and Rāma who came and freed her. At the very South of India lies Vivekananda Rock, a small island beyond Kanya Kumari to which Swami Vivekananda swam, having walked the entire length of India. He meditated and held vigil there, finally deciding to accept the invitation to travel to America and speak at the Parliament of the World's Religions in 1893, an event that changed the religious history of the world. The West, the direction of the sunset, saw great maritime trade, receiving ships from China and Arabia and eventually Portugal, France, and Britain. The Western port city of Mumbai boasts the world's most productive film industry, and the Northwest of India abounds with cultural and religious pluralism, serving as home to Vaiṣṇavas, Śaivas, Jainas, Sikhs, and Muslims in abundance.

For India, food constitutes life. With famine as the catalyst that inspired Gandhi's nonviolent campaign to insist that the British quit India, and with the memory of food shortages in the 1950s still fresh in the minds of many, scientific ingenuity has been employed to guarantee a seven-year surplus of grains and other foodstuffs. Cattle, rather than being seen as primarily a source for meat, are used in India for a total of five gifts: dung is burned for fuel, urine harvested for its ammonia and used as a cleanser, milk helps nourish more than a billion Indian souls, the hide of a departed cow yields sandals and shoes, and certain groups, even within the Hindu tradition, consume beef when the cow expires.

> 11. O Earth!
> Sacred are your hills, snowy mountains, and deep forests.
> The [soil] of your Land is brown, black, and red.
> Earth, you are protected by Indra.
> May I stand on the Earth unconquered, unharmed, uncrushed.
> May you be fertile, arable, and sustainer of all.

This verse gives a sense of the varieties of Earth's forms and the diversity of her soils. People seek protection on the earth, and implore the Earth to be fruitful.

> 16. O Mother Earth!
> You are the world for us and we are your children.
> Empower us to speak in one accord,
> steer us to live in peace and harmony,
> and guide us in our behavior
> so that we have cordial and gracious relationships with all other people.

This verse calls for peace rooted in an understanding of shared humanity. The precept of nonviolence (*ahiṃsā*) suggests that humans have the capacity to gain self-control over behaviors that otherwise could lead to confrontation and violence. The notion of being "guided in our behavior" as offspring of the same mother indicates a feeling of fellowship and solidarity arising from recognition of shared origin.

18. You are great.
Ruled by your own natural forces,
your movements are swift and astonishing.
You are forever protected by the great strength of Indra.
Dazzling like bright gold, may we get illumined by the Land,
and may no one hate us.

As a text within the larger corpus of Vedic literature, the *Pṛthivī Sūkta* resides within the narrative frame and philosophical methodology of the *Ṛg Veda*. Building on earlier insights of such illustrious scholars as Norman Brown, Antonio deNicolas has provided a fourfold analysis of the *Ṛg Veda*[14] that can be readily recognized in the *Pṛthivī Sūkta*. According to deNicolas, the overall narrative of the Vedas takes place in the context of a cosmic, meteorological struggle. Each year, India suffers withering heat with no rainfall, eagerly anticipating the arrival of the monsoon. The dry period, like the dry flaming breath of a dragon, takes the name Vṛtra, a therianthropic or animal form that embodies and encapsulates this difficult time. Indra ends the dry period by hurling thunderbolts, dismembering the dragon and releasing life-giving waters. Indra, like Hercules and Thor in parallel mythologies, casts aside the dragon and allows the rains to fall. Once Indra has done this work, order emerges from the preceding chaos. From the merely possible, Indra creates structure. Within this structure, humans then create sacrifice, inviting different gods and goddesses to bring a wide variety of boons and gifts, including wisdom, wealth, and happiness. The array of human desires results in an abundance of deities: the goddess Sarasvatī brings wisdom; Lakṣmī, wealth; Ganeśa, happiness. Through dedication to one or more of these symbolic powers, humans seek to attain a sense of fulfillment aptly expressed with the Sanskrit term *ṛta*. This indicates a culmination of effort exerted over a long time and brings completion through human creative effort. The *Pṛthivī Sūkta* follows this pattern of invoking the deity and celebrating her greatness. By moving the world from the unknown and barren domain (*asat*) into a productive agricultural cycle with reasonable societal norms (*sat*), Indra allows for sacrifice (*yajña*) that culminates in a vision of the world at its very best, an artistic expression of harmony and completion (*ṛta*).

22. Oblations and sacrifices are duly performed by the Gods of the Land.
The human race dwells on the Land, receiving the life-sustaining nourishment.
May the Land grant us the foundational breath of life.
May the Earth give us longevity.

The earth as mother receives offerings and bestows blessings. Food, physical abilities, long life, and wealth all arise from and depend upon the earth. The temples in which sacrifices are offered become the locale at which the power of the earth is honored. Many Hindu temples include a shrine to the earth goddess, Bhū Devī. Jain temples often include a shrine to the earth god, Bhū Deviya. Buddhist sculptures include an oft-repeated image of Siddhartha Gautama touching and invoking Mother Earth as his sole witness during the night of his awakening and transformation into the Buddha. In Thailand, one finds abundant images of the Mother Goddess coming to the rescue of the Buddha by gathering the waters into her hair and then setting its power free by squeezing her tresses, effectively drowning the forces of darkness represented by Māra.

> 23. O Mother Earth!
> Instill in me with abundance that fragrance which emanates
> from you
> and from your herbs and other vegetation, as well as waters.
> This fragrance is sought by all celestial beings.
> May there be no hatred against us.

The relationship between agriculture and the earth, as well as the relationship between earth and fragrance, can be found in this verse. Additionally, the association between the gods and fragrance is made explicit. The gods are known as Gandharvas and the goddesses as Gandharvis, beings who subsist and receive pleasure not from fleshy contact but by the particles of earth carried on the wind that hold sufficient power to satiate hunger and erotic desires. Gandhārī, the wife of Dhṛtarāṣṭra, who renounces her sight to honor her blind husband, and Gandhi, the champion of India's independence from British colonial rule, both hold names rooted in this important sense.

> 24. O Mother Earth!
> May that perfume come to us in abundance,
> the perfume that is in the lotus,
> the fragrance worn by gods when the sun marries the dawn.
> May there be no hatred against us.

This verse identifies the quality of freshness found in the air in the early morning.

> 25. The fragrance that you have granted to men and women
> and which is also present in horses, deer, and elephants,

shines like radiance in maidens throughout the Land.
May that radiance come to us and may there be no hatred
against us.

In traditional times, the musk of animals would be known to every farmer and every city dweller who relied upon horses for transport. Likewise, the scent of deer and elephants would be part of everyday life in India, though elephants would be known only through circuses and zoos outside of India and Africa. Feeling solidarity with all beings who carry scent, including our own species, can bring a sense of common good will.

26. I pay homage to the Earth.
This Land holds firmly together
goldmines, rocks, stones, and even dust.

This verse reminds the reader of the many forms of earth. In the western deserts of both India and the United States, one sees the magnificence of naked outcroppings of rocks and minerals, particularly in places such as the Grand Canyon and Death Valley, where the varieties of color and the immensity of the formations evoke awe. Josiah Whitney, after whom Mt. Whitney, the tallest mountain in the lower forty-eight states, is named, traveled often to India and, while exploring the Grand Canyon, named the formations viewed from above after the Hindu gods Brahmā and Viṣṇu and Śiva.

27. We venerate Mother Earth,
the sustainer and preserver of forests, vegetation,
and all things that are held together firmly.
She is the source of a stable environment.

The forest even today in India remains an important resource. Some 17 percent of the forest cover of India is under some form of protection. The Chipko Movement has inspired many similar actions to protect watersheds and rivers against the effects of deforestation. Afforestation movements have found success in such places as Mount Arunachala, as will be described in the chapter of this book on fire.

28. If we are standing, sitting, or walking,
or whether we run, and even if we start with the right or left
foot,
may we never cause pain and misery to others in this Land.

This verse invokes the human body in relationship to the earth. The human person can run, walk, sit, or stand. Regardless, this presence always relies upon and in some cases lies upon the earth. By remembering her endless and uncomplaining support, one can cultivate a sense of humility and a desire to inflict no harm.

> 29. I invoke you O Mother Earth!
> You give shelter to all seekers of truth.
> You provide us the strength-giving food and ghee.
> You give us nutrition.
> You are the source of all creative energy.
> Render us safe on this Land.

The Upaniṣads proclaim Brahman Annam, food is god. By acknowledging utter human reliance on earth for all food, this verse expresses deep appreciation for both sustenance and the potential for creativity.

> 35. May the crop grow faster when we plow and seed the land.
> But, while doing it, may we never harm your vital parts.

The earth, when cultivated, gives crops for food. Land not well managed, however, will begin to break down. Repeated monocropping can result in loss of nutrients to the soil. Clear cutting of forests can cause desertification. Mismanagement in the American heartland produced the Dust Bowl of the 1930s. The devastation of the Malagasy rainforest has decimated countless species of plants and animals. Good management ensures a stable agricultural system. Disrespect for the earth invites famine.

> 36. May each part of the cycle of seasons, O Land,
> the summer, the rains, the autumn, the winter, and the spring,
> which constitute a year,
> pour happiness on us here on Earth.

The rhythm of the seasons in India require the repeated return of the monsoon. If the monsoon fails, disaster can follow.

> 37. This earth who is a purifier,
> who carries the fires within her waters;
> who moves like a serpent;
> who has chosen Indra as her companion rather than Vṛtra;

and who has driven away the enemies of Gods,
may that one make us strong and mighty.

This complex verse also alludes to the climatic cycle as well as to Indra's struggle to renew order within the world through battles with the dragon of uncertainty. Heat within the water ensures rain-laden clouds. The waters rise up from the ocean to create serpent-like clouds, resembling the dragon. Indra comes forth with his thunderbolt to break open the dragon cloud and deliver the life-giving rains of the monsoon.

40. May the Land fulfill our desire for riches.
May Providence assist us!
May Indra lead us!

Without Indra, the thunderstorms fail; without the rains, life cannot flourish; riches cannot be gathered.

42. We pay homage to that Land
that is the source of all grains: rice, barley and wheat.
The five races of human beings live here.
Here the rains make her fertile.

The well-being of human persons relies utterly upon the agricultural cycle. The diversity of grains, rice, barley, and wheat, demonstrate the author's familiarity with the different regions of India. Vandana Shiva has championed barley and millet as the overlooked grains that hold great potential for withstanding the stresses of climate change due to their hardiness. This verse also alludes to ethnic diversity. India sits at the crossroads of many civilizations. Africans have long lived in India; the people of the northeast carry distinctly East Asian features; the central Asians to the north hold strong physical resemblance to the people indigenous to the Americas; in the northwest, strongly Caucasian features can be seen; in the south, the Dravidians exhibit yet another set of distinct physical attributes.

43. May the Lord of Creation [Prajāpati]
grant upon this Earth continued splendor and exquisiteness
unto her in all regions for our enjoyment.
Cities were built here by the gods
and fields were cultivated.
She is the universal mother of them all.

This verse affirms the importance of village and urban life in India. As Anthony Cerulli has noted, a robust, healthy life requires a balance between "outward focused action (*pravṛtti*) and inward focused action (*nivṛtti*)."[15] The health of the human person requires time for inward devotion as well as engagement in the activities of the world. This verse celebrates enjoyment and work.

> 44. May the Goddess Earth,
> the bearer of many treasures like gold, gems and other riches
> that are hidden in her secret places,
> be generous and bountiful to us,
> and bestow upon us her special favors.

Continuing with the theme of celebration, this verse praises the precious stones and metals that can be found in the earth.

> 45. O Mother Earth!
> You care for the people who belong to different races,
> practice various religious and spiritual beliefs,
> and speak different languages.
> Like the wish fulfilling cow,
> may you bless us all in thousand-fold manner.
> Please do not become outraged by our destructive tendencies.

Diana Eck's study of the geography of India affirms the pluralist nature of Indian cultures, wherein one finds more than two hundred languages,[16] large Sanskrit narratives that praise gods and goddesses known throughout the subcontinent and beyond, local deities, diverse food practices, and, as this verse states, "various religious and spiritual beliefs." Multiplicities abound on Mother Earth. This verse makes reference to the bounteous cow with her many gifts as well as to the number *one thousand,* indicating great plenty. It also acknowledges the "destructive tendencies" that define and plague human experience and capacity.

> 48. The Earth which bears both the good and wicked
> permits wild animals such as boar and deer, to move freely around.
> 49. O Mother Earth!
> Although various wild animals
> such as the lion, the tiger, the wolf, the jackal, the deer, and others

are nurtured in your forests,
keep all menacing animals away from harming us.

The earth welcomes all manner of goodness as well as darkness. By listing various forms of animal life, the text acknowledges a variety of large animal species, asking that those who might prey upon humans be kept away.

52. May the Mother Earth graciously grant us
a suitable abode where the bright light and darkness are
recognizable,
where the day and the night can be distinguished in this Land,
and where rains make the land richer and fertile.

Returning from fear and danger, the text turns to praise and delight, rejoicing in the simple joy of the night and the day and the coming of the monsoon.

53. May I be blessed with power and energy
derived from heaven, earth, and space.
May I draw inspiration from the fire, the sun, the waters, and
the gods
so that I may act with wisdom.

This verse hails the natural world as the source of wisdom, a sentiment echoed later in the Upaniṣads.

54. People, behold!
I am the accomplisher of great deeds.
I am victorious everywhere, the ruler of all.
May I have the strength to subjugate those who poison our Land.

From this connection, one can gain the power to prevail over travail. The next three verses pay obeisance to the four directions, to the eternality of the earth, to the various enterprises and endeavors undertaken on the land. The earth is asked to destroy anyone who commits acts of disrespect toward her.

55. When requested by gods, O Goddess,
you revealed your grandeur and charm.
Thereafter, the four geographical directions were evidently
established.
O Earth! May your timeless magnitude continue to be with us.

56. Irrespective of the place and region in this Land,
whether in a rural area, in the woods,
in the battleground, or in a public place,
may we always sing your praises.
57. O Mother Earth!
You are the protector and the keeper of the Creation.
You are the sustainer of forests and vegetation.
Since you came into being, you have been the leader of all.
If anyone tries to harm you,
destroy them with the same ease as when a horse shakes off the dust on it.

Protection from harm remains a constant concern. One gets a sense of the imminence of impending tragedy, whether a monsoon that is too strong, monsoon that fails, pestilence, disease, the threat of being killed by wild animals, and so many other dangers.

58. Give us the strength so whatever I speak is pleasant like honey.
Whatever I see, my glances are met with respectful return from others.
May I have the ability of swiftness and strength so that I am able to vanquish those who exploit you.

Just as the writer asks for protection from Mother Earth, so in turn this verse puts forth a vow to return the favor. Harmful practices might include overuse of resources or fouling the water or air.

59. O Mother Earth!
May you bless us with milk that flows from your full breasts.
Bless us with other nourishments from your Land
including grain, agricultural produce,
as well as with fragrance.
Grant us peace, tranquility,
[clean] fragrant air, and other worldly riches.

From the Land arise all riches. With sufficient and hopefully abundant food, society can be made stable, bringing peace and tranquility.

61. O Primeval Mother!
You are the wish fulfilling cow.

You are borderless.
You are the world-mother of all beings.
You are the provider of all things in life.
Let Brahmā [Prajāpati], the first among all born,
replenish any deficiency you might have.

This verse addresses Mother Earth as if she were an older sister, suggesting that she make an appeal to the creator of all things if she feels in any way deficient.

62. O Mother Earth!
May all those who dwell upon you
be free from diseases, especially from Yakṣmā [tuberculosis],
and may they all flourish.
Be watchful over them, and grant them a long life,
so that they continue to be healthy, and always offer you their tributes.

Tuberculosis looms large in the psyche of the Vedic sages. As part of the *Atharva Veda*, this verse makes a connection with the more medical portions of the larger text. The sixth story of the *Yogavāsiṣṭha* tells the tale of a "gluttonous cannibal woman named Karkaṭī" who transforms herself into the form the size of a needle and becomes known as Viṣucikā, the goddess of cholera."[17] The local king tames her through his wisdom, making his kingdom safe for the righteous; she is said to have fed only on the bodies of criminals.

63. O Land!
With your gracious kindness and intellect,
bless us with prosperity and fortune,
so that we live in harmony with the powers of Heaven.
O All-knowing Mother, establish us in the most appropriate manner.

This final stanza takes the same versification as that found in the Gāyatrī Mantra. It also uses the verb *dhī*, which in the Gāyatrī is used to express the sentiment "may we reflect upon" and here is used to ask that the vision of Mother Earth result in stability, intelligence, and wealth.

This early example of Vedic literature conveys a sense of the majesty of the earth, referring to her with two primary words: Pṛthivī, rendered here as Earth and Bhū, translated here as Land. Temples to the latter goddess abound throughout India. Through these verses one gets a sense of the primacy of the earth as an all-pervading presence and ground, in both senses of the word. Whereas the Buddhist literature to be explicated below, particularly the *Dhātu Vibhaṅga*, emphasizes nonidentity with the earth and the other elements, the *Pṛthivī Sūkta* celebrates her abundant fullness.

Buddhism: The Dhātu Vibhaṅga, the Mahārāhulovāda Sutta, and the Visuddhimagga

Buddhism arose in robust conversation with the philosophical traditions active in northeast India 2,500 years ago, including Brahmanism and Jainism. Both Buddhism and its earlier cousin faith Jainism critiqued Vedic ritualism as practiced by the Brahmins. A widespread form of Jaina asceticism was taught by the Buddha's contemporary, Vardhamāna Mahāvīra, also known as the Jina. Both the Buddha and the Jina criticized Vedic sacrifices that entailed the taking of animal life. The Buddha developed a modified form of asceticism, less rigorous in some ways than Jaina monasticism. All three systems patterned their worldview on what has been called proto-Sāṃkhya, an assessment on how to find happiness and freedom by understanding and purifying one's emplacement within the physical and psychological worlds. Hinduism, Buddhism, and Jainism share in common the acknowledgment that human happiness relies upon a healthy mental relationship with the material world. To achieve this happiness, one must understand the physical elements as well as the emotions in order to live an ethical life free from troubles.

The Pāli Canon, the foundational text for all schools of Buddhism, includes as its third basket an exposition of all the aspects of physical and mental reality known as the Abhidharma. Two Suttas of the Buddha in the Majjhima Nikāya include detailed instructions for progressive meditation on the five elements: the *Dhātu Vibhaṅga* or the Exposition of the Elements (MN140) and the *Mahārāhulovāda Sutta*, the Greater Discourse of Advice to Rāhula (MN 62). In the *Dhātu Vibhaṅga*, the Buddha requests to take shelter in a shed owned by a potter in Rajagaha/Ragagṛha. The potter, named Bhaggava, agrees, but notes that someone is already staying there. The Buddha introduces himself to Pukkusati who makes space for him and they spend the night in meditation. In the morning, the Buddha asks Pukkusati where he learned to meditate and in reply Pukkusati says that he had learned this technique from followers of the Buddha, whom he one day hoped to meet. Without letting on his true identity, the Buddha provided Pukkusati instruction in the sequential meditation on the five elements, beginning with earth and ending with space. At the conclusion of the tutorial, it dawned upon Pukkusati that he had been in the presence of the great master. He begged to be given initiation as a monk. The Buddha asked him to obtain proper robes and a begging bowl. While in search of these items, Pukkusati was killed by a runaway cow. When asked by his followers what happened to Pukkusati after he died, the Buddha replied: "Monks, the clansman Pukkusati was wise. He practiced the Dhamma in accordance with the Dhamma and did not pester me with issues related to the Dhamma. With the destruction of the first five fetters, he has arisen spontaneously [in the Pure Abodes], there to be totally unbound, never again to return from that world."[18] Pukkusati was one of the five hundred arhats who achieved freedom during the lifetime of the Buddha, and did so immediately upon learning the elemental meditations.

The Buddha explained to Pukkusati that the human person has six faculties: smell, taste, seeing, touching, hearing, and thinking. These six connect through the sense organs and the mind with earth, water, fire, air, and space. The Buddha explained the internal and external forms of each property, and urged Pukkusati to not identify with them, freeing himself from all attachment. The ultimate proclamation, "No Self, No Doer, No Owner" *(nāhaṃ, nāsti, na me)* signals the Arhat state for each successful meditator. This phrase also marks the culmination of the *Sāṃkhya Kārikā*, indicating that one has reached the freedom of *kevala*.

Here are the words of the Buddha in regard to understanding the earth property as translated by Thanissaro Bhikkhu:

> These are the six properties: the earth property, the liquid property, the fire property, the wind property, the space property, the consciousness property. "And what is the earth property? The earth property can be either internal or external. What is the internal earth property? Anything internal, within oneself, that's hard, solid, & sustained [by craving]: head hairs, body hairs, nails, teeth, skin, flesh, tendons, bones, bone marrow, kidneys, heart, liver, membranes, spleen, lungs, large intestines, small intestines, contents of the stomach, feces, or anything else internal, within oneself, that's hard, solid, and sustained: This is called the internal earth property. Now both the internal earth property and the external earth property are simply earth property. And that should be seen as it actually is present with right discernment: "This is not mine, this is not me, this is not my self." When one sees it thus as it actually is present with right discernment, one becomes disenchanted with the earth property and makes the earth property fade from the mind.

This process repeats for each element as we will see in successive chapters, signaling that this process for meditation was both effective and well known, though it does not seem to reappear in Buddhist literature for several hundred years.

The identical instructions appear in the *Mahārāhulovāda Sutta* when the Buddha instructs his own son, Rāhula, who had become a monk. However, the Buddha adds special encouragement regarding facility in these meditations, noting that this helps to stabilize and protect the mind:

> Rāhula, develop meditation that is like the earth; for when you develop meditation that is like the earth, arisen agreeable and disagreeable contacts will not invade your mind and remain.[19]

Although the element itself has been deemed empty of abiding qualities, this exercise produces a sense of mastery over any attachment that might arise in regard to the element or things made of the element earth.

The *Visuddhimagga* (ca. 430 CE) provides a comprehensive guide to Buddhist ethical practices and meditation techniques. The author Buddhaghosa (ca. 370 to 450 CE) was born near Bodhgaya, traveled south to Kañcipuram, the site of the earth temple described at the start of this chapter, and later moved to Sri Lanka. He was said to have been a Brahmin who converted to Buddhism. According to one account, he recited Patañjali, which could be a reference to either the grammarian or the philosopher; in another, he recited a "Vedic text." He then discussed the content of Patañjali's work with a Buddhist monk who challenged him to become a monk and learn Buddhism, which he did.[20]

Though most contemporary Buddhist traditions do not teach the process of meditating on the elements, this practice is emphasized in the *Visuddhimagga*. The *Visuddhimagga*, whose title may be translated as "The Path of Purification," provides instructions for the practice of forty forms of meditation. Unlike the earlier *Satipatthana*, which progresses from body awareness to breath awareness to mind awareness to the central teachings of Buddhist dharma including the Brahma Vihāra (see list below), the *Visuddhimagga* outlines a meditation that begins with externals and moves toward inner awareness. It also highlights the importance of loving kindness toward the community of monks and mindfulness of death.[21] After describing the six kinds of temperament (greedy, hating, deluded, faithful, intelligent, and speculative),[22] Buddhaghosa describes the proper places for each personality type to take up the practice of concentration. For instance, the greedy person would concentrate best in very difficult conditions, "ugly and unsightly,"[23] while the speculative person would find a cave to be most conducive.

The text lists the forty possible meditation subjects in seven groupings. The first four of the first set, plus the tenth, are of particular interest for this study. The list of forty is:

1. Ten *kasiṇas* (elements and colors delineated below)
2. Ten kinds of foulness (bloated, livid, festering, cut up, gnawed, scattered, hacked, bleeding, worm-infested, bare skeleton)
3. Ten recollections (Buddha, Dharma, Saṅgha, virtue, generosity, deities, and mindfulness of death, body, breathing, and peace)
4. Four divine abidings (Brahma Vihāra: Mettā, Karuṇā, Muditā, Upekkhā)
5. Four immaterial states (boundless space, boundless consciousness, nothingness, neither perception nor non-perception)
6. One perception
7. One defining[24]

Without going into the details of each, it is noteworthy to mention that the final, fortieth category, defining, brings one back to the first four of the first group, the four elements, underscoring the theme of this study. Meditation on the four elements is said to be appropriate for people of all temperaments,[25] though the defining of the four elements, the fortieth meditation subject, is said to be suitable only for one of intelligent temperament.

For the early Buddhists, and within certain forms of Yoga to be described below, the observance of the elements, referred to by Buddhaghosa as the *kasiṇas,* held a key place within the training and cultivation of consciousness. Meditation on the earth, water, fire, air, and space served several functions. It reminded the practitioner of the commonality of elements: all persons and all things are composed of these essential components. A particular configuration, when seen in its glorious individuality, might seem appealing. It might become an object of desire or lust, whether it be an attractive house or car or even body. But when seen from the perspective of its sharing its basic composition with all other entities in the universe, it might be viewed with a bit more reserve, with a bit more care. When a perception of common origin colors one's perspective on, or perception of, things in the world, then one is less likely to be overcome by infatuation or attachment.

In the traditional Buddhist and Yogic way of meditating or concentrating on the elements, the practitioner fashions in succession a series of supports for honing in on the element under contemplation. In the case of the earth, the meditator is advised to gather together a lump of " 'pure dawn-colored clay,' somewhere in size between a saucer and bushel in diameter, and shape it into the form of an even disk."[26] One then gazes at the earth mound for an extended period of time, reciting various epithets for the earth: *pathavī/pṛthivī,* an ancient term used to refer to the Earth goddess; *mahī,* the Great One; *medina,* the Friendly One, *bhūmi,* the Ground, *vasudhā,* the Provider of Wealth; and *vasudharā,* the Bearer of Wealth.[27] In this process of concentration, the body is held stable in a meditative pose; the sense of sight is restricted to the mound of earth; the mind is held in check by repeating various terms associated with earth. After repeated practice with eyes open, one then masters the ability to visualize the earth *kasiṇa* with eyes closed. At this point, the practitioner enters into the "production phase" and is able to recreate this meditation regardless of place or circumstance. Restriction of the external senses leads to the strengthening of inner resolve and the ability to overcome such obstacles as distraction and attachment. Patañjali describes the effects of meditation as follows: "The *saṃskāra* born of it restricts other *saṃskāras.*"[28]

Detailed descriptions for this practice begin with advice for finding a suitable monastic residence. Once the monk takes up residence there, he or she creates a disk either the size of a bushel (*suppa*) or saucer (*sarava*).[29] This disk is to be crafted from "clay like that in the stream of the Ganga, which is the colour of the dawn."[30] It is to be constructed in a screened place away from public view or under "an overhanging rock or in a leaf hut," "either portable or as a fixture." To create a portable *kasiṇa,* one smears the clay onto rags or leather or onto four sticks; a fixed one will be created on top of stakes pounded into the ground. In either case, a stone trowel is used to "make it as smooth as the surface of a drum."[31] The text goes on to say that the practitioner should take a seat approximately thirty inches away so that it comes into sufficient focus without revealing too much detail, and so that one does not need to bend the neck to gaze upon it. The seat should be sufficiently raised (approximately ten to twenty inches) to prevent the knees from aching.

The meditator then gives mental homage to the three jewels of Buddha, Dhamma, and Sangha and begins to fix the gaze upon the circle of dried yellowish clay. The eyes are not to be opened too wide, as they "get fatigued and the disk becomes too obvious" nor too little, as the "disk is not obvious enough" and the "mind becomes drowsy."[32] The ideal is to gaze lightly, as if looking at one's image in a mirror. The mind is not to dwell on the color of the clay, but to review various names that indicate the earth, including "earth (*pathavi/pṛthivī*), Great One (*mahi*), Friendly One (*medini*), ground (*bhūmi*), the Provider of Wealth (*vasudhā*)," and so forth.[33] By gazing and invoking these words "a hundred times, a thousand times" one develops "the learning sign," which indicates that one can recreate the visualization of the *kasiṇa* whether the eyes are opened or closed. The monk is then urged to go back into private space and "go on developing it there . . . striking at it with thought and applied thought."[34]

The benefit of this concentration is that it serves to reduce hindrances in the mind: "[T]he hindrances eventually become suppressed, the defilements subside, the mind becomes concentrated with access concentration, and the counterpart sign arises." This latter phenomenon is described as a purified visualization of the *kasiṇa,* appearing "like a looking-glass disk drawn from its case, like a mother-of-pearl dish well washed, like the moon's disk coming from behind a cloud, like cranes against a thunder cloud" but with "neither colour nor shape."[35]

In the first Jhāna or mind-state cultivated by concentration on the Earth Kasiṇa, one experiences applied thought and sustained thought leading to "happiness, bliss, and unification of mind."[36] In the second Jhāna, one abandons applied and sustained thought, automatically dwelling in happiness, bliss, and unification of mind. In the third Jhāna, one abandons happiness, replacing it with equanimity. In the fourth Jhāna, one moves beyond the dualities of pleasure/pain, joy/grief that adhere to bliss. This fourth is characterized as "purity of mindfulness due to equanimity."[37] The four Jhānas, though distinct from one another, all include the unification of mind.

This process is then followed in succession by the water, fire, air, and space *kasiṇas,* as will be described in successive chapters. When each of these is cultivated, benefits are said to accrue: "The hindrances eventually become suppressed, the defilements subside, and the mind becomes concentrated."[38] This power wears away conventional constructs of the mind that see things in their particularity rather than in their shared essence.

This practice was documented by the early scholars of Buddhism T. W. Rhys Davids (1843–1922) and Caroline Augusta Foley Rhys Davids (1857–1942) and F. L. Woodward (1871–1952). T. W. Rhys Davids transcribed and published a manuscript text called the *Yogāvacara* in 1896. It was the first such work rendered into Roman script from the Sinhalese. C. A. F. Rhys Davids wrote the introduction to Woodward's translation, which was published in 1916. The translator renders the word *kasiṇa* as "device" and provides little more than a list: earth, water, fire, air, their aggregate, blue-green, yellow, crimson, white, space, light.[39] The Rhys Davids and Woodward speculate that the manual, which cites no author, might have been part of an attempt in eighteenth-century Sri Lanka (then Ceylon) to revitalize the Buddhism being practiced in Thailand (then Siam).

C. A. F. Rhys Davids likens the *kasiṇa* practice to a description of rapture by the Christian mystic Jakob Boehme (1575–1624) who describes "gazing at a surface of shining pewter" and then declaring "to behold the inward properties of all things in nature."[40] She states that the author of the *Yogāvacara* feels "a sense of keen interest or zest rising to transport, enthusiasm, rapture, as the presence of a part of the reality of things is unveiled."[41] She goes on to describe the mindfulness (her translation of *sati* or *smṛti*) as "pseudo-physical *localization* of ideas,"[42] a rather apt description of the concentration process.

Woodward, in his prefatory note to the translation, states that one of his informants in Ceylon, Doratiyāveye, who flourished in the year 1900, had been offered instruction in the Yogāvacara techniques by his guru but declined, protesting that they would free him from all possibility of rebirth, and that he wished to return as a bodhisattva to help others. Woodward goes on to write, "Be that as it may, the elder was content to teach the practice to one of his pupils who went mad and died. . . . There is no one, now, as far as I know, in Ceylon who either knows or practices these strenuous exercises."[43] This perhaps accounts for a very interesting response to a question that I posed to a contemporary teacher of mindfulness, Trudy Goodman. I had shared with her that these practices described in the *Visuddhimagga* were seemingly identical to those described in the *Gheraṇḍa Saṃhitā* that I had learned in Yoga training. She said they were considered too dangerous, and that the practice of mindfulness (*sati, smṛti*) being transmitted was restricted to the *Satipatthāna*, the canonical text, which emphasizes focus successively on body and breath, feelings, thoughts, and "dharma," which also includes reflection on all the constituents of reality, including the elements and the mental factors. When I asked Jack Kornfield if any contemporary Buddhist teachers include the *kasiṇa* concentrations as part of their teaching, he referred me to a book by Bodhipaksa (Graeme Stephen) titled *Living as a River: Finding Fearlessness in the Face of Change*,[44] which includes a chapter on each of the five elements, citing the *Dhātu Vibhaṅga* as quoted above, and giving examples from contemporary science in regard to each of the five elements.

In my own direct experience of cultivating the earth concentration, all sorts of material objects, from dishes to automobiles to electronic equipment, appear to be none other than variations on the same primal matter: different configurations and usages of Mother Earth. This perception helps to hold back the tendency to send the five senses outward (*prapañca*). A shift occurred wherein I no longer automatically saw worldly objects as inherently desirable, but came to see them in terms of their root origins. Upon reflection I came to see that the arising of objects cannot take place without the power of intentional awareness. Once seeing that an object depends radically upon the subject's own structures of mind, the sending forth of that mind to the object becomes optional. In this way, hindrances of karma can be reversed. The mind and its experience and relation to things in the objective world becomes purified.

Jainism: The Ācārāṅga Sūtra and the Jñānārṇava

The cosmology of the Jaina tradition also embraces the elements, but construes them in a markedly different manner. Vardhamāna Mahāvīra, the twenty-fourth and most recent Tīrthaṅkara or Great Teacher of this tradition, lived approximately 2,500 years ago, contemporary with the Buddha. Rather than lauding the power and beauty of the earth writ large, he examined it in minute detail, developing the foundation for a powerful indigenous biology. The earliest surviving text of Jainism, the *Ācārāṅga Sūtra*, recounts Mahāvīra's grand experiment, which yields the following premises regarding nature and the universe: life can be found in multiple forms, each charting its own course, energized by a life force (*jīva*) at its core and defined by the karmic particles that surround and constrict its innate energy, consciousness, and bliss. According to Jainism, even clods of dirt, drops of water, bursts of flame, and gusts of wind are alive in their specificity. Each possess the sense of touch. Each exerts its own will for a period of time before moving from one body to the next, perhaps from elemental form to microbial form to plant or animal or even human. This living universe is also an ethical universe. As we will see in the animal chapter, even animals can and do make ethical decisions that will determine future experience, life after life.

For Mahāvīra, this feeling universe moving toward compassion began with his careful observance of the natural world. "There are beings living in the earth, living in grass, living on leaves, living in wood, living in cowdung, living in dust-heaps"[45] that merit protection. Rather than gazing on the goods of the earth with greed, Mahāvīra exhorts his followers to develop an affectionate eye, even toward a well-formed tree: "These trees are noble, high and round, big; they have many branches, extended branches, they are very magnificent."[46] Likewise, monks and nuns are advised to praise vegetables with their speech: "[T]hey are grown up, strong, excellent; they have spread their seed, they are full of sap";[47] as well as food itself: "[I]t is excellent, it is well seasoned, it is most delicious, it is most agreeable."[48] With this attitude and approach of regarding the world born of the earth, a sense of compassion can arise. The hallmark of the Jain worldview may be summarized as follows: by developing sensitivity to the myriad beings within the world, the heart can incline toward protection rather than exploitation. By developing an attitude of care, one's own fettering karmas diminish, advancing one toward a state of moral and practical freedom.

Jainism has charted its own course since its inception, distinguishing itself from Buddhism by asserting the eternality of individual souls and from Hinduism's Advaita Vedānta by rejecting the existence of a singular unified consciousness. At the same time, it shared a common interest in technologies of worship and meditation, utilizing techniques common to all three traditions, including ritual worship (without animal sacrifice) and meditation, including visualization and recitation of mantra. Like the Buddhist and Yoga traditions, it incorporated elemental meditations into these practices, which find full expression in two texts: the *Jñānārṇava* of Subhacandra (ca. eleventh century), and the *Yogaśāstra* of Hemacandra (ca. 1150). Select verses from the former text are quoted below, most of which appear verbatim in the *Yogaśāstra*. The *Jñānārṇava*'s author was a prominent philosopher within the Digambara or Sky Clad group, while Hemacandra represents the Śvētāmbara or White Clad denomination, underscoring the universality of these meditation practices within Jaina communities.

The *Jñānārṇava* describes elemental meditations in two different chapters, and places the elements in two different sequences. Chapter 29 sets forth the four elements (earth, water, air, fire), four corresponding geometric forms (square, crescent, sphere, triangle), four colors (ochre, white, blue-black, yellow), and four mantras (*laṃ, vaṃ, yaṃ, raṃ*) to be performed. In chapter 37, the order is altered: earth, fire, wind, water, and space. Both diverge from the standard order found in Buddhism and in Hindu Yoga texts, which proceed from earth to water to fire to air to space.

> 17. This *maṇḍala* of the four elements
> is inconceivable and beyond characterization.
> Through the legendary great practice (Mahābhūta Dhāraṇā)
> the perception of this by oneself can occur.[49]

This stanza exhorts the reader to focus attention on the elements in such a way that one becomes rendered speechless, no longer able to conceptualize or characterize them as merely physical objects. In the poetic journey that follows in this chapter of the *Jñānārṇava*, earth is linked to color, geometry, and mantra, demonstrating the innate complexity of the "great practice."

18. The first element to be experienced
is the earth, followed by water.
From there one expands into the city of the wind,
all the way to the limits of the fire *maṇḍala*.

The order is similar to that found in the *Visuddhimagga* as indicated above and the *Markaṇḍeya Pūrāna* as described in the first chapter of this book. However, two profound differences must be noted. First, fire appears in the final position, moving air or wind to position three. Second, the fifth great element is not listed here, for reasons that will become clear as we move into the space chapter of this book.

19. (The earth) is to be internalized through the earth seed
mantra (*lam*).
Equal in splendor to melted gold,
approached through the mark of the lightning bolt,
this city carries everything on its square.

This verse communicates details about how to proceed with building the meditative experience. It requires the utterance of a mantra, in the case of earth, the mantra *laṃ*. One is to visualize a golden color when meditating upon the earth, as well as the marker of the lightning bolt and the geometric shape of a square.

Chapter 37 of the *Jñānārṇava* gives more explicit directions in terms of the technique and results of a slightly different meditative sequence. In this later section, the order of concentration on the elements is switched, with water rising to ascendancy as a culminating practice that cools the burning fires generated by the breathing practices that have eradicated karmas. Space enters the list, recognized as the container of the other four elements. One reconfigures the gaze upon the earth to visualize the earth as taking the shape of a lotus. The "stuff" of the earth becomes correlated with mountains seen in the distance at dusk. This meditation then promotes fires to burn, scorching the eight downward petals of the lotus that represent the eight Jaina karmas. The four negative karmas, to be purified and expelled through this practice, are karmas that (1) obstruct knowledge, (2) obstruct intuition, (3) obstruct energy, and (4) cause delusional thinking and action. The four remaining categories of karma, which are also ultimately left behind, are karmas that enable (5) feeling, (6) lifespan, (7) physique, and (8) social status. This fire that is used to incinerate the karmic petals leads to effortful breathing that frees the practitioners from all constraints. The visualization on water leads to a reflection on the presence of the liberated soul and great teacher Mahāvīra, seen externally on his Lion Throne as well as internally within one's own body. As will be seen in the chapter on Space, this final meditation exercise reconfigures the space of personal identity as well as allows one to enter into an experience of the Siddha Loka, the realm of freedom that hovers at the top of the Jaina cosmosphere.

The following verses invoke the earth variously as a mountain, the filaments of a lotus, the color of melted gold, and the murmuring of all sixteen seed syllables:

> 37. 2. Those who are well controlled (*samyamis*)
> and who are totally conscious overcome the snare of birth
> using the five concentrations on substances.
> These are to be known as explained below by the heroes.
> 3. (These substances) would be earth,
> then fire, breath, and eventually water,
> all contained within the form of space.
> These are then to be understood in steps.

The above two verses introduce the order of the elements and state that the practice of meditating upon them must be followed in sequence. The phrase uses the term *samyama,* a technical term from the *Yoga Sūtra* to describe adepts in Yoga who have mastered the triple practices of concentration, meditation, and *samādhi,* the last three limbs of Yoga through which one gains mastery over the elements, the senses, and the mind.

> 5. The Yogi should move his or her well-formed focus
> toward the middle of the thousand petaled lotus,
> bringing to mind its blazing immeasurable splendor,
> shining as brilliantly as melted gold.
> 6. Like filaments rising up in the lotus,
> and like the brilliant mountains
> that surround the earth,
> (these experiences) delight the bee-like mind.

The visualization of the lotus, accompanied with the color of molten gold, seems to perhaps evoke the color of the sunrise, with the petals perhaps representing the reach of sunbeams at the start of the day.

7. (While gazing at these mountains)
one should focus on the crown of the lotus
as the golden heavenly Mount (Meru),
emitting a web of yellow light,
tinging the horizon in reddish brown.

Continuing the sunrise theme, this particular verse reminds me of morning walks on the Westchester mesa, gazing east, where the rays of the risen sun illumine the San Gabriel, San Bernardino, and San Jacinto Mountains, creating a hue of reddish brown.

8. One should think of oneself
seated comfortably and tranquil
(high on a white throne)
similar to the autumnal moon.

This verse directs the focus away from the splendid external landscape, asking the meditator to see oneself in the special position of sitting upon a throne (according to the commentary) and assuming a mood of ease, comfort, and tranquility. If the "autumnal moon" refers to the equinox that occurs each September, then the full moon would be setting to the west while the sun rises in the east.

9. Marked with qualities of abstinence, patience, and discipline,
free from attraction and aversion,
one cuts off the flow of karma
at its very origin.

That meditative state brings a state of equipoise, a moment where the haunting thoughts of the past and the anxious anticipation of the future are held in abeyance. One dwells in a state of moral purity.

10. Then, using the practice of meditation
on the lotus in the *maṇḍala* of the navel,
one focuses on the beautiful
uplifted sixteen petals.

With the mind calmed, one is able to bring the focus within the body upon the navel, the source of sound at the base of the diaphragm. In this relaxed and balanced mode, one turns to the array of sounds that may be emitted from the body.

> 11. One should reflect upon the vibration
> of the great mantra at the crown of the lotus,
> its petals nested within one another
> as a glorious garland of (sixteen) syllables.
> (From the commentary: a, ā, i, ī, u, ū, ṛ, ṝ, ḷ, ḹ, e, ai, o, au, aṃ, aḥ)

The sequential uttering of the sixteen syllables lifts the energy from the lower part of the abdomen to the crown of the head,

> 12. Through the murmuring of the sixteen seed mantras
> comes a state of abeyance adorned with the emptying of sound.
> (This experience is like) the glowing of a pendulous moon at its fullest,
> its white face extending beauty (everywhere).

Like the classic Tantric image of the sun and moon flanking the minaret-like temple, this verse suggests that the chanting of mantra provides a moment of catharsis as beautiful as the full moon.

The luxuriant language from chapter 29 invites the reader to visualize the earth as suffused with a golden hue, murmuring the syllable *laṃ*. As its abstract representation, one contemplates the shape of a lightning bolt, inscribed upon a square. Chapter 37 adds a bodily interiorization of a sixteen petal lotus, feeling it in a sense echoed by the density and immensity of a real and imagined mountain. The golden-hued earth turns a reddish brown in this contemplative practice. This first installment connecting earth, a palette of yellow and brown, the lotus, the mountain, and the utterance of mantra within the human body will find fuller development in subsequent chapters, which link the concentration on elements with the transformation and elevation of consciousness.

Consciousness and Activity: Reciprocity in Sāṃkya

The environmental process begins with consciousness. To be aware of one's ecosystem, one must begin with the body, the seat of consciousness. For this segment of the chapter, we turn to the Hindu tradition in its classical phase. Whereas the Vedas and the Upaniṣads brought forth stunning imagery and speculation, by the time of the Buddha and Mahāvīra some 2,500 years ago, philosophers began to organize their thinking in a manner that brought forth six distinct ways of viewing the world (*darśanas*). Sāṃkhya, reported to be the oldest, will be examined in detail below. Its companion schools are Vedānta, which emphasizes a sense of oneness and unity, and Yoga, which provides methods through which to attain the insights of Sāṃkhya and Vedānta. All three posit the possibility of human freedom or *mokṣa*. The other three schools are less certain of the attainability of this lofty goal. Nyāya claims that logical thinking is the best human achievement. Vaiśeṣika opts for a comprehensive physical description of the world. Mīmāṃsā asserts that the best path to follow is the proper performance of ritual. All six figure in the tradition and in the consideration of the five elements in this book, which seeks to convey a ritual, aesthetic sense of the world within the structures of reasoned and reasonable thought.

In ancient India, the person or *puruṣa* was regarded as a reflection of the world: eyes were the sun and moon; breath, the wind; feet, the earth. By looking closely at one's own body, the cosmos itself could be discerned. The relationship between the microphase of one's body and the macrophase workings of the universe provides a root metaphor for seeing the world from a holistic perspective, leading to environmental awareness. By seeing the universe as reflective of and relating to body functions, one sees oneself not as an isolated unity but as part of a greater whole.

The *Ṛg Veda* speaks of consciousness in terms of two birds sitting in the same tree: one eats sweet berries on one branch, while the other gazes dispassionately from a different branch. This twofold analysis of reality led to a philosophical system known as Sāṃkhya. The active bird, associated with the feminine principle, comes to be known as *prakṛti,* while the inactive bird is referred to as *puruṣa,* linked with the masculine principle. *Prakṛti* manifests her creativity through three all-pervasive modalities (*guṇas*) of light, activity, and dullness (*sattva, rajas, tamas*) that in turn divide into twenty-three concrete realities (*tattvas*). These realities are brought to life through the power of consciousness, for whom the manifestations of *prakṛti* dance alluringly.

These twenty-three begin with operations of the mind: emotion (*buddhi*), ego (*ahaṃkāra*), and thought (*manas*). Four sets of five then issue forth from one's mental structures and predispositions: the senses, the body, the subtle elements or capacities, and the gross elements. Smelling, tasting, seeing, touching, and hearing (the senses or *buddhīndriyas*) attach themselves to walking, grasping, talking, excreting, and sexual capacity (the action organs of the body or *karmendriyas*). This bundle then goes forward through its subtle powers of perception (*tanmātras*) to make contact with the earth, with water, with fire, with air, with space (the gross elements).

In the articulation of Sāṃkhya philosophy during the classical era (ca. 200 CE), the feminine principle, known as Prakṛti, lies at the root of all manifest existence.[50] From her creative, dancing powers, the building blocks of experience arise. Prakṛti's field serves as the repository for all karmic impressions (*saṃskāras*) and inclinations toward particular states of being in the world (*bhāva*). From this constellation of forces arises a fixed identity (*ahaṃkāra*) and the operations of the thinking mind (*manas*). The sensory organs and the action organs coalesce to bring the subtle body into contact with the external world of the five great elements. Reality and experience make themselves manifest (*vyakta*) through the operations of this matrix clearly designated with the marker of the feminine. Prakṛti serves two purposes. She provides experience for the enjoyment and perhaps amusement of consciousness. She also, when her dance comes to an end, allows consciousness to reside in its own nature of nonjudgmental awareness, referred to as a state of liberation (*mokṣa*). Without the feminine creative principle, life would be impossible. Some have argued that the Sāṃkhya system and its Vedāntic successors remain skeptical and critical of the manifest world.[51] I have argued that the reciprocity between the feminine, creative realm of manifestation and the male-gendered "aloof" state of pure awareness, indicates a recognition of the importance of enjoying the bodily and sensory realms as a key feature of Indian philosophy. This celebration of the manifest world is expressed in aesthetic theory and is abundantly evident in India's rich traditions of color, flavor, movement, and an overall appreciation of beauty.[52]

In Sāṃkhya and Tantra, the five great elements (*mahābhūtas*) appear when in proximity to the five subtle elements within the human body (*tanmātras*). The world is experienced through the five great senses or gods of perception (*buddhīndriya*). The earth (*pṛthivī*) reveals itself through the sense of smell (*gandha*) linked to the human nose (*nasa*). Water (*jal/āp*) reveals itself through taste (*rasa*) found in the mouth (*mukha*). Fire (*agni/tejas*) reveals form (*rūpa*) experienced through the eyes (*akṣa*). Wind (*vāyu*) unveils touch (*sparśa*) known through the human organ of the skin (*tvak*). Space (*ākāśa*) contains all sound (*śabda*), which is perceived through the ears (*karṇa*). The outer world only emerges when the sense organs are directed by the mind to identify them as such. The particulars of physical reality obtain fruition only on contingency. They only take shape in the context of human presence. Without the basic orientation and directionality and intentionality of the mind, no world can be known. The world and consciousness exist in reciprocity.

Simply put, according to Sāṃkhya, the world begins with structures of consciousness that unreel themselves such that they construe and engage physical reality. Emphasis is placed not on the world as a given, external reality, but as an expressive experience of each individual's propensities and attachments.

The world hinges on taste and preference; one sees what one intends to see, and engages the world according to one's own predilections.

The world in this system is intimate to one's own sense of being. Without the sense of smell, there could be no crisp scent of autumn leaves, no gentle wafting of the ocean breeze. Without the sense of taste, there could be no soothing drink of water or startling spiciness. Without the eyes and the light that bathes them, there could be no color or form. Without the garment of skin that cloaks our bodies, there could be no caress of human contact. Without the ears, no sound could be heard or sent forth as communication with others. In the most intimate of ways, the world cannot exist without the body in which we dwell.

Reflecting on the power and glory of the body, practitioners of Yoga developed techniques by which one could finely tune the body's capacity for sensory experience and also for directed thought. Through the application of postures that imitate animals and through the controlled use of breath, the human person is guided through Yoga to experience the world from the perspective of other living beings. By holding the lion's pose, one approximates the experience of ferocity and fullness. But standing in the tree posture, one gains the stability and rootedness of the tree. By mastering the breath, one learns the origin and control of thought.

This intimacy of thought with body, and of body with the world, can be seen from an ecological angle. This outlook does not allow for a world to exist outside of one's perception of it. It can help us recognize and remember that our very sustenance must not be taken for granted. The food we eat is part of the same elemental structure of which we are composed. Furthermore, we depend on the labor of other humans who produce and transport food for our consumption. These people, in their work, must rely upon soil, sunshine, and rainfall to produce our food. We cannot conceive of anything in the universe that does not rely on and relate to the creative expression of the five elements; nor can we have access to any item without the power of our own sensuality.

When one can see and smell a flower in such a way that the flower becomes a celebration of the creative powers of the universe manifested both internally in human biology and externally in the botanical realm, then a true sensitivity to life can be cultivated. An environmental ethic emerges from a sacred attention (*puruṣa*) to the needs of one's body and the earth itself, both of which become manifest through the creative matrix (*prakṛti*).

The *Yogavāsiṣṭha*: Sāṃkhya, Tantra, and Yoga

In the tenth century, the Kashmiri philosopher Abhinavagupta interpreted the creative reciprocity of the Sāṃkhya system in a new way, transforming seminal aspects of Indian philosophy into an expression of a near Sufi-like celebration of spiritualized consciousness, in which all phenomena provide an occasion for an experience of bliss.[53] This aesthetic suggests that all interaction between awareness and objectivity contains the potential of revealing "non-dual Ultimate Reality."[54] Notably, unlike Advaita Vedānta, which refers to the world as illusory, the Śāktā philosophy associated with Tantra, building on the principles of Sāṃkhya, "posits the world of plurality as real."[55] This affirms the importance of knowing the nature of the world as key to the discovery of consciousness and hence liberation.

Abhinavagupta seems to have relied somewhat on the *Yogavāsiṣṭha*, a text of more than 29,000 verses that grew into its current form, building on an earlier text called the *Mokṣopāya*, nearly a thousand years ago.[56] It consists of sixty stories within a frame narrative wherein the sage Vasiṣṭha offers words of wisdom to the young prince Rāma, whose mind has become overwhelmed at the prospect of armed conflict. In story after story, Vasiṣṭha seeks to stabilize Rāma's thinking and teach him about the ephemeral nature of all attachment.

Contrary to a more Buddhist approach that emphasizes the putrid nature of decaying flesh in addition to prescribing fixed attention on the elements (see above), Vasiṣṭha celebrates all that emanates from and remains connected with his body. He enters into an experience of the anthropocosmic, a term used by Eliade from the 1940s through the 1970s "to account for the correspondences between microcosm and macrocosm that appear throughout the history of religions" and more recently used by Tu Wei Ming "to describe the dynamic interconnectedness of Heaven, Earth, and humanity."[57] This episode, titled "The World within the Rock," occurs toward the end of the last book of the *Yogavāsiṣṭha* and indicates his own profession of enlightenment to Rāma. The examples given in other stories are about the experiences of other people. Because this is about Vasiṣṭha's own enlightenment, it merits close consideration.

The *Yogavāsiṣṭha* helps to demonstrate the importance of feminine creativity in Indian tradition. As noted by Karen Pechilis, this text provides a prototype for the emergence of Hindu female gurus in the story of Queen Cūḍālā, the young woman who achieves highest spiritual knowledge and then becomes the teacher of her husband.[58] Stories of female spiritual prowess and creativity can be found laced through this epic-sized tale,[59] indicating that the affirmation of the reality of the world results in the espousal of a reverent attitude toward the role of the feminine, the emblem and expression of manifest reality. One particular story sequence, which extols the power of the feminine, can be found in the second section of the *Nirvāṇa Prakaraṇa*, the last book of the *Yogāvasiṣṭha*. In "The World within the Rock," Vasiṣṭha narrates his own vision of how the goddess Kālarātrī or Bhagavatī created and held under her power the world of cities, forests, and mountains. Vasiṣṭha then describes discovering these creative abilities within himself as he performs progressive concentration (*dhāraṇā*) on the elements and senses within his own body.

The sage Vasiṣṭha narrates how a celestial woman, identified as Kālarātrī or Kālī, brings him into a great rock (one can visualize perhaps the great sculptures of Mahabalipuram), where she shows him her husband, a sleeping "creator," identified as Rudra or Śiva. In proximity to her husband, the goddess begins to dance, emitting from her body the entire world while deep within the recesses of her husband's meditation cave, now known as Vasiṣṭha's cave, a short drive from Rishikesh. My daughter and I visited this cave in 2008, perched above the green flowing waters of the Ganges. We were drawn through the darkness to an oil lamp illuminating a small statue of the dancing Śiva and sat in reverent silence, punctuated gently by women chanting mantras softly invoking the luminous presence palpable in this sacred place.

The goddess Kālī who takes Vasiṣṭha on this remarkable journey comes by many names in this narrative:

> VII.84.10. She is called by the names Jāyā and Siddhā because
> she is accompanied by victory and prosperity at all times.
> She is also designated as Aparajitā or the invincible,
> 11. Viryā the mighty, Durgā the inaccessible,
> and is likewise renowned as Umā,
> composed of the powers of the three syllable Aum.
> 12. She is called the Gāyatrī from being chanted by every body
> and Sāvitrī from being the matrix of all things.
> She is named Sarasvatī for giving us insight
> into what appears before our sight.[60]

The goddess is not portrayed here as unconsciousness, inert, or carrying any negative connotation. To the contrary, Vasiṣṭha states that

> VII:84.20. All cities and continents, mountains and islands,
> Hang on her agency as a string of gems around her neck.
> She holds together all parts of the world
> and influences her force as vibration (*spanda*) in them all . . .
> VII:84.22. She is the one great body of the cosmos.
> It is this power which supports the earth, with all its seas
> and islands, and its forests, deserts, and mountains.

With elegant phrases, Vasiṣṭha describes the creation and maintenance of the world through the dance of Kālī:

> VII.85.1–4. Dancing with her outstretched arms
> which looked like a forest of tall pines . . .
> She contains the world in the vibration of her mind (*cit-spanda*).

This vision of the goddess caused Vasiṣṭha to observe that "the world was seated in his own heart."[61] He saw that his spiritual nature was purely *ākāśa* or space;[62] from this space came the movement of the intellect (*buddhi*), the sense of self (*ahaṃkāra*), then the mind (*manas*); from this emerges the five senses and five organs, and then, from the subtle elements (*tanmātras*), the world.[63]

At first, Vasiṣṭha watched Kālī generate the world through her body and senses. He observed Kālī's creation of the world as external to himself. He then saw the world emerge from his own body. He saw that whatever arose in the world was not different from his own body.[64] He then saw himself manifest in his own body the creative powers he had seen in the goddess. He became the goddess, playing with the creation of the world. On the one hand, he declared the world to be empty (*śūnyameva*), an epithet for space or *ākāśa*; on the other hand, he saw himself fill the world.[65] On the other hand, he saw the manifestation of the world arise through the careful and sustained practice of the progressive elemental meditations on earth, water, fire, air, and space, to be pursued one by one in each of the following chapters.

Vasiṣṭha's descriptions rejoice in the beauties of nature. Like the Buddhist Sukkapati who learned from the Buddha the emptiness of all elemental realities, Vasiṣṭha repeats again and again that ultimately all things are empty (*śūnya*) and that all things are constructed by the mind. But with wild exuberance and pure enjoyment, he revels in describing the results of the creative process. He proclaims being united with valleys and forests of the earth, as will be seen in the translation shared and explicated below.

The story of the World within the Rock carries a fascinating account of how Sāṃkhya categories came to be employed within the larger stories of the Śaiva tradition. Śiva is depicted as a remote, meditating figure, like a king who has lost interest in his domain. The goddess Kālī, in ghostly form, emits the world as a shadow when she comes close (*saṃyoga*) to her beloved. In poetic detail, Vasiṣṭha articulates the relationship between senses (*buddhīdriyas*) and the subtle elements (*tanmātras*) and the gross elements (*mahābhūtas*) of earth, water, fire, air, and space. He sees the entire manifest world within his own body. He receives wisdom from a sage and then returns to the court, taking up his task of offering instruction to Rāma.

This particular story is noteworthy because Vasiṣṭha is not telling a story about someone else. He is telling Rāma about his own meditation experiences, and in the process instructing Rāma how to meditate in succession on the different tattvas of the Sāṃkhya system. By gaining intimacy with the fundamental functions of nature in the form of the five elements, Vasiṣṭha describes in detail how to experience meditation by concentrating upon and appreciating the beauties of nature.

In this story, Kālī shows the processes through which the world emerges and demonstrates the dynamic, living relationship between the material of the world and the processes of sense perception, all of which are in service of consciousness (*cit*). The story of the World within the Rock tells of a repeated return to the world of manifestation and creativity, followed with yet another ascent into a state of abeyance and removal from worldly entanglements. In each instance of creative engagement, the world of the senses and elements is described in loving detail, a constant reminder of its beautiful yet chimerical and fleeting quality.

This story takes the reader into a space and state of purified, powerful awareness (*cit-śakti*, *Yoga Sūtra* IV:34). It provides an interpretation of how the elements of Sāṃkhya fit with the Kashmir Śaivaite teaching of vibration (*spanda*). By having the dance of the goddesses reveal the power of consciousness itself, the *Yogavāsiṣṭha* revises Sāṃkhya and brings it into its own special form of nondualism. It affirms and celebrates the story of the world by spinning a beautiful tale about the process of its emergence. While affirming, almost reluctantly, the importance of the solitary, aloof, detached meditating yogī, it simultaneously delights in the wondrous beauty of the goddess and the elemental world she creates. It draws the reader into a sense of immediacy and rapport with the elements. The poetic exuberance of this narrative account underlines the unwillingness of the *Yogavāsiṣṭha* to denigrate and reject the lessons to be learned by a close observance of and intimacy with the natural world. The telling of the *Yogavāsiṣṭha* stories themselves can perhaps be sufficient to establish one in an imaginative space that effects subtle transformation, into a state appreciative of beauty and the creative powers of the goddess.

Earth in the *Yogavāsiṣṭha*

Concentration on the elements or *mahābhūta dhāraṇā* plays a central role in guiding Vasiṣṭha's spiritual journey, a journey that leads from the world into reverie, and from reverie back into the world. In "The World within the Rock," we have seen Vasiṣṭha enter into a darkened cave where he sees Lord Śiva in meditation. A shadow calls his attention to the presence of the goddess. As he gazes upon her body, she dances, creating the world, carrying mountains and forests on her shoulders and arms. When she ceases to dance, the world stops and begins to dissolve. Her magical presence intrigues Vasiṣṭha. She instructs Vasiṣṭha about how she creates the material universe from her body. She inspires him to take up a sequence of concentration exercises (*dhāraṇā*) through which he sees how his own body is connected with the fundamental elements that comprise the world.[66] He seems delighted, surprised, and even overwhelmed as he discovers that the powers of the elements themselves reside in his own body. The adventure culminates when Vasiṣṭha encounters an ascended sage who gives advice on how to maintain purified consciousness while moving about in the world. The sage tells him:

> The infinite consciousness (*cid-ākāśa*) is I,
> it is the three worlds,
> it is the *puruṣa* (cosmic being)
> and it is you.[67]

This philosophy affirms the validity of the constructed realm and hence forms a foundation for Vasiṣṭha to exhort Rāma to resume his duties, similar to Krishna's counsel in the *Bhagavad Gītā*.

In order to capture a sense of the rich imagery employed by the author in praise of nature, new translations of portions of successive chapters describing Vasiṣṭha's encounter will follow. In this narrative, Vasiṣṭha undergoes a shift in awareness. He assumes the position of a sovereign king, overseeing the landscape of his domain from a birds-eye view. What begins as rhapsody about the beauties of nature becomes a celebration of the material powers contained within his own body. Vasiṣṭha, as we will see, becomes anthropocosmic.

The Earth

In volume VII, chapter 89, Vasiṣṭha describes looking down upon the earth. From this vantage point, he sees soil, plants, mountains, rivers and relates them to his own body:

> 58. Through performing concentration on the earth (*pṛthivī dhāraṇā*),
> I dissolved into the form of the earth.
> While still retaining this expanded consciousness,
> I became like a universal ruler (surveying his domain).

59. And indeed, through my concentration on the earth,
I went to the mines at the root of the earth.
I came to understand my body as the trees,
the grasses, the mountains, the continents, and more.

Through these verses, we begin to see the expansion of Vasiṣṭha's awareness as he feels the intimacy between his own body and the various aspects made of earth and made from earth.

60. As I took possession of the throne of the earth,
forests sprouted from my body.
I became adorned with cities
as if laced with strings of pearls.
61. I was endowed with forests separated by villages.
The regions of the netherworld were sunk deep in my bowels.
My arms embraced the mountain ranges
and my continents were encircled with oceans like bracelets.

Vasiṣṭha's experience of earth includes the many cities and villages that can be seen, separated by forests. It is as if he were seeing the planet from a satellite.

62. I felt my body covered with grasses like hair,
as well as tree-tangled mountains,
held up by the heads of ten elephants
and the hundreds of heads of the primal serpent Śeṣa.
64. The beautiful ridges of the Himalayas and the Vindhyas,
the clouds high on Mount Meru,
the abundance of the rivers such as the Ganges:
all this evokes a delicate string of pearls.
65. Caves and thickets and marshes
appear to encircle the ocean.
The white salts of the desert
shimmer like a beautiful garment.
66. In ancient times (of the great flood)
the ocean purified all things.
When it receded, the flowery forests
were resplendent with fragrant pollen.

This bird's eye account of the planet includes seeing mountain ranges, coastlines, and vast deserts and forests.

> 67. Repeatedly, the ground is plowed and turned:
> cooled by the winds of the winter,
> warmed by the heat of summer
> and moistened by the waters of the rainy season.

From his elevated vantage point, Vasiṣṭha seems to see not only the earth but also the changing of the seasons, and gained appreciation for the all-important agricultural cycle.

> 68. My chest became the expansive plains.
> My eyes became pools of lotuses.
> My crown was the light and dark clouds.
> My body (*mandiram*) contained the ten regions.

His body becomes connected and inseparable from the landscape, including the solidity of earth in his chest, the fluidity of water in his eyes, and the levity of space surrounding his head.

> 72. Filled with floods, deserts, farms, kingdoms, as well as people,
> on named continents of stone with rivers, forests,
> and oceans to the end of the horizon,
> the Earth is an assemblage of vessels and designs
> connected with various adorning marks,
> as if flecked with groups of lotuses in a raging river,
> or like a pond laced with vines.

Vasiṣṭha describes the planet with great precision and emotion. He sees mountains, forests, deserts, caves, plains, and oceans. He describes the seasons and, like the anthropocosmic sections of the *Bṛhadāraṇyaka Upaniṣad*, makes correlations between his body and the body of the world. He feels vegetation sprout from his body. His arms embrace the mountains. His chest becomes the broad plains, his eyes become lotus pools, and clouds gather around his head. He becomes entranced and absorbed into the beauty of the earth.

Gheraṇḍa Saṃhitā on Earth

The literature we have surveyed and the temple mentioned at the start of this chapter all date from more than a thousand years ago, with the *Atharva Veda* being composed by 1000 BCE, the *Ācārāṅga Sūtra* by 300 BCE, the *Visud-*

dhimagga by 430 CE, and the *Jñānārṇava* and *Yogavāsiṣṭha* by 1000 CE. Each of these texts in its own way presents a sustained reflection upon the earth, with the latter three providing specific instruction on how to fix one's gaze and thoughts on the elements in sequence. This technique, though not specified in the *Yoga Sūtra*, does appear in the *Gheraṇḍa Saṃhitā*, a late–seventeenth-century text that conveys the key practices of Haṭha Yoga. The practices echo the earlier descriptions in the *Jñānārṇava*: visualize the color yellow, repeat the mantra "*laṃ*," and mentally place oneself upon a lotus on top of a square. In keeping with Haṭha Yoga practice, one must "hold the breath and mind in abeyance" for a long period of time in order to achieve the connection that results in a transformative state. The *Yogavāsiṣṭha* describes great reveries that accompany the practice. The benefits in this text are perhaps overstated as well as understated: through Pṛthivī Dhāraṇā one can overcome death and also learn to move freely on the earth.

> 70. For the earth element (*tattva*),
> One generates the color yellow,
> repeating the syllable "*laṃ*"
> while seated on a lotus placed on a square.
> Having done this, one is supported
> and stabilized in the heart.
> The steady adept should hold
> the breath and mind in abeyance
> for two and a half hours.
> Doing this concentration on what is beneath
> always leads to victory on the earth.
> 71. Now the benefits of the practices of earth concentration are told:
> The one who practices concentration on the earth regularly
> conquers death and would become indeed
> an adept at moving on the earth.

This text includes descriptions of each of the elemental meditations, which will be considered in sequence in the chapters that follow on water, fire, air, and space.

Feminist Ethics and Earth Meditation

This chapter began with reflections on the practice of Pṛthivī Dhāraṇā as taught at Yoga Anand Ashram in the 1970s. The technique required preparing a plate with soil upon it, and to gaze on this soil twice a day, at sunrise and at sunset, for twenty minutes each sitting. Though in some ways simpler than the technique offered in the *Gheraṇḍa Saṃhitā*, the Ashram training carried with it a deeply ethical message. The first Earth Day had convened just two years prior, and the founder of the Ashram, who had participated in Gandhian Salt Marches as a youth, felt the urgency of the environmental movement. Gurāṇi Añjali cared deeply about the earth and encouraged her students to see connections between environmental degradation and human neglect of the foundations of a life such as the elements. She composed a song that laments the current state of affairs:

> The earth is burning
> The sky is ablaze.
> Thoughts of the past haunt us every day.
> We turn to the day
> We go into the night
> Pollution on the land, in the waters, in the air
> Where are the fathers?
> Where are the mothers?
> Like little children we scream now and then
> To be heard once again
> We scream now and then
> Hypocrites abound all around and around
> Taking issue everywhere
> No one cares, who will care?
> Where is the embrace and that loving care?
> We keep looking for that place
> With that embrace
> Stranded in this world, you and me all alone
> You are my hope
> I am your hope[68]

A critique is offered here of apathy, along with acknowledgment of the fundamental human need to connect with one another in order to bring about positive change.

This plaintive song written by a woman calls attention to the earth. Connections may be seen between the representations of nature as the manifestation of the goddess, and the role of contemporary women in the environmental movement in India, as well as the emergence of Green Yoga in the United States. The passages we have encountered from the Vedas and the *Yogavāsiṣṭha* underscore the sanctified role of the feminine in understanding nature. The idea and ideal of "Mother Earth" finds expression in the *Atharva Veda*'s goddesses Pṛthivī and Bhū, Sāṃkhya's Prakṛti, and in Kālī's dance in the *Yogavāsiṣṭha.* Sāṃkya, Tantra, and Purāṇic cosmology refer to the manifest world as an emanation of Prakṛti, the creative principle and matrix of all things apart from consciousness. In Jainism, the cosmos, consisting of hell realms, the earth (Jambudvipa), and the heavens, is depicted in the form of a woman.[69] The body of the mother provides the context for all experience, from the smell of the earth to the power of human memory. Consequently, women logically can be seen as having a primal connection with the earth, and hence a deep sense of responsibility for her well-being.

Vandana Shiva is perhaps India's most well-known environmental activist. She has championed the remembrance of the Bishnoi movement three hundred years ago, led by Amrita Devi, a woman who inspired a movement of three hundred people, some of whom "sacrificed their lives to save their sacred *khejri* trees by clinging to them."[70] Vandana Shiva has brought attention to the Chipko Movement, which worked at forestation projects in the Himalayas, and is herself an international spokeswoman on the topic of seed preservation.

Vijaya Nagarajan of the University of San Francisco, in addition to founding a nonprofit organization for the promotion of nature awareness through backpacking, has documented the role of women's domestic art in giving praise and acknowledgment to beauty and nature's evanescence. Each morning throughout Tamil Nadu, women adorn their thresholds with intricate designs crafted of rice flour. These *kolam* designs are inspired by the Yantra patterns that celebrate the intersection of the Yoni (symbolized by the downward triangle) with the Liṅgam (symbolized by the upward triangle). The Yoni represents the manifest, visible aspects of the earth and of Prakṛti; the Lingam stands for consciousness or Puruṣa. By bending toward the earth before the glimmer of dawn, these women humble themselves, making an offering to be consumed throughout the day by ants, keeping the house pestilence-free while inviting all guests to cross over a sacred space to enter the home. In describing their work, one woman commented on the connection between the decline of the ozone layer and the increasing neglect of the *kolam* due to the pressures of modern life: "We are losing the ability to give to each another and to give to God. We are forgetting that we need to practice giving constantly. . . . We used to give to each other. We used to give to the gods, goddesses. . . . We have to learn to give again."[71] The women of Tamil Nadu see the earth as Bhū Devī. Nagarajan comments that "Bhū Devī acts as a reminder of the fragility of the soils and the earth; she is a mnemonic device serving to shape the conceptualization of the natural world." Another of her informants states that "Bhūmi Devī is our mother. She is everyone's source of existence. Nothing would exist without her. The entire world depends on her for sustenance and life. So, we draw the Kolam first to remind ourselves of her."[72]

Commenting on the adaptation of traditional nature-based rituals to modern life, Madhu Khanna of the Indira Gandhi National Centre for the Arts in New Delhi sees Dūrga Pūjā, widely practiced throughout Bengal, as a way to invite seasonal agricultural festivals into the city. She notes that "the ritual, as it exists today, has the potential to inspire urban dwellers to use symbols rooted in the earth for ecological activism."[73] Similarly, Vasudha Narayanan of the University of Florida writes about the use of the performing arts to convey an environmental message, "communicating the tragedy of ecological disasters using such art forms as Bharata Natyam."[74] She cites in particular Mallika Sarabhai's dance drama about the Chipko Movement performed in "Shakti: The Power of Women" and Sujatha Vijyaranghavan's work, choreographed by Radha in Chennai, that condemns pollution by dramatizing the rescue of a poisoned world by Lord Śiva, whose throat turns blue as a consequence.

Each of these women has brought to public awareness ways in which the contemporary issue of environmental degradation is being addressed through making a connection between the earth goddess and the current state of the world. From the Himalayas to the north, Rajasthan to the west, Tamil Nadu to the south, and Bengal in the east, women in all corners of India are drawing upon the imagery of the goddess to communicate a modern message. According to traditional Indian philosophy and cosmology, the world is a gendered, feminine place. Throughout the Indian story tradition, women have embodied the power symbolized by numerous goddesses. By giving honor to the earth, women give honor to the goddess and recognize the power of the goddess who resides in themselves. Just as the dancing Bhagavatī Kālī brings forth the world and stirs the sage Vasiṣṭha into deeper awareness and appreciation, so also devotion to the goddess, in both traditional and contemporary forms, can stir the world to an increased sense of urgency in regard to the plight of Mother Earth.

Conclusion

Buddhists of long ago developed a meditation to cultivate appreciation of one's ephemerality, advocating visualization first of oneself and then all others as nothing more than rotting flesh giving way to bare bones. Through applying this technique, one was empowered to overcome attachment to one's own physicality and the attractiveness of others. Rather than stripping away our corporeality, modes of meditation need to be developed and practiced that can re-enflesh our reality and reveal our intimacy with universal process. Just as Thomas Berry has advocated turning away from Christianity's obsession with personal sin toward a celebration of creative processes in the universe, so also in the Asian traditions there is now room and a need for applying their profound interiorities in such a way as to heighten awareness of the earth's postindustrial dilemma. Gurāṇi Añjali has stated that Americans need to wake up to their senses in order to see the world; it is only by clearly seeing the world that wisdom can be attained. Through breathing deeply, walking quietly, tasting delicately, hearing keenly, lessons can be gleaned from the world about the world. As our perceptions become clarified, thoughts become still. As our thoughts become still, our tendency to acquisitiveness begins to subside; a contentment arises that can serve as the perfect antidote to the overconsumption that currently chokes our culture. By centering ourselves, we turn away from the outward-moving immaturity that seeks constant gratification. To center ourselves, we need to return to the power of our senses and their relationship with the elements that compose both our bodies and the planet itself. As our attachments weaken, our consumption will diminish. The diminishment of consumption in turn is the key to an environmentally sensitive lifestyle.

In this chapter we have seen many ways in which nature has been articulated in Indian philosophy through the five great elements (*mahābhūta*): earth, water, fire, air, and space. The Earth has been lovingly described in the *Atharva Veda*'s *Pṛthivī Sūkta*. The Buddha instructs Pukkusati to regard the elements closely and proclaims that success in this technique brought him to freedom. Buddhaghosa taught a successive reflection on the elements, beginning with earth. The elements are carefully listed in the *Sāṃkhya Kārikā*. The Jainas prescribed careful rules about how to interact with the earth, and how to gaze upon it transcendentally. For Vasiṣṭha and for the Haṭhas Yogis, contemplation on the earth serves as the gateway to self-knowledge. Seeing the elements and their relationship with the senses and the body constitutes the foundation for knowledge in Indian thought and literature, a knowledge that leads to wisdom and freedom.

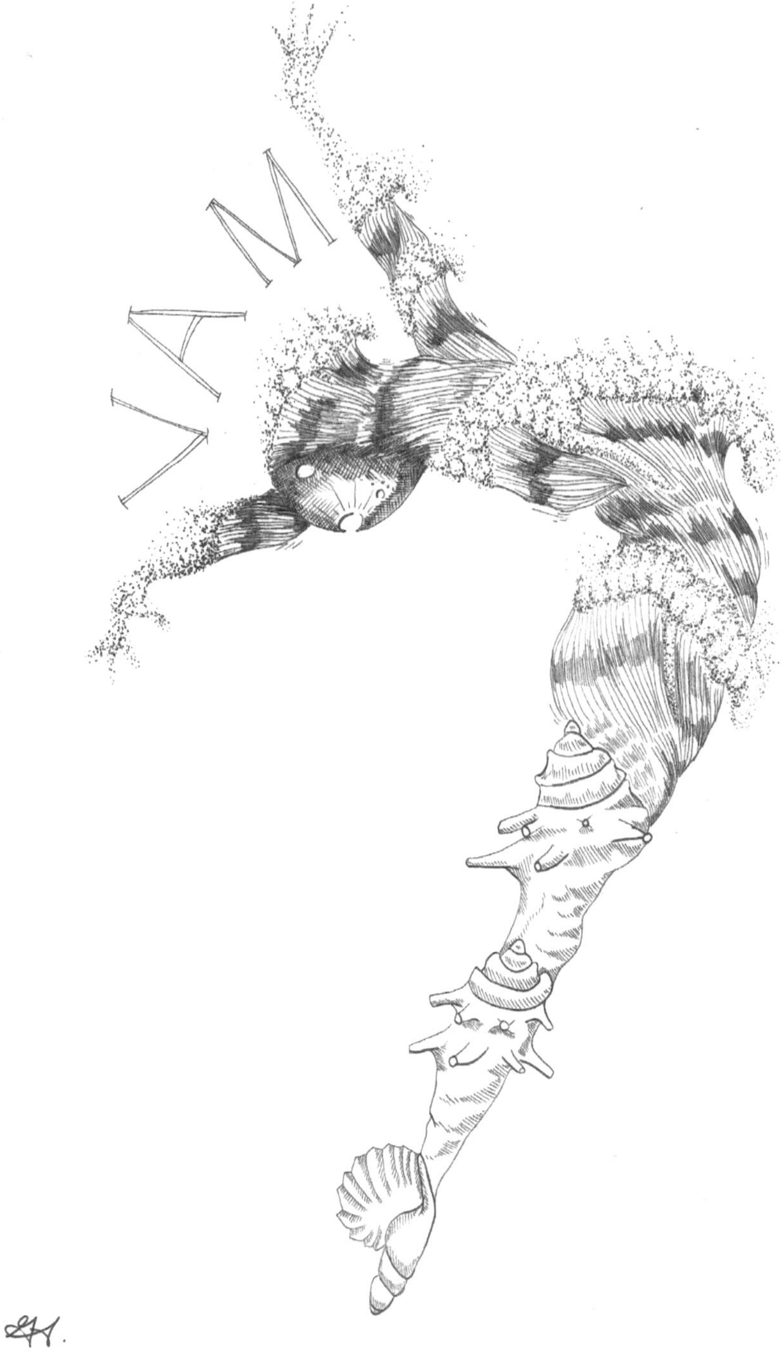
VAM

3

Water

Life-giver and Purifier

Water provides the most basic needs for all forms of life. Knowing one's water means to know the stuff of one's body. Water evokes clusters of memories and meanings. Learning about the source of one's water helps one understand the local watershed and hence the surrounding ecosystem. As a child, our family's water came from a shallow well just four feet deep. When we moved to a different geological site, away from the Lake Ontario sediment plain to the glaciated Genesee Valley, our well had to be sunk more than sixty feet, and also required softening to lessen the mineral content. On Long Island, our water was seriously tainted with industrial effluent, requiring activated granulated charcoal reverse osmosis treatment. And in Los Angeles, our water comes from multiple sources: the Eastern Sierras, the Colorado River, and underground aquifers. Beyond its utility, water can inspire and terrify. Learning to swim in Lake Ontario and Johnson's Creek instilled a healthy sense of respect for the water and its temperature fluctuations, its currents, and startling surprises such as the occasional dead fish. Learning to body surf on Fire Island during the heat of the Long Island summer, and to negotiate the rockiness of North Shore beaches brought different pleasures, as did discovering the Nissequogue and Amityville Rivers. Whether at the Great South Bay or Long Island Sound or Peconic Bay, or even New York Harbor, the glint of light on the water and its great flowing expanse evoke an energy of calm and awe. Moving to Southern California, where all beaches welcome visitors and no bridges must be crossed, brought new vistas of endless blue, seen from the beach itself, as well as from hills, mountains, and even my office.

At Yoga Anand Ashram, our practice of concentration on water (*jal dhāraṇā*) began in November. For the month we were asked to gaze upon water in a clear glass bowl, approximately five inches in diameter, fixing our eyes in *tratakaṃ,* the practice of holding the gaze steady until tears begin to well. Gurāṇi Añjali told us not to practice this at the beach or to visualize rolling waves, as one of her Yoga classmates back in Calcutta had tried this with negative results; she felt as if she were flailing about in the surf! However, we did explore new mysteries within and around water during that month, including frequent visits to the beach and the discovery of glowing diadems in Stony Brook Harbor late at night, a phenomenon known as bioluminescence. Additionally, we came to appreciate the capacity of the body to generate tears as we held our gaze, as well as the fluidity of blood coursing through our veins and more. Some months later, my wedding included a water ceremony. Añjali reminded us that from water we are born, and in water we conceive new life. She poured blessed water from a sacred vessel known as a lothal over our joined hands, which were wrapped in marigold garlands.

Water blessings in India carry the name *arghya,* a ceremony wherein a person gathers water in the hands or fills a conch shell or a purpose-shaped vessel called the *arghyapātra* and pours it into a river or on a threshold or into another container to be returned to the earth or to the sea.[1] In the early morning one can see people engaging in this ritual at the opening of a business, as well as in morning ablutions that also serve as a morning bath. In a poetic description of this ritual, the novelist Shivaji Sawant describes in first-person narrative the daily practice of the warrior Karṇa, son of the Sun:

> One day I happened to be at the bank of the Ganga. I had finished my bath, and scooped a palmful of water for the *arghya* ritual. On my right, about twenty steps away, was the river bank. Its stone steps were dim in the soft, hazy dawn-light. My *añjali* water fell drop by drop into the river and became one with the Ganga again. I kept re-filling my empty *añjali* palm, and devotedly offered it . . . the east was slowly blushing a light pink. A little later the golden emperor of the blue kingdom raced his chariot, pulled by a thousand sun-rays for horses, and stood laughing atop the eastern horizon. The birds and beasts welcomed him with sweet calls. . . . Dewdrops glittered silvery on dry grass. . . . The myriad waves of the Ganga, in spangly golden dresses, humming dances-melodies, performed circular choreographies. All moving and unmoving life woke into consciousness and throbbed.[2]

At the banks of the Ganges, in the square ponds known as tanks that adjoin temples, and even at the beach, people congregate to perform this solitary ritual in solidarity, sometimes in silence and sometimes accompanied with sacred chants. Water purifies. In the summer of 2013, my wife and I lived on the island of Spetses in Greece. Each morning at dawn my colleague Katharine Free and I would swim in the Aegean Sea, watching the sun rise from the water, spilling its golden glow, illuminating the darkened, wine-like water. One day the three of us swam off Hydra after a splendid boat ride and reveled as beams of light mysteriously emerged from the depths. The gleaming followed us like the eyes of the Mona Lisa, an illuminated hologram provoking delight. For Katharine, the light sent messages from her sister, who passed away that same morning in California, unbeknownst at the time.

The Water Temple in Tamil Nadu

The Jambukeśvara Temple, located in Thiruvanaikaval, also known as Tiruchirapalli, honors water (*jal, āp, vāri*). The water temple rises up from a lush jungle with green stretching in all directions. Tiruchirapalli sits near the world's oldest operative dam, the Grand Anicut, constructed by a Chola king in the second century. Due to year-round irrigation, the leafy environment of the Water Temple stands in stark contrast to the drier, dustier site of the Earth Temple.

During our entry into town, Karthik, Chris, and I drank and ate from luscious coconuts, freshly hacked and cracked. We descended into a broad river valley for our visit to the water temple. As we entered the temple compound, a wonderful mural greeted us, depicting the story of the spider and the elephant. At this particular temple, Pārvatī, known at the water temple as Akhilaneshwari, had not yet married Śiva, so their shrines were separate, not back to back as in the prior temple. The spider-elephant mural depicts a beautiful woman bathing the Śiva lingam. A spider had woven a web overhead, to help protect the Lingam, and the spider did this every morning. But every afternoon a hulking elephant would come and perform *abhiśheka,* sprinkling water from his trunk onto the lingam, wrecking the spiderweb. So each morning the spider wove a new web, harboring great enmity toward the elephant. Finally the spider died and reincarnated as a great king. He built the water temple to protect the Śiva lingam and made the entrance to the inner sanctum very small, to ensure that no elephant could enter. Sure enough, we had to duck low as we entered the sanctum, illumined with many oil lamps. This particular temple differed from the others in that it was cooler, surrounded with gardens and dense groves of banana, coconut, and palm trees.

As we wandered through the Water Temple, we closely examined the many pillars adorned with vignettes from the Purāṇas. One particularly stunning tableau depicts the Avatāra Dattatreya carrying the three heads of divinity: Brahmā, Viṣṇu, and Śiva, with four dogs at his feet, each representing one of the four Vedas.

Water in the Vedas: *Pṛthivī Sūkta*

The *Pṛthivī Sūkta*, examined in the prior chapter, includes several verses that extol the power of water, noting the many forms that water takes upon earth.

> 3. Upon her lie the oceans, many rivers, and other bodies of water.
> Her agricultural fields produce grain.
> All those that live, move, and breathe [depend upon the Earth];
> May the Land confer upon us all riches.

The earth supports the vast oceans, small ponds, lakes, rivulets, and mighty rivers. The fresh water that falls as rain helps nourish crops. Lakes, canals, and reservoirs help guarantee that water can flow when needed for agriculture. All beings need food. The Earth provides the soil, the water, and the wind to receive the energy of the Sun, ensuring the continuity of life.

The ecologist and lawyer M. C. Mehta has taken to heart the great challenge confronting the purity of water in India. He seeks to cleanse the water of the Ganges River, the lifeblood and spiritual purifier for hundreds of millions of people in North India. Mehta has filed 200,000 lawsuits against polluters who dump untreated waste directly into the river. Others have enacted local pollution control initiatives, including the late Dr. Mishra, a trained hydrologist and Hindu priest who regularly drew attention to the foul state of many of India's great rivers.

> 8. In the beginning, the Earth was inside the water of ocean.
> She was discerned by the sages whose hearts are enwrapped in Truth.
> She resides in space.

May She make our nation strong, powerful, and studded with
splendor.

This verse indicates a triune relationship between Earth, water, and space. The waters part, allowing the Earth to emerge. Space stretches infinitely beyond the boundaries of these two. The combination of the three allow the human nation to flourish.

9. Just as waters are flowing everywhere,
hermits move on the Earth without any restriction.
The Earth is multitudinous and bountiful with all kinds of food
and milk.
May that Earth grant us abundant splendor.

The wandering mendicant, known in India since the time of the Vedas, serves as a reminder that beyond the confines of societal norms, iconic figures wander freely. To relate their lifestyle with the flow of water indicates the ease with which these "others," these reminders of freedom, are accepted by those who choose a more sedentary path. The Earth provides sustenance to both. Milk merits mention here, indicating the special life-giving properties of water.

30. May our bodies enjoy only the clean (pure) water.
May you keep away from us that which is polluted
and may we always do only the good deeds.

The earth carries the waters that provide the pure, fresh water needed for human flourishing. By fouling the waters, humans do harm to themselves. This verse gives encouragement to be mindful of the vital need for clean water.

60. When you were shrouded in the depths of the ocean,
Vishwakarma [the Cosmic Architect] created you by offering
oblations.
On appearing out of the ocean,
you revealed all your hidden hunger-fulfilling items
and other valuable materials for the enjoyment
of those who are devoted to you, Mother.

This verse describes how the earth emerged from the ocean. It indicates a connection between the performance of ritual, in this case ablutions, and the maintenance of the cosmic order. Just as human beings emerge from water, so also the earth itself rises from the ocean. John Cassian (360–435 CE) suggested that Christian scripture merits a fourfold reading: literally interpreting the words; seeing what might be intended allegorically or analogically; discerning any ethical intent; and finally, how the words might speak to the heart and mind of the listener. These five verses from the *Pṛthivī Sūkta* describe water as life giving, flowing, productive of food. Analogically, the descriptions of water not only allude to the essentiality of water, but also point to the freedom of water's flow as a metaphor for the life of the wandering renouncer and meditator. Ethically, these hymns chide the reader to never pollute the water. Finally, at a deep personal level, the *Pṛthivī Sūkta* urges understanding of the interconnections between the oceans and the earth, water and food, flow and happy abundance.

Buddhism: *Dhātuvibhaṇga, Mahārāhulovāda,* and the *Visuddhimagga*

As we have seen in the prior chapter, the Buddha gave explicit instruction on how to meditate on the elements, starting with the earth. His second set of instructions to the monk Pukkusati advise focusing on the water element, seeing its internal bodily manifestations as well as its external aspects, and then learning to regard it with dispassion:

> And what is the liquid property? The liquid property may be either internal or external. What is the internal liquid property? Anything internal, belonging to oneself, that's liquid, watery, and sustained: bile, phlegm, pus, blood, sweat, fat, tears, oil, saliva, mucus, oil-of-the-joints, urine, or anything else internal, within oneself, that is liquid, watery, and sustained: This is called the internal liquid property. Now both the internal liquid property and the external liquid property are simply liquid property. And that should be seen as it actually is present with right discernment: "This is not mine, this is not me, this is not my self." When one sees it thus as it actually is present with right discernment, one becomes disenchanted with the liquid property and makes the liquid property fade from the mind.[3]

The liquids of the body and the watery aspects found in nature are to be understood not as an object to be desired or reviled, but simply acknowledged dispassionately.

As with the discussion of earth, the Buddha adds a hint of positivity when describing this practice to this own son, Rāhula. He states:

> Rāhula, develop meditation that is like water; for when you develop meditation that is like water, arisen agreeable and disagreeable contacts will not invade your mind and remain. Just as people wash clean things and dirty things, excrement, urine, spittle, pus, and blood in water, and the water is not repelled, humiliated, and disgusted because of that, so too, develop meditation that is like water; for when you develop meditation that is like water, arisen agreeable and disagreeable contacts will not invade your mind and remain.[4]

This passage praises water for its dexterity. It can clean all manner of substances. It also praises water because it does not complain. It does not feel humiliated while being subjected to foul substances. Nor does water feel disgust. With equipoise, it accepts what is given and moves on. This, according to the Buddha, is the desired demeanor for the Buddhist monk.

Many centuries later, Buddhaghosa gave detailed instructions on how to practice concentration on water. He states that for one who has undertaken this *kasiṇa* in a past life, a state of blissful concentration will arise spontaneously when one is near "a pool, a lake, a lagoon, or the ocean."[5] The example is given of Elder Cula-Siva, who entered this state while on a ship in the ocean.

The instructions state that one should "fill a bowl or a four-footed water pot to the brim with water uncontaminated by soil, taken in the open through a clean cloth strainer, or with any other clear unturbid water." One should take it to a place as described earlier in the section on the earth *kasiṇa* and sit comfortably. Without focusing on specific details, one begins to repeat various names for water (*apo*) such as rain (*ambu*), liquid (*udaka*), dew (*vari*), fluid (*salila*): water, "water." One then obtains the "learning sign" when the presence can be detected as with the counterpart sign, "like a crystal fan set in space, like the disk of a looking-glass made of crystal."[6]

The use of language is particularly interesting here and in the other segments that describe the *kasiṇa* concentrations. Rather than assigning a mantra, as we will see in later Jaina and Hindu practice, Buddhaghosa urges the meditator to employ the cogitative mind, reciting various names used to describe water. As we have seen in the method taught by Vasiṣṭha in the *Yogavāsiṣṭha*, it is also possible to visualize the element in all its various manifestations, adding to the recitation of names and mantra.

Water in Jainism: *Ācārāṅga* and *Tattvārtha Sūtras*

The *Ācārāṅga Sūtra* boldy proclaims: "There are living beings in water, many lives; of a truth, to the monks, water has been declared to be living matter."[7] The author proclaims that one must recognize the life in water bodies and protect it. A person should drink only water that has been filtered to avoid harm to the more complex bacteria (*nigoda*) that resides in water. If one protects all forms of water, then one will earn "the splendor, honor, and glory of this life for the sake of . . . final liberation."[8] The care taken to do no harm to water extends to the meager daily implements used by a monk or nun for survival. Clear instruction is given not to use one's begging bowl until "the water has dried up and the moisture is gone."[9] At the most minute level, this early text of Jainism accords water a special place in the ethical life of Jaina monks and nuns, requiring its constant and careful attention and protection.

The *Tattvārtha Sūtra* specifies that water exists in three primary modes: souls that inhabit water as described in the *Ācārāṅga Sūtra*, bodies of water such as oceans and lakes and rivers, and heavenly beings associated with bodies of oceanic water. First, the text lists the three forms taken by souls that inhabit water bodies: snow, rain, and ice. Every water soul's body possesses the sense of touch. As an individual soul or life force (*jīva*) it may exist as a water body only a short time before taking a new form.[10] However, the lifespan of a large body of water may be as long as seven thousand years.[11]

Traditional Jaina geography as given in the *Tattvārtha Sūtra* includes the following oceans: Lavaṇa, Puṣkara, Varuṇa, Kṣīra, and Svayambhūramaṇa, before the text states that the oceans are innumerable. The *Tattvārtha Sūtra* lists six mountain ranges of six hues, and places upon them the following lakes: Padma on the golden mountain, Mahāpadma on the white mountain, Tigiñca on the crimson mountain, Kesarī on the blue mountain, Mahāpuṇḍarīka on the white mountain, and Puṇḍarīka on a second golden mountain. Fourteen rivers are named, with seven flowing to the west and seven to the east: Gaṅgā, Sindhu, Rohit, Rohitāsyā, Harit, Harikāntā, Sītā, Sitodā, Nārī, Narakāntā, Suvarṇakūlā, Rūpyakūlā, Raktā, and Raktodā. The first two rivers, India's largest, are said to be joined by fourteen thousand tributaries.[12]

The third association with water can be found in the description of one of the categories of gods that live in the lower heavens. These "mansion gods" are headed by Jalakānta and Jalaprabha, who rule over the Oceanic Youths (Udadhikumāra). This class of gods enjoy sexual pleasures and live a minimum of ten thousand years. These divine beings are said to be "loved by water" and to be the color of water.[13] The commentary on the text states that "Oceanic youths are blueish black with graceful thighs and waist. They have an unyielding manner and their emblem is the crocodile."[14] These and the other gods are said to travel in special air chariots around Mount Meru, the highest mountain of the Himalayas. Jaina temple art depicts these heavenly beings in whimsical detail.

In three ways, and in three realms, Jainism depicts water. First, particles of water are unique and distinct forms of life, potentially destined for future births in other bodies. As such, one seeks to protect water bodies in order to avoid the accretion of karma that can occlude one's own energy, consciousness, and bliss. In the aggregate, these life forms gather together to form the second expression of water, the flowing and still waters of rivers, lakes, and oceans. As a geological feature, water surrounds and in a sense supports the land and, in the case of mountain lakes, is contained by earth. Water takes a third form in the heavens. One might interpret descriptions of the oceanic youths as remarkable cloud formations that rise and swirl above and around the mountains, earning the rewards for a life lived in virtue. It must be remembered, however, that for Jainism the heavens are a temporary state, and that eventually one must descend from heaven to regain a human state, the only form through which one may find release and ascent to the Siddha Loka, the realm of freedom far above and beyond the hellish, earthly, and heavenly realms.

This brings us to the discussion of the Jaina Yogi and his or her relationship with the world of water. As we saw in the prior chapter, elemental meditations play an important role in the path toward freedom in the *Jñānārṇava* and the *Yoga Śāstra*. The ethical care accorded to water becomes transformed into an active embrace of the presence of water. Water here becomes a focus of meditation, wherein the practitioner regards the outer beauty of water as well as experiences its bodily presence.

The *Jñānārṇava* suggests that the Yogi contemplate the timelessness of waves within the ocean:

> 37.4. The Yogi, with equanimity while in the world,
> focuses on the milky ocean.

The mist of each silent, peaceful wave
resembles a garland of pearls.

One can imagine the Yogi sitting on a hill above the ocean, watching the waves lap against the shore, mesmerized by their constancy and brightness.

The Yogi then turns his or her mental focus to the geometry, color, and mantra associated with water:

37.20. (Water), represented by the crescent moon,
is signified with the Varuṇa syllable (*vaṃ*).
Its pulsing sprinkles nectar.
This city of Varuṇa is the color of the moon (white).

The shape associated with water is the crescent, as if the moon itself holds water like a delicate, elongated vessel. Second, one murmurs the mantra *vaṃ* repeatedly, forming a wave of sound that connects one's attention with the vibratory qualities of water itself. This practice generates a sensation within the body of releasing a pulsation that "sprinkles nectar," a simultaneously metaphorical and emotional reference. Finally, one visualizes and associates water with the color white, similar to the waves one sees in the ocean. This concentration on water brings the mind to a place of focus and calm and, as we will see in the chapter on space, allows for an elevated state of purification within the Jaina journey to freedom.

Water in the Yogavāsiṣṭha

In the ninetieth chapter of the *Yogavāsiṣṭha*'s *Nirvāṇa Prakaraṇa*, Vasiṣṭha explores various forms of water. He again performs *dhāraṇā,* defined by Patañjali as "the binding of the mind to a place" (*deśa-bandhaś-cittasya dhāraṇā*, *Yoga Sūtra* III:1). This practice, when extended, moves one into a state of meditation (*dhyāna*) and ultimately into *samādhi,* generating the triple state of concentration known as *saṃyama*. Vasiṣṭha proclaims:

90. 9. Just as I experienced the earth-plane
by earth contemplation (*pṛthivī dhāraṇā*),
then, just as I saw those many worlds
held in the form of the earth,
so also I became water, which was seen
by me in the same way (as from above).

10. By concentration on water, I became water,
as if this unconscious (substance)
took on consciousness
inside the abodes of the oceans with its quiet gurgling.

Hindu thought, unlike Jaina perspectives, does not see the elements as holding life as an intrinsic quality. The term for the inertness of water, *jaḍa,* referring to "inanimate, lifeless matter,"[15] stands in contrast to the term for conscious awareness, *cetana.* Due to his elevated state of concentration, Vasiṣṭha seems to project life into various forms of water through the intensity of his gaze.

15. [Water] takes the form of drops of dew
asleep in the beds of leaves,
constant at all times,
tirelessly gleaming in all directions.

By carefully observing the glimmer of morning dew, Vasiṣṭha paints with his words a description of being enthralled with the sublimity of an everyday occurrence.

16. Along its endless journey,
[water] takes a home in various lakes and rivers,
occasionally resting gracefully by a bridge,
like an old friend.

This particular description reminds me of a practice called Shambhavi Mūdra, mentioned in the *Haṭha Yoga Pradīpikā* and taught at Yoga Anand Ashram. In this practice as taught at the Ashram, one visualizes a beautiful place from the archive of memory. This image evoked for me Smith's Pond in Lyndonville, New York, a place of great beauty constructed and maintained by the local family who had pioneered the mass production and distribution of applesauce. With their wealth, they created a large pond surrounded with mown green grass on the border of a forest, with a delicate fieldstone bridge arching its way over the small creek that brought a constant flow of fresh water. In the summer, a family of swans always nested there, gliding across the lake with regal comportment, their long white necks stretching toward the sky, topped with brilliant beaks. Beneath the water, schools of goldfish clustered, awaiting the crusts of bread that we tossed into the water.

19. Having arisen from the woods in the form of mist
into the ocean of the sky,

this indwelling gem stuck
as tear drop jewels in the blue stars.

Just prior to my marriage, Eastman Kodak hired me as part of the team that cleaned their Marketing Education Center nightly. The Center was set away from River Road overlooking the banks of the Genesee. As our crew departed each morning at 1 a.m., mists would arise from the river, creating an aerial snake echoing the meandering of the river, catching the gleam of our headlights and inviting us to look upward, into the midnight blue sky, marked with constellations and the Milky Way.

20. [Water] took rest in the thrones of the clouds,
accompanying Lady Lightning
whose blue sapphire light
illuminated Vasudeva on his Snake Throne.

Electric storms bring a jolt of energy and a sense of danger. In India during the monsoon, in the northeastern American states year round, in the Midwest particularly in the summer, thunder and lightning create a mood of relief and excitement, altering the heavens and evoking a sense of human smallness.

21. Atoms of water gush forth in tiny drops.
Each holds its essential nature,
like Brahman is found in all souls.

Vasiṣṭha makes a theological proclamation here, noting in the language of Advaita Vedānta that a unitary consciousness vivifies all reality. He uses a simile rather than metonymy, indicating that the omnipresence of rain reminds us of the ubiquity of Brahman, rather than stating that Brahman is found in the rain itself.

26. In the form of a rising mist,
[water] ascends on the chariot of the winds,
bestowing joyous fragrance in the channels
of the pure sky.

The images of this verse conjoin the fragrance arising from the earth with the mist carried by the wind up into the vast expanse of sky.

27. Rāma, by dwelling in that [water concentration]
from the smallest particle
to the ultimate experience of it,
the whole world comes into existence.
31. This knowledge shines forth as the highest purity.
It indeed appears to us as empty.
This vast space, in its expansiveness,
is who you were and who you are.

Vasiṣṭha experiences water in its various forms. It becomes the vehicle for his self-realization. He describes dew, drops of rain, the gathering of moisture in clouds, mist, rain, rivers, oceans, and lakes. He also discusses how the beauty of water brought him again to a deep appreciation and awareness, stilling his thoughts and revealing vast empty space. This process reveals how the mind can be trained through cultivated awareness to experience states of joy and bliss.

Jal Dhāraṇā in the *Gheraṇḍa Saṃhitā*

The *Gheraṇḍa Saṃhitā* offers instruction for the practice of water concentration, similar to that found in the Jñānārṇava text of Jainism. The geometric form, the color, and the mantra are identical: crescent, white, and *vaṃ*:

72. Now we will discuss practicing water concentration.
This element resembles a conch or a half moon.
Its color is white like jasmine.
It is associated with the seed syllable "*vaṃ*"
such as generated by a bee seeking splendid nectar.
It is always linked with Viṣṇu.

However, rather than associating water with the Vedic god Varuṇa, this text, which arises much later, invokes Viṣṇu, a deity widely worshipped at the time of its composition.

The breath and mind should be held in abeyance
for two and a half hours.
The adept at water concentration
would overcome sins and difficulties.

The period required to achieve full effect is quite a bit longer than the 40 minutes required each day at Yoga Anand Ashram.

> 73. Now we will tell the benefits of the water mudra.
> Whoever knows this highest water mudra,
> that knower of Yoga will not die
> even in deep terrifying water.

This verse perhaps suggests that one can learn to swim even in rough waters if well trained in this technique, a hopeful promise.

> 74. But this highest mudra must be carefully concealed.
> Otherwise, if revealed, its power will be destroyed.
> This is the truth; I say this from direct experience.

The author ends the discussion with a hint of mystery. Did boasting about this accomplishment jinx the author in some way?

Reflections on Water

Wildlife abounds in watery areas: crayfish in the stream beyond the meadow down the country lane; dolphins in the Pacific and in the Ernakulam canal in Kerala; white egrets worldwide; whales on a journey that never stops. On one magical flight from Los Angeles to Monterey, the pilot invited us to look down into the ocean and observe a pod of Great Blue whales making their way northward. From thousands of feet in the air, we could see them blowing air through their spouts, churning the water white with their flukes, creating a vortex of commotion with their sheer size and power.

The cascade of thoughts that can be generated about water seems endless. A large percentage of hospitalizations arise due to dehydration. Without water, human life ends in forty days or less. More than three-quarters of the human body consists of water. The flow of water provides reassurance that life continues. The stoppage of water, whether in the world or in the body, signals the disruption of life itself.

As with the concentration of earth, sustained attention to water stirs up thoughts and emotions of appreciation. These first two elements, earth and water, anchor the person and the world in a place of stability, a place referred to in the *Maitri Upaniṣad* as *bhūr,* the earth upon which waters flow: "The feet are the earth."[16] Earth and water, as seen in the first chapter, correlate to the lower reaches of the body, the feet and legs, the anus and reproductive organs. Grounding and watering keep the human person alive and connected with the wider world. In the next chapter we will address heat and warmth, the awakening like the dawn of higher aspects of human potential.

RAM

4

Fire

Locus of Desire

The element fire, known as *agni* and *tejas,* stands in the middle, above earth and water, below air and space. Its creative and purifying aspect generates a heat known as *tapas*. It also resides in the middle part of the body, energizing the diaphragm and the solar plexus. The fire in the belly digests food. The heat of desire arising from the midpoint of the body pushes people to express themselves in words. Agni causes people to act.

The *Ṛg Veda* Hymn of Creation X:129 extols heat as the origin of the One, who then moves among and creates the many:

> Darkness was concealed by darkness there,
> and all this was indiscriminate chaos.
> That ONE which had been covered by the void
> through the heat of desire (*tapas*) was manifested.[1]

Heat in the form of *tapas* provides the will power that allows engagement and creativity. It represents the inner fire generated through exertion and concentration.

Stories about and invocations of Agni, the god of fire, abound in the Vedas. More hymns praise Agni than any other deity. The very first hymn of the *Ṛg Veda* gives honor to Agni, asking for blessings and acknowledging Agni's link with sacrifice and the sunrise. Agni is the "king of the sacrifice, radiant protector of the cosmic order (*ṛta*)."[2] Agni's light illumines darkness. Agni's heat cooks food. Both priest and householder kindle the flames of Agni to gain auspiciousness.

For the month of Agni Dhāraṇā we were asked by our teachers at Yoga Anand Ashram to light an oil lamp or candle every morning and every evening, gazing upon its golden glow for twenty minutes at each sitting. We held our gaze in *trāṭakaṃ,* the technique where the eyes are held open until tears form. We then closed our eyes to experience the afterglow behind closed eyelids. This practice brought heightened awareness of electric lights and change of light in the sky at dawn and dusk.

This twice-daily sitting concentration supplemented other practices related to heat. As part of our general training in Yoga, we were invited to generate internal, purifying heat by practicing *tapas* on a weekly basis. We kept silent one day, usually on Saturday, navigating daily chores by using hand signals and writing notes. On Sunday we fasted, imbibing only fruit juice and herbal tea. This weekend *tapas* practice stretched for years.

As with the practice of the Earth and Water Concentrations, we were invited to let our minds wander to thoughts of the past. Campfires, fireplaces, bonfires, and country barns on fire arose from my memory. Central to this concentration was appreciation for the warmth provided by the furnace, the car heater, and the winter sun, especially because it was a very cold northeast winter. The electricity went out during a memorable ice storm while engaging in this practice, making the conservation of warmth and light all the more vital. Gurāṇi Añjali shared with us that her own studies took place under the light of an oil lamp, as her childhood home in Calcutta had no electricity.

The rising and setting of the sun played a central role in the *sādhana* of the overseer of ritual, the Pujārī of Yoga Anand Ashram. Each morning before dawn, I would run the two blocks in darkness from our home to the Ashram, unlock the door, climb the stairs, warm the ghee, refill the lamp, and kindle the flame as the morning's light would begin. As the sky started to glow, I would light one or three or five sticks of incense and sing the Gāyatrī Mantra, once at the brick altar on the floor, the *havan*, and then in each of the four corners of the room, returning once again to the *havan,* which I also washed every day, replenishing the flowers every three or four days. Agni expressed itself during this twice daily ritual in three ways: the kindled lamp, the heat in my body and voice, and the brilliance of the rising and setting sun. As Pūjārī, I remained ever mindful of the presence of Agni at all ashram events, refilling the lamp with ghee and lighting fresh sticks of incense when the others had burned out.

Downstairs from the Ashram loft, in the main body of the original barn, we created a restaurant and acquired a new mastery of Agni. We became cooks, working first with hot plates and teapots, and eventually with a full service range and oven. The heat generated by this bold entrepreneurship undertaken by young people in their early twenties was not limited to the stove but arose in all manner of human interactions: vendors, customers, fellow cooks, and servers. The crucible of food preparation steels one for all manner of business and emotions. Santosha Vegetarian Dining operated from 1977 until 2003, arising from the heat of desire, serving thousands and cultivating a worldly and sublime wisdom within its many workers. The heat of desire, rather than being rejected in the Ashram, was to be cultivated and understood and put to good use. Creative fires produce music, art, movement, penetrating insight, and even families. Agni lights the way in all these endeavors.

Arunachala and Fire

The Annamalaiyar Temple in Thiruvannamalai honors fire (*agni*). Its compound spreads out at the base of Mount Arunachala. As we entered the temple we encountered what seemed to be a wall of heat. We noticed camphor fires burning on the ground in honor of the powerful force of fire. The contrast between cool and hot became inescapable. The Gopurams, the seven-to-ten-story towers that mark the four directions, create a great stir of cooling winds that signal the transition into sacred space. One enters the Fire Temple from the east, walking straight from the cool breeze into the area of the burning camphor fires, which elevate the temperature dramatically. Hot and cold: the *Gītā* advises enduring both, whether they cause pleasure or pain.[3] One's highest self remains steadfast in conditions of cold, heat, pleasure, and pain.[4]

The temple deities are set back from the entrance several hundred feet in a central hall. The Śiva image faces east, the direction of the rising sun. As we entered the Śiva *liṅga* room, we walked once again into a vault of fire, a wall of radiant heat, generated by the many *deepas,* the oil lamps illuminating the room. We then circumambulated to the opposite side, reaching the shrine in honor of Pārvatī. She faces west. The Śiva and Pārvatī images in this temple, as well as in the wind and earth temples, are back to back, indicating their full union and coproduction of the world. Pārvatī is called Unnamalai Devī at the fire temple.

After departing from the central shrine, we lingered at a sandalwood altar in honor of Ganeśa, noted for its cooling powers. Ganeśa was made by Pārvatī as she sculpted sandalwood paste from her own body, crafted during a period of wistful desire she felt due to Śiva's long absence away far in the northern Himalayas. As she breathed life into the image she created, Ganeśa's calm and comical presence brought cooling and joy to her circumstance, qualities that devotees of Ganeśa continue to enjoy.

Our continued circumambulation took us to the southern side of the compound where Ramana Maharshi took refuge more than one hundred years ago. He was born in 1879. As a teenager in Madurai, he fell into a state of inquiry, asking again and again, Who am I? When he did not receive an answer, he began to wander. An attendant at the Annamalaiyar Temple discovered him half-dead in the subterranean Ganeśa shrine where we stood and nursed him back to health. Many years later, perhaps twenty years after his disappearance, his mother heard of a sage who resembled her son living in a cave near the Thiruvannamalai Temple. She traveled there immediately and cooked and cared for him as people flocked from all over the world to receive his wisdom. He was a confidant and spiritual advisor for many, including the scholar Walter Evans-Wentz, who had written his doctorate under the supervision of William James on traditional Irish lore and wrote several books on the great Tibetan masters.

As we moved our way to the exit, a family friend of Karthik told us about growing up just outside the western Gopuram. As a child he regularly played cricket in the western yard at the foot of the mountain before the temple regained popularity after years of relative neglect. This happened with the rise of the Indian middle class in the 1990s and the resulting temple revitalization movement.

In the heat of the late afternoon when we arrived, we felt relief under the Gopuram with its cooling breezes. We experienced intense heat as we walked by the camphor fires and even more intense heat within the temple. We felt some relief as we lingered with Ganeśa. We welcomed the cooling breeze of the eastern Gopuram as we exited the Fire Temple and slipped into the coolness of the night.

The next morning we were serenaded by loudspeakers from the temple intoning "Oṃ Namaḥ Śivāya" and "Oṃ, Oṃ, Oṃ." We traveled to the other side of town to visit the Ramana Maharshi Ashram. After seeing the main gathering hall and reading his remarkable story, we walked the wooded path up to the cave where Ramana lived for many years. We sat in meditation in the hall where he lectured. All through the extensive compound a deep pervading silence could be felt. Hiking up the side of Arunachala Mountain we caught breathtaking vistas of the Fire Temple below, with expansive views of the surrounding countryside.

Australian environmental activist John Seed became deeply involved with this sacred place, creating an early instance of modern on-the-ground conservation in India. In 1987, Seed received a plea from Apeetha Aruna Gin, an

Australian nun living near Arunachala mountain in Tiruvannamalai, near what was then called Madras. She lived at Sri Ramana Maharshi Ashram, mentioned above. She noticed that the surrounding areas had become stripped clean of vegetation due to local scavenging for firewood and fodder to feed the goats. Seed raised money for the development of a new NGO established by Apeetha: the Annamalai Reforestation Society. Through the efforts of this organization,

> the space between the inner and outer walls of the vast 23-acre temple complex has been transformed from a wasteland into what became the largest tree nursery in the south of India. Hundreds of people have received environmental education, and a 12-acre patch of semidesert was donated to the project and transformed into a lush demonstration of permaculture and the miraculous recuperative powers of the earth, Hundreds of Tamil people have been trained in reforestation skills—treeidentification, seed collection, nursery techniques, watershed management, erosion control, sustainable energy systems. Shiva's robes are slowly being rewoven.[5]

Seed himself speaks and writes of his own affirmation of the importance of this preservation work through a special quiet moment he experienced in the Arunachala forest with a troop of scores of monkeys:

> They groomed each other, they made love, mothers breast-fed their babies, children played and cavorted, utter unself-consciously living their everyday lives in my astonished and grateful presence. . . . I had never felt more accepted by the nonhuman world. I knew that Shiva had answered my prayer, had acknowledged my efforts, and was giving me his sign of approval.[6]

For Seed, this moment established a link between his work and the life of the mountain, arising from the heat of desire to help save a degraded environment.

Atharva Veda

Just as the *Ṛg Veda* celebrates the power of fire in hundreds of verses, so also the *Atharva Veda* devotes numerous stanzas in acknowledgment of the presence of Agni.

The first mention comes in the context of the Land, who carries upon her the presence of fire:

> 6. O! All sustainer of all!
> Bearer of rare treasures and sacred universal fire,
> Land of all moving life,
> possessor of gold, whose consort is Indra,
> may you give us wealth and good fortune!

The element of fire sustains the life of human beings, who possess and control fire. This verse speaks of the fire that allows for warmth and the cooking of food, and the god Indra, the master of the thunderbolt who brings the monsoon rains. These two deities, the most frequently invoked in the Vedic literature, work in tandem to ensure human prosperity. Indra uses lightning to release the waters from the heavens and bring the monsoon. Agni kindles the flames needed for illumination and cooking in each and every household every day.

M. C. Mehta, mentioned in the earlier sections on earth and water, has seen the urgency of addressing the overuse and misuse of fire with the rise of industrial economies and overuse of fossil fuels. M. C. Mehta is deeply worried about climate change and global warming. In a conversation with him in December 2006, he lamented the rapid disappearance of the Himalayan ice pack, narrating a harrowing adventure in Gangotri. He and his colleagues had hiked up into a pilgrimage site. On the way back, a huge chunk of ice had collapsed, endangering some Europeans down below. The meltdown of the glaciers will certainly mean trouble for India in the years to come. Some scientists estimate that all the glaciers might dissolve by 2050. Currently, the bulk of precipitation in the Himalayas comes in the form of snow. This snow gathers all through the winter months, and during the summer, slowly melts, feeding the great rivers of Asia all throughout the year. These include the Ganges, the Indus, the Irawaddy, the Brahmaputra, and even the Yangtze River of China. If the water does not take the form of snow and ice, it will rush down to the plains as soon as it falls, causing flooding at times of rain and drought during the hot, dry periods. Billions of people will be affected. Human industry has caused the warming of the earth. If nothing is done to rectify the situation, humans will lose their "wide and limitless domain." M. C. Mehta is contemplating appropriate action to stem this problem.

The Vedic seers discerned that the force of Agni takes many forms. It vivifies plants, is released in thunder, and is stored in stones.

19. Our Earth is full of Agni (fire).
It is the same Agni through the herbs and other medicinal plants.
The clouds carry it in the form of thunder; and the stones store it.
The same energy, in the form of hunger,
flows through human-beings and animals.
May that energy sustain us all along.

Agni suffuses the world with energy. It takes shape in animals, minerals, and vegetables. Without fire, no movement could exist, no being could subsist. This verse echoes back to the repeated mention of Agni in the *Ṛg Veda.* It also repeats the refrain of solidarity through the recognition that just as all beings arise from the earth, so also all beings share in the same energy of fire.

As mentioned above, the kindling of Agni starts and maintains the daily rituals of *pūjā*.

20. The fire [Agni] needed for sacrifice (*yajña*) and worship (*havan*)
comes from the sky where it exists in the form of sunrays
brightening the entire space.
That Agni is also found in many other forms.
May that energy help us to dissipate diseases.
Let it be available to us all the time.

Fire rituals were developed to be performed in alignment with the change of seasons. These rituals imitate and give honor to the power of the sun. With the advent of Modern Postural Yoga, Surya Namaskar has become a popular global recognition of the power of the sun, coupled with the generation of heat within the body. The rigor of this exercise energizes and loosens the body, as will be described in the appendix of this book.

The great power of fire can energize and it can incinerate.

21. May She, the Earth,
who is saturated with fire and blackened by it,
enlighten me and make me glorious.

This verse alludes to the destructive power of fire. Not only does this power give energy and facilitate sacrifice and allow the cooking of food, it can bring about tremendous destruction, as will be discussed in the *Yogavāsiṣṭha*'s analysis of fire later in this chapter.

The Puruṣa Sūkta of the *Ṛg Veda* makes an important correlation between the eyes and the power of the sun. The Atharva Veda also makes a similar connection.

> 33. With the help of the Sun,
> may my vision survey a vista as wide as yours, O Land.
> May my eyesight never get diminished year by year.

The Sāṃkhya philosophical system links the subtle element of the capacity to see form (*rūpa*) with the eye (*akṣa*). Light from the sun, whether directly or indirectly, enables the eye to operate. Indirect forms of sunlight include the reflected light of the moon and the release of solar energy through the burning of fuels and the surging of electrical current. Whether from coal, petroleum, or even vegetable oil and ghee, all energy owes its origin to the sun.

Buddhism: The *Dhātu Vibhaṅga*, the *Mahārāhulovāda*, and the *Visuddhimagga*

In his instructions to Pukkusati, the Buddha emphasizes that this element, like the others, once engaged and understood, must be seen as not holding any abiding essence. It must be disaggregated from one's sense of self.

> What is the fire property? The fire property may be either internal or external. What is the internal fire property? Anything internal, belonging to oneself, that is fire, fiery, and clung-to: that by which [the body] is warmed, aged, and consumed [with fever]; and that by which what is eaten, drunk, consumed, and tasted gets completely digested, or whatever else internally, belonging to oneself, is fire, fiery, and clung-to: this is called the internal fire property. Now both the internal fire property and the external fire property are simply fire property. And that should be seen as it actually is present with right discernment: "This is not mine, this is not me, this is not my self." When one sees it thus as it actually is with right discernment, one becomes disenchanted with the fire property and makes the fire property fade from the mind.[7]

This passage specifies two internal forms of fire: the positive capacity of digesting food and the negative aspects that cause illness and the fire of fever within the body.

For his own son, the Buddha gives the same teaching, with one important difference. He states that concentration on fire can provide a "firewall" against attraction and repulsion. All defiled things and all pure things can be burned by fire.

> Rāhula, develop meditation that is like fire. . . . Just as people burn clean things and dirty things, excrement, urine, spittle, pus, and blood in fire, and the fire is not repelled, humiliated, and disgusted because of that, so too, Rāhula, develop meditation that is like fire, for when you develop meditation that is like fire, agreeable and disagreeable contacts will not invade your mind and remain.[8]

Meditation on fire and meditation like fire purifies the mind, bringing it to the desired state of equanimity.

The *Visuddhimagga* provides instructions on how to perform concentration on fire. It gives an example of someone who mastered this practice in a past life, and then tells how to prepare a method for gazing upon fire:

> For those with experience with this practice in a past life, "it arises in any sort of fire, not made up, as one looks at the fiery combustion in a lamp's flame or in a furnace or in a place for baking bowls or in a forest conflagration."[9] The text cites the examples of Elder Cittagutta who entered this Jhāna while looking at a lamp. Others have work to do: "split up some damp heartwood, dry it, and break it up into short lengths . . . go to a suitable tree root or to a shed and make a pile in the way done for baking bowls and have it lit. Make a hole a span and four fingers wide in a rush mat or a piece of leather or a cloth, and after hanging it in front of the fire, sit down in the way already described. Instead of giving attention to the grass and sticks below or the smoke above, one should apprehend the sign in the dense combustion in the middle."[10]

The text lists words to be repeated to reinforce this concentration:

> The words used to support this form of fire concentration are: fire (*tejo*), Bright One (*pavaka*), Leaver of the Black Trail

> (*kanhavattani*), Knower of Creatures (*jataveda*), Altar of Sacrifice (*hutasana*) . . . fire, fire.[11]

As with the other elemental concentrations, Buddhaghosa notes two accompaniments to this practice: a learning sign and a counterpart sign. The former indicates that the practice remains with one throughout the day, and when one sees something related to fire, then remembrance of the practice arises. The counterpart sign is like the afterglow mentioned above, when the field of vision carries the mark of the elemental focus, in this case, an abiding presence of red or gold:

> One becomes reminded of this practice and carries the learning sign when seeing "any firebrand or pile of embers or ashes or smoke. . . . The counterpart sign appears motionless like a piece of red cloth set in place, like a gold fan, like a gold column.[12]

These two signs indicate that the *kasiṇa* has been effective, and that its effect lingers. Because of its enduring presence, it serves to protect the mind, girding it from wayward or distracting thoughts, as told to Rāhula by the Buddha.

Jainism: The *Ācārāṅga Sūtra* and the *Jñānārṇava*

Whereas the presence of fire in Hindu traditions marks the large Vedic rituals and the smaller temple and home *pūjās,* fire presents complications for the Jaina faith. Fire has great destructive power. Upon full initiation, Jaina monks and nuns are not allowed to kindle fire or to cook their own food. They generally refrain from participating in ceremonies that require the use of fire. To light a fire causes great disturbance. To snuff out a fire requires smothering its vital energy. The most nonviolent behavior would be to avoid fire whenever possible, though as we will see, the practice of inner purification (*tapas*) serves a central role in the dispersal of fettering karmas.

The *Ācārāṇga Sūtra* warns that one should be mindful of fire, that if one "denies the world of fire-bodies, one denies the self; if one denies the self, one denies the world of fire-bodies."[13] The text states that one should not hurt others through the use of fire. Care is to be exerted not to do harm to fire nor to allow fire to harm others. The author notes that

> [t]here are living beings living in the earth, living in the grass, living on leaves, living in wood, living in cowdung, living in

> dust-heaps . . . which, coming near fire, fall into it. [They are] touched by fire and shrivel up, lose their senses, and die there.[14]

The destructive power of fire must be avoided. "A wise person should not act sinfully [in regard to] fire, nor cause others to act so, nor allow others to act so. The one who knows the harm caused by fire is called a sage."[15] Great respect must be accorded to fire.

The *Jñānārṇava* takes a different approach to fire and sees it as a prime candidate for focus and purification. Chapter 29 describes the geometry, mantra, and color associated with fire:

> 29. 22. The fire *maṇḍala* is approached through the *svāstika* triangle
> with the seed (*bīja*) mantra (*ram*),
> shining like one hundred fires arising,
> pulsing with awe-inspiring yellow.

The repetition of the mantra, accompanied with focus upon the color and form of fire results in a flow of positive sensation:

> 37. 13. From the murmuring (of that mantra *raṃ*)
> one should then focus afterward
> on the emerging gentle result,
> an uninterrupted succession of endless pulsing fire.

This state of meditation undoubtedly is accompanied with a slowing of the breath and the generation of the brain wave state that indicates success in mastering the technique.[16] The next step indicates the distinctly Jaina mark of this practice:

> 14. By this, the eternal Jina (is visualized) within these flickering flames.
> Then, when that fire burns continually,
> one becomes steady,
> situated in the white lotus of the heart.

During a visit to the Jaina complex of temples in Hastinapur in 2013, Ganini Pramukh Shri Gyanmati Mataji, the founder, explained that within the blazing sun resides the perfect image of the Tīrthaṅkara, and that one can learn how to internalize this perfection. In order to accomplish this herculean feat, one must first destroy all the fetters of karma, delineated in Jainism within eight groupings and conceptualized in the form of a lotus. In this instance, one invokes the purifying powers of fire:

> 15. The eight upside down petals,
> representing the eight kinds of karma,
> are to be burnt completely by the fierce fire
> that arises with the great mantra and meditation.

The four negative karmas, to be purified and expelled through this practice, are karmas that obstruct knowledge, that obstruct intuition, that obstruct energy, and that cause delusional thinking and action. The four remaining categories, which are also ultimately left behind, are karmas that enable feeling, lifespan, physique, and social status.[17]

From an internal visualization, one turns to an external seeing of fire:

> 16. Then the triangular mandala of fire (is visualized)
> outside of the body.
> One should focus on those flickering flames
> as if they are bioluminescence.

The *svāstika* represents the cycle of birth, life, death, and rebirth in the realms of humans, gods, animals, and hell beings. It signals the possibility of release, of freedom from the karmic cycle. As related to fire, it works with mantra to advance one on the path toward great purification.

> 17. Marked by a svastika located at the edge,
> the fire seed *bīja* is approached (with the syllable *ram*).
> It is smokeless and glittering with gold
> as it ascends in the rising wind.

The dramatic power of this combined application of focus on the triangular flames of fire and the mantra *ram* results in rapid progress in the eradication of karma:

> 18. The inner fire of the mantra burns
> like a brush fire burns city after city,
> running and resounding swiftly,
> spreading radiance from its flames.

The end of the conflagration brings a state of peace, somewhat akin to the final peace found as the embers stop glowing on the funeral pyre.

> 19. This state reduces both body and lotus to ash.
> Burning itself out, the fire gently, softly
> goes into a state of peace.

As we will see in the space chapter, this state does not end with empty finality, but with a glorious ascent to the realm of the Siddha Loka.

The Fire Chapter of the *Yogavāsiṣṭha*

In the chapter on Agni Dhāraṇā, Vasiṣṭha celebrates fire in myriad forms, from the sun and moon and stars to the simple oil lamp. Through his meditation on heat and light he experiences deep delight and a feeling of safety and security. The correlated sense, seeing, can only function through the presence of light. For Vasiṣṭha, light becomes truly revelatory:

> 91.1. Then I disappeared into fire
> through the brilliant concentration on fire.
> I became linked with its various parts such as
> the moon, lightning, stars, flames, and so forth.

He draws parallels between stable government and the security afforded by life well-lit:

> 2. From its essential nature as eternally luminous,
> it spreads light like a beloved prince.
> It makes all things visible. It makes all things right.
> Thieves fail to conceal themselves in its glow.
> 3. Through its gentle, friendly lamps
> it provides thousands of delights.
> It allows all purposes to be seen
> in every house, like a good prince.

In addition to sociological commentary, Vasiṣṭha refers to the function of the moon and the sun in the vastness of the sky:

4. It brings good cheer to all the world
through the sparkling rays of the moon and sun.
Through its singular delights it casts light
into the distance, lifting up and pervading
the circumference of the sky.

He also talks about the clarifying power of light, which dispels ignorance. He proclaims it to be like the best of gems:

5. Light destroys the combined qualities
of blindness and affliction.
It possesses the quality of
revealing all truth and awakening.
6. The people proclaim with gusto:
"[Fire] is the axe [that cuts] the tree of darkness.
It provides the foothold for making things exceedingly pure.
It is golden, the ruby among gems."

Referring to the colors attributed to the three *guṇas* of Prakṛti, red for activity (*rajas*), black for lassitude (*tamas*), and white for purity (*sattva*), he draws parallels between the light and the relationship between fathers and sons:

7. It [energizes] reds, blacks, and whites;
it abides eternally through its gleaming limbs,
like a father gives shape to the bodies
of all his sons.

The powers of fire to restrain itself from going out of control, and to warm living spaces in cold weather are praised.

8. Fire, through its blessings, chooses
to spare the house of children from destruction.
It also protects [the people] from piercing winds
throughout the land.

Through his gaze, Vasiṣṭha sees fire buring below and above, in the hells and the in the heavens, on the earth and in the radiant sky. Fire bridges all worlds.

9. I saw the master [burning] brightly
in the darkest forms of the hell region.

With eyes half open, I saw its active form,
on the surface of the earth and at the crown of existence.
10. I saw [fire] in the abodes of the gods,
where illumined souls are eternally in great splendor,
as well as the light on the ruined huts of the people
and in the recesses covered in great darkness.
11. [I saw] that stainless radiant virgin sky
become smeared with the color of saffron [at sunset],
making way for the illumination of the moon and stars,
as well as the winds that bring night dew.

Vasiṣṭha comments on the agricultural cycle and its reliance on the light of the sun, as well as the ability of light to bring illumination to all circumstances:

12. Her grace causes the fields of corn each day
to ripen and grow up out of the darkness.
Her radiance [draws water up] into the clouds
that fill the vast crystal dome [of the sky]
and bring cleansing rains.
13. By her, meaning is bestowed.
Through her, comes illumination.
Like a younger sister, she reveals the highest truth:
there is consciousness only.
14. Her lustre on the lotus pool reflects
the actions of living beings on the earth and below,
just as from consciousness emerges
the wonderment of thought, perception, and form.

The cosmic aspect of fire and light can be seen in this acknowledgment of the seasons and the movement of heavenly bodies:

15. A necklace of innumerable jeweled stars
is called together from the mist.
Light increases with the days and seasons throughout the year
and froths in fires under the ocean.
16. The moon and sun move briskly
inside the great darkness of the night sky,
just as the one who stands deep in the great universe
is the one eternally moving and imperishable.
Fire marks personal qualities of strength and beauty:

17. Fire is the brilliance in gold,
the strength in men,
the crystal gleam in all jewels,
and the flash in lightning storms.
18. It is the splendor in the phases of the face of the moon.
It is the mark of beauty in long eyelashes.
Its undying love flows abundantly.
It glitters in the laughter of friends.
19. Fire is in the love that arises and shines forth
and can be found in the innate allure of the movement
of a face, an arm, an eye,
an eyebrow, a hand, or a lock of hair.

Fire also inspires fear, due to its power of incineration and its presence on the battlefield:

20. Fire shows that these three worlds are as flimsy as straw.
It burns in the slap of one's worst enemies.
It starts the thunderclap
and dwells in the heart of the strong lion.
21. Among excellent, active warriors,
fierce fire can be found in the sound
of their clashing swords, breaking through armor,
and in their harsh, noisy battlecries.
22. It emboldens the gods to fight the Dānava demons
and the demons to resist the gods.

In mid-verse, Vasiṣṭha describes one aspect of the miracle of chlorophyll, which causes a plant to grow up toward the light, attracting and elongating cells through its allure.

Fire is the force that moves all beings.
It causes plants to sprout upward.

Vasiṣṭha praises the light and heat of the sun for revealing all that can be seen, and the rays of the sun for their capacity to reach all directions, north, east, west, south, northeast, northwest, southeast, southwest, up, and down. The sun gives measure and rhythm to the passing of time.

23. Bright-eyed one, I experienced those things
in these coverings of space that make up the world
as if they were shimmering in the desert.
24. I saw the phoenix sun as its streams of light
scattered over all ten points of the horizon.
I saw its limbs flash on chosen mountains,
making them appear as if they were villages on the face of the earth.
25. The wheel of the sun is filled with treasure
like the desire within a flower's blossom.
Light sits within the universe like phosphorescence in the darkened sea.
Its continuous line of days unfolds just as fruits ripen on the tree.
Similarly, Vasiṣṭha expresses love and admiration for the moon.
26. The face of the moon in the sky
forms a pool of elixir.
Each evening it smiles cheerfully
on the people of the night.
27. (The moon's) power reflects all lovely good fortune in the world.
His wife, Rohini, (shines) in the night
as the most beloved white lotus flower.

The stars do not escape notice. The following description reminds this reader of moonless nights in Joshua Tree National Park, where the Milky Way marks and charts the sky with its brilliance.

28. To me appeared a gentle trail of stars,
arrayed like nectar flowing through the heavens,
like a web of shining flowers on a vine,
twisted and heaped together.

Another favorite outdoor California pastime, the beach walk, often reveals what the next verse describes, particularly toward sundown, where the slanting rays backlight the waves, revealing pearl-like white and radiant gold, rising up from the deep blue sea.

29. I saw jewel-like waves in the hands of the oscillating ocean,
as if merchants' hands were tossing them
on their scales to weigh them.

Fish catch the glimmer of sunlight like no other being; clouds, illuminated by lightning, tell of imaginary worlds, and hint of possible trouble.

> 35. I saw the gleaming flash of those little fish in the waves,
> standing transfixed in the roar of the water of a beautiful
> whirlpool.
> 30. I see whirlpools of fish in the water of the ocean,
> multitudes of sunbeams on that water,
> and in the delicate clouds,
> (portents of) lightning igniting a forest fire.

The voracious appetite of fire cannot be ignored. Fire can devour all things, as happens with frequency in the American West.

> 31. I saw the beautiful burning of the sacrificial fire,
> its tenacious flames devouring the wood,
> spreading throughout all that can be burned,
> roaring, strong, and crackling.
> 32. I saw the brilliance in gold and rubies
> that is called great in things made of jewels.
> I also saw things reduced to ash by fire
> just as knowledge is destroyed by the wicked.

Agni also carries erotic connotations, stoking the heat of sexual desire.

> 33. The wives of the rulers of men,
> as well as those of the Asuras, Uragas, and Gandharvas,
> are adorned, each of them, with strings of pearls
> placed on the summits of their breasts.
> 34. Just as a bride applies the marriage mark to her forehead
> delicately
> as if treading a path without causing harm,
> so also my wavering vision
> catches glimpses of flickering fireflies.
> 36. Tender stalks of flowers engaged in amorous activities
> in the women's quarters of the palaces, rising as if illuminated by
> lamps.

37. Having given forth their radiance
under the cover of darkness,
they then retreated, exhausted, wilted,
like the steady turtle draws its limbs inside its shell.
38. Due to weariness at the end of these times,
when all the world wanes as if sinking into a whirlpool,
I sat as the clouds disappeared into space
with a flash like that of a roaring elephant.

As this beautiful chapter reaches its climax, Vasiṣṭha first observes the magnificence of the sun setting over the Arabian Sea, and then, having absorbed the lessons of Agni, feels its destructive potential. Just as Śiva and Kālī trample the world in their apocalyptic dance, so too does Vasiṣṭha quell the world with the passing of the day.

39. The sun expanded at the end of the day
as its fires were absorbed into the waters,
into the skies at the end of the world's horizon,
dancing in endless waves of water.
40. With my teeth like kindling sparks
and my arms aflame, my tangled hair ablaze,
I generated a powerful roiling whirlpool of smoke.
41. I burned the towns made of wood.
My flaming mouth chewed on all creatures.
I devoured all things made of the eight forms of wood
and brought them to their ultimate dissolution.
42. Through striking forth fire as with axes, spears, and knives,
I caused a furious arc of sparks to fly forth,
giving vent to the purpose of fire.

Vasiṣṭha explores various metaphors of fire and light including its ability to dispel ignorance, its ability to provide comfort "like a good prince," its ability to protect and illumine. Like a Buddhist, he proclaims that fires remind us that all things are fleeting. Like a Vedāntin, he hints that just as fire can be found in all manner of things, so also resides the soul. Through thinly coded language he applauds the sexual power associated with fire, and celebrates the beauty not only of the passing of each day at sunset, but the stark beauty of fire's destructive power.

Concentration on Fire in the *Gheraṇḍa Saṃhitā*

The practice of focusing on fire can be seen in many aspects of Haṭha Yoga. The practices of *āsana* generate heat and warmth, particularly the forward bend (*paśćimatāna*) and the peacock (*mayūra*) poses.[18] Additionally, *prāṇāyāma* generates heat and sweat, particularly with slow deliberative practice of the moon and sun breath through repeated rounds of alternate nostril breathing. The left nostril activates the moon or Iḍa channel or river (*nāḍī*), while the right activates the sun or Piṅgala.[19] References to the moon and sun, beacons of heavenly light within the body, demonstrate the correlative and cosmic aspects of Yoga practice. The generation of heat through the practice of *āsana* purifies the body, releasing impurities.

The *Gheraṇḍa Saṃhitā* provides instruction on how to practice the Agni Dhāraṇā from the perspective of Haṭha Yoga. It begins by referring to this practice as a *mudrā,* a gesture or seal and locates its efficacy in the stomach. Its mantra is *raṃ*; its color is red.

> 75. Now we will tell about the fire concentration mudra.
> This is located in the stomach.
> Its seed syllable sounds like an Indragopa insect (*raṃ*).
> Its geometric form is the triangle.
> This element burns like the red lamp of Rudra.
> It gives success.

One is advised to practice this concentration for more than two hours, holding the mind in place of steadiness.

> One should hold the breath and mind in abeyance
> for two and a half hours there.

The one who practices this concentration stays safe, and gains intimacy with the power of fire.

> Concentration on fire keeps one safe
> from the dark deep danger of death.
> 76. The practitioner rises up into
> the shining light of fire.
> Through the blessings of this mudra,
> one lives and does not die.

The fire of desire ensures that action will continue. Fire holds the capacity to create and purify. Yoga practice honors both aspects.

Conclusion

In this chapter we have discussed the practice of Agni Dhāraṇā from several perspectives, starting with the twice daily practice at Yoga Anand Ashram, its temple manifestation in Tamil Nadu, the celebration of Agni in the *Pṛthivī Sūkta*, the Buddha's teachings on Fire Concentration, and Buddhaghosa's instructions on how to prepare the Fire Kasiṇa. We also explored the Jaina respect for the destructive and purifying powers of fire, Vasiṣṭha's rhapsodic encounter with fire, and the practices and benefits of fire in the context of Haṭha Yoga's *Gheraṇḍa Saṃhitā*. Agni manifests desires (*kāma*), burns away impurities through its *tapas,* illumines the world, and provides safety and warmth. Agni also destroys. In the next chapter we will explore the life-giving powers of the wind and its connection with breath.

YAM

5

Air

Wind and Breath

Wafting trails of incense reveal the movements of air as they traverse a room. For more than a dozen years, a group of meditators assembled early each Sunday morning at the Hill Street Center in Santa Monica, often practicing the elemental concentrations. The light angled into the room directly during the winter months, entering through the windowpanes, spilling upon the golden pine floor, glancing up to catch the billows of fragrant smoke. Sometimes the incense seemed to chase down one person or another. The play between the incense and the currents of wind had a sense of humor.

One year, the group received a special opportunity to concentrate on the mysteries of life borne by the wind. A hummingbird nested just outside the window, knitting a nest among the delicate boughs of a pear tree. Over the course of several months we tracked her flitting movements as she glided upon the air, returning to the nest to incubate her eggs and eventually to hatch and feed her young brood. The movements of a hummingbird seem to defy the laws of gravity. Born more of the air than of the earth, the hummingbird provides lessons on how to remain nimble, how to keep moving.

During the month of Vāyu Dhāraṇā at Yoga Anand Ashram, we were encouraged to be mindful of the wind, through observing the incense and the swaying of the trees. Portions of Long Island remain thickly forested, particularly on the north shore, but also near Great South Bay. Even in the winter, the Long Island scrub oaks tend to keep their leaves. Pine trees can be found in abundance, as well as majestic large oaks and maple trees. The Stony Brook campus harbors stretches of forest preserve that includes dogwood, scrub oak, and pine. During stormy weather, the wind along the winding roads and in the preserves bends the trees from side to side, and in times of ice storms, many trees splinter and fall. The rustling of the wind through the trees can be gentle or at times of high winds, thunderous. Making a connection between the rhythm of the breath and the movement of clouds and trees caused by the wind brings an aliveness to the body and world.

We were also taught to be mindful of our own breath through the daily practice of *tribandha, anuloma viloma,* and other forms of *prāṇāyāma*. Diaphragmatic breathing stabilizes the mind. Daily practice of breath awareness, combined with observing the movement of the wind outside and the stirring of air inside, creates a feeling of protection and well-being.

Kalahasti

Our 2013 elemental temple pilgrimage began in the state of Andhra Pradesh. Karthik, Chris, and I had landed in Chennai, met with friends from Pondicherry and Chennai, and engaged the services of a driver to bring us northward to the air temple in the Chittoor district, located on the edge of a mountain. As we ascended from the low-lying lands of Tamil Nadu, we entered a higher, cooler, breezier locale. We moved swiftly onto newly built country roads in Andhra Pradesh and drove by a huge new temple in honor of a couple renowned for their spiritual teachings on the oneness of all things. From there we proceeded to Kalahasti.

Kalahasti welcomes its visitors with a gigantic polychrome statue of Śiva and Pārvatī, sitting back to back. We walked up the hill to the Śaiva temple in honor of the element air/breath/wind/Vāyu, just in time for the evening *pūjā* and *darśan*. An orchestra of musicians with cymbals, drums, gigantic clarinets, and chanting priests invoked the Śiva *liṅga, deepa* oil lamps dancing to the rhythms of chants from the Atharva and Yajur Vedas. We then processed around the reverse side for an invocation in honor of Pārvatī. A kindly old gentleman tended a side shrine in honor of Ganeśa, and invited us to give the small statue a push on its swing. The many pillars in this temple are adorned with various images, including Yoga postures and an abstract representation of Śiva/Śakti in the form of a yin/yang design. The stories of Śiva and Pārvatī associated with Kalahasti depict a mature couple, in the prime of life, kindly administering their domain.

Vāyu and the Maruts in the *Ṛg Veda* and the *Pṛthivī Sūkta*

The lauding of the elements in early Sanskrit literature includes praise and a healthy respect for the power of the wind (Vāyu) and thunderstorms driven by the wind, referred to as the Maruts. In the first maṇḍala of the *Ṛg Veda*, an analogy is drawn between horses drawing a chariot and the wind: "Vāyu yokes his chestnut pair, Vāyu his ruddy pair, Vāyu the two nimble ones to the chariot . . ."[1] The wind pulls forward the dawn and readies the cows for milking. The verse proclaims "You, Vāyu, with no one ahead, have the first right to the drinking of these soma drinks of ours," a seeming reference to all manner of abundance.[2]

> The Maruts bring rain with the wind:
> The Maruts scatter mist; they make the mountains tremble,
> when they drive their course with the winds . . .
> The rivers hold themselves down for your expansion
> and for your great gusting.
> You at night we invoke for help, you by day,
> you when the ceremony is proceeding.
> Up they rise, bright with ruddy breath, along their courses,
> bellowing on the back of heaven.[3]

The Maruts ensure that the rains will return, operating with Indra to beckon the strong monsoon.

The tenth and final *maṇḍala* of the *Ṛg Veda* includes four verses that give praise to the wind. The first describes the invisible hand of the wind:

> 1. Now (I shall proclaim) the greatness of Wind and of his chariot:
> Shattering as he goes. Thundering is his sound.
> Touching heaven as he drives, turning things red,
> and tossing up dust from the earth as he goes.
> 2. The dispersed eddies of the Wind press forward together.
> Following him, they go to him, like girls to a festive gathering.
> Yoked together with them on the same chariot,
> the god speeds on as king of this whole world.
> 3. Speeding along the paths in the midspace,
> he does not settle down on any single day.

> Comrade of the waters, the first-born abiding by truth—
> Where was he born? From where has he arisen?
> 4. The breath of the gods, the embryo of the world,
> this god wanders as he wishes.
> Only his sounds are heard, not his form.
> To him, to the wind, we would do honor with our oblation.[4]

This elegant description bears resemblance to the Hymn of Creation, which also invokes the waters and asks, "From where has he arisen?"

A shorter verse in the last book of the *Ṛg Veda*, as noted by Jamison and Brereton, credits the wind "with the ability to provide healing and . . . to keep us alive and prolong our lifetimes."[5]

> 1. Let the wind blow hither a remedy,
> which is luck itself, joy itself, for our heart.
> 2. O Wind, you are father to us, and brother,
> and comrade to us. Make us live.
> 3. What deposit of immortality has been deposited
> yonder in your house, O Wind.
> Give us of that for us to live.

This brief poem celebrates the wind as family and friend and giver of long life.

In the Pṛthivī Sūkta of the *Atharva Veda* the wind has many tasks. It supports the flight of birds, swirls billows of dust, and stokes fire:

> 51. The two-winged swans, falcons, eagles,
> and birds of all kinds fly fearlessly
> where the wind comes rushing,
> raising dust storms and uprooting trees,
> as well as fanning fire.[6]

The wind also holds the power to make things calm and pleasant:

> 59 . . . Grant us peace, tranquility,
> fragrant air, and other worldly riches.[7]

From Vedic literature, we see many qualities of the wind: its potential to bring storms and the blessings of rain; its destructive capacity; and its ability to heal.

Buddhism: *Dhātu Vibhaṅga, Mahārāhulovāda Sutta,* and *Visuddhimagga*

The Buddha urges Pukkusati to understand the function of the wind in all its forms, externally and internally. The Buddha in particular emphasizes the need to know the various ways that gases circulate throughout the body, both in terms of respiration and digestion. These gases, known as *prāṇas,* serve as markers for health. Traditional Indian medicine takes care to understand and regulate them for maximum health.

> And what is the wind property? The wind property may be either internal or external. What is the internal wind property? Anything internal, belonging to oneself, that is wind, windy, and sustained: up-going winds, down-going winds, winds in the stomach, winds in the intestines, winds that course through the body, in-and-out breathing, or anything else internal, within oneself, that is wind, windy, and sustained: This is called the internal wind property. Now both the internal wind property & the external wind property are simply wind property.[8]

As with the other elements, the Buddha tells Pukkusati to ultimately disengage any ego investment in the wind.

> And that should be seen as it actually is present with right discernment: "This is not mine, this is not me, this is not my self." When one sees it thus as it actually is present with right discernment, one becomes disenchanted with the wind property and makes the wind property fade from the mind.[9]

The "fading from the mind" refers to the process of overcoming attachment and quelling the compulsion to obsess about the particularities of air or breath.

It is important to keep in mind that this statement does not in any way condemn the air or the breath. Instructing his own son, the Buddha urges Rāhula's meditation to become like the air:

> Rāhula, develop meditation that is like air; for when you develop meditation that is like air, arisen agreeable and disagreeable contacts will not invade your mind and remain. Just as the air blows on clean things and dirty things, on excrement, urine, spittle, pus,

> and blood, and the air is not repelled, humiliated and disgusted because of that, so, too, Rāhula, develop meditation that is like air; for when you develop meditation that is like air, arisen agreeable, disagreeable contacts will not invade your mind and remain.[10]

The air does not protest if it encounters foul smells, nor does it rejoice at the presence of perfume. Just as with the other elements, the air retains its equanimity at all times. The Buddha calls upon his son to emulate the air.

Some centuries later, Buddhaghosa provides detailed instructions for setting up the air *kasiṇa*. The wind cannot be placed in a bucket or framed. It cannot be contained. Hence, the instruction advises to watch the effects of the wind:

> To develop the air Kasiṇa, one need not create a disk of dried clay nor collect clear water in a bowl nor build a fire to be viewed through a hole in mat. One merely "notices the topics of growing sugarcane moving to and fro, or the tops of bamboos or of trees, or the ends of the hair."[11]

The text also advises that one can "establish mindfulness where the wind strikes a part of the body after entering by a window or a crack in a wall, using . . . names for wind (*vata*) (such as) breeze (*maluta*), blowing (*anila*) . . . and air, air."[12] The use of words reinforces attention and helps focus the mind. The learning signs that arise include seeing wind as if seeing swirls of steam arising from hot rice and an eventual state of "quiet and motionlessness."[13] The description of the different forms taken by the air indicates an attentiveness to detail that characterizes sustained meditative practice.

Jainism: *Ācārāṅga Sūtra, Jīva Vicāra Prakaraṇam,* and *Jñānārṇava*

The Jaina tradition developed its own biology. Its earliest surviving text, the *Ācārāṅga Sūtra*, discusses the life and intelligence found within plants immediately following its description of the life within fire, then continues with the presence of life within the air. First it lists the many ways in which animals are born: from eggs, a fetus, a fetus with placenta, from various forms of liquid, from a chrysalis, and from "regeneration" in the case of humans, gods, and hell-beings.[14] The text alludes to the classical grouping of animals in light of the numbers of senses they possess. Whereas elemental beings, plants, and microbes have the sense of touch, worms add the sense of taste, insects add the sense of smell, flying insects add the sense of sight, while higher-order fish, birds, and mammals add the hearing and the mind. For the sake of one's own ethical propriety and to thin out the karma that accrues due to acts of violence, the text proclaims: "A wise person should not act sinfully towards animals, nor cause others to act so, nor allow others to act so."[15] Life must be known and respected in all its forms.

After this delineation of complex forms of plant and animal life, the *Ācārāṅga Sūtra* describes the presence of life within the air. In grand language the author proclaims, "For the sake of the splendor, honor, and glory of this life, for the sake of birth, death, and final liberation, for the removal of pain . . . if a man acts sinfully towards wind . . . this deprives him of happiness and perfect wisdom."[16] This first lecture of the *Ācārāṅga Sūtra* ends with the reminder that no person should act sinfully to any of the six kinds of lives, whether found in the earth, water, fire, plants, animals, or the air. Observant Jaina monks and nuns are not allowed to tread upon green grass or to shout loudly or to use a fan, or to kindle or extinguish a fire, out of concern not to disturb elemental or plant bodies.

The *Jīva Vicāra Prakaraṇam*, written by Śāntisūrīśvara in the twelfth century, provides extensive details on the nature of life according to Jainism. In regard to the wind, it delineates winds that blow up, that blow down, that come from the mouth, that carry a "melodious humming tune," that are dense and rarefied.[17] The text also specifies the lifespan not only of air bodies, but of all the elements:

> The duration of life of the earth (an earth body) is twenty-two thousand years; that of the water-bodied souls is seven thousand years; that of the wind-bodied is three thousand years while that of the trees is ten thousand years and that of the fire is three days and three nights.[18]

The text provides greater detail on specific forms of soil, stating that earth body life can exist for a thousand years in the desert, rich soil for twelve thousand years, with the hardest of stones lasting the maximum of twenty-two thousand years.[19] Following the same logic, life within a particular body of air might last as long as three thousand years, while most air bodies abide for a much shorter period.

Jainism distinguishes itself from Buddhism and Advaita Vedānta due to its staunch adherence to the teaching of the real presence of entities in the world. Souls exist, karmas exist, and through the practice of ethics, karmas, which are particular and real, can be expunged, leading to freedom. The path to this freedom taught in the *Jñānārṇava* and repeated in Hemacandra's *Yogaśāstra* uses the same techniques found in the traditions of Tantra, which developed in both Buddhism and in Hinduism. As with the practices of the other elements, concentration on the wind is supported by a specific geometric mark, in this case a sphere, the color of bluish black, and the mantra *yaṃ*.

> 29.21. The Vāyu *maṇḍala*, subtly marked,
> is approached by the wind syllable (*yaṃ*).
> It glows like blue-black ointment,
> gathered into the shape of a perfect sphere.

The practice of focusing on the wind, according to the author, moves more quickly than the prior three and seems to favor people of a spiritual disposition.

> 29.23. Thus, in these (four practices)
> the wind moves quickly and incrementally.
> This is to be known at the right time
> by those devotional highest people

The twenty-ninth chapter of the *Jñānārṇava* describes concentration on the four elements of earth, water, fire, and air. These take four corresponding geometric forms, the square, crescent, triangle, and sphere. Four colors are associated with these four: ochre, white, yellow, and blue-black, respectively. Four mantras correlate with the four elements, starting with *laṃ* and extending through *vaṃ* and *raṃ* to *yaṃ*.

Chapter 37 states that concentration on the wind allows one to travel widely, experience passion, and settle into calm:

> 22. In this state, one finds enjoyment in moving about the world
> with one's countenance travelling with the wind,
> wandering to the abodes of people,
> settling down on the face of the earth.
> 23. With the powerful wind,
> one can speedily rouse oneself up into passion.

> Then, through firm, accomplished practice,
> one can calm the breath (the inner wind).

As with the Buddhist and Hindu texts, the Jaina approach to wind, air, and breath interconnects.

The *Yogavāsiṣṭha*

As Vasiṣṭha drew near the end of his spiritual journey, he ascended into the winds, feeling the breath within the body as inseparable from the wind that plays with "the people, the trees, and the beautiful blooming flowers." As he practiced concentration on the wind (*vāyu dhāraṇā*), he proclaimed:

> VII.92.1. Next I came to concentrate on the operations of the wind,
> spreading my thoughts resolutely
> to examine the world and satisfy my curiosity.
> 2. I rose up into the wind [that surrounds] the earth,
> playing with the people, the trees, and the beautiful blooming
> flowers,
> protecting the water lilies.

Continuing with the erotic theme that began during the Agni Dhāraṇā, he sees a way to extend coolness to those who have been heated by the throes of desire:

> 3. Desiring to bring some relief
> to the exhausted bodies of these amorous ones,
> I sprinkled down drizzle and mist
> with the higher purpose of bringing them joy.

Each of these meditations took place as if from above. As Vasiṣṭha looks down from his elevated perspective, he sees that he can guide and educate vegetation, and that in return, vegetation sends blessings of sweet fragrance.

> 4. I became the teacher of the dancing leaves
> on grasses, trees, and tender vines.
> I was adorned with the fragrance of flowers
> and the splendor of medicinal plants and fruits.

He feels the movement of wind in times of love and in times of great distress on and within the earth. As wind, he embodies gentle adoration and destructive power alike.

> 5. At times of quiet and celebration
> I fondly caressed the worlds of beautiful women.
> At times of calamity (such as earthquakes)
> I tossed rocks as if they were feathers.

Vasiṣṭha also experiences the movement of the wind in the heavens and in hell and in the ocean and sky. The wind seemingly forms a bridge between all these worlds.

> 6. In heaven, I carry the earth's honey and pollen,
> Arising from the jasmine that adorns the trees in paradise.
> In hell, my gathered fires illuminate the thick fog.
> 7. In the ocean my undulating movements
> can be seen in the pounding of the surf.
> In the sky, I move the clouds to hide
> and then reveal the mirror of the moon.
> 8. I support that beneficial vehicle,
> the powerful army of stars,
> moving perfectly through the three worlds
> on their powerful, speedy chariot.

Breath and wind relate closely to thought, as elegantly expressed in the following verse:

> 9. Closely resembling how thought quickly appears and disappears,
> it touches the body though it has no body,
> inducing bliss through its movement (*spanda*)
> like the fragrance of sandalwood.

Vāyu provides an extended metaphor for stages of human life, providing succor and relief from exhaustion.

> 10. [The wind drives] the hard showers of rain and snow.
> It brings infirmity to the old.

It makes the young drunken with joy.
For the gentle ones, it brings silence and innocence.
11. Its course lifts up sweetness,
and brings the nectar of happiness to the heavens.
The beloved [winds] of March take away
the fatigue that comes with long love making.
12. Though tired from the incessant
swinging and swaying and undulations of the Ganges,
the wind [in the mountains] does not recognize its own fatigue
and fends off extended exhaustion.

The wind adorns the world with beautiful movement, causing plants to sway and stirring thoughts and actions of love and love-making.

13. Through its caresses, it bends the abundant flowers
and the vines waiting like wives in springtime.
It incessantly shakes and moves the palm fronds.
It dislodges bees from the plants.
14. Having enjoyed pleasures for a long time under the face of the moon,
the full cloud of sleepiness comes upon the bed.
Exhausted from making love, [the wind] is taken away
to that splendid lotus that throbs in the heart.
15. The wind, like a horse, moves through the sky,
established in and combined with the clouds.
It resembles a dancing elephant
in the throes of sexual desire.

The wind comes from on high, bringing cleansing to the pure and curses to those without virtue. It is the power that moves the other elements into action.

16. (The wind) as herdsman of the clouds at the top of the mountains
energetically casts down lightning and rain.
He extends soothing rain to the liberated ones
and destructive dust over the enemies of dharma.

Images of flowers, fragrance, space, sound, pulse, the heart, and oneness create a cascade of wonderment.

17. The fragrance of flowers pervades
space as if it were sound.
Devoted to the limbs of each being as well as the earth itself,
[the wind] rises up as the pulse of breath.

The wind carries the fragrance of the flower. It cradles the movement of each and every being.

18. (This breath) is the one self behind all actions,
hidden in the heart of this splendid body.
It serves as the guide to eternal oneness.
Educated families know its essence.

The breath, like a hidden key, allows one to understand the body and its connection with the universe.

19. (The wind) steals away the treasured fragrance
that traverses cities and rivers.
(It beckons) the cool moon, that orb shining in the darkness,
rising from the ocean of milk.

The winds that stir up upon the setting and rising of the sun in coastal places also can be discerned with the rising of the moon.

Vasiṣṭha continues to enumerate the powers of the wind and of the inner wind (*prāṇa*). It energizes animals, surrounds islands and continents (92:20), it moves the ocean and moves sediment to form sandy beaches (92:22), it brings music to reed instruments and appears as if it were an elephant in the sky (92:25). The wind cools and dries (92:26). It enters every channel (*nāḍī*) of the body; it is the essence of life's biological functions (92:28–29). From this dawning realization, Vasiṣṭha comes to see that all bodies, including those of the gods named as Moon, Sun, Hari, Indra, and Brahma rely utterly upon the presence of wind. From his vaunted perspective, he saw

. . . the seas and oceans, the islands and mountains,
stretching to the limits of the horizon. . . .
heaven and earth and the underworld regions
with all their inhabitants, their births and their deaths. (YV VII:92:33–34)

In this exhilarating, airy realm, Vasiṣṭha sees that all things are made of the five elements (*bhūtapañcarūpiṇā*, YV 92:35). He communes with their various forms as animals and trees and travels to the land of snow and ice. He ascends to the billowy clouds, describing them as white as talc (*śubrābhram*) and as luscious as fresh butter (*navanīta*, YV 92:39). He cavorts with lilies and lotuses, geese and swans, rippling across lakes, flowing with streams (YV 92:41–42). He comes to feel that:

> The earth with its rivers of pure waters
> and its solid hills and rocks
> were as the veins and blood
> and flesh and bones of my body.[20]

After these realizations, Vasiṣṭha nears the end of his quest for freedom, as will be explored in the chapter on space.

Air in the *Gheraṇḍa Saṃhitā*

In Haṭha Yoga as described by Gheraṇḍa, the concentrations provide a seal (*mudrā*) for the emplacement of yogic experience within the body. By holding the gaze upon the effects of air, by visualizing the color black, and by reciting the mantra *yaṃ*, mastery can be gained over the operations of the body and the mind. Gheraṇḍa links this practice with Īśvara, acknowledging the power that comes with the mastery of wind, air, and breath.

> 77. Now we will tell about the air concentration mudrā.
> It is black like ointment.
> This element (*tattva*) is made of lightness (*sattva*).
> Its syllable is "*yaṃ*."
> Its deity is Īśvara.
> One should hold the breath and mind in abeyance for two hours.
> The adept at air concentration would be able to move through space.

The training at Yoga Anand Ashram included a *prāṇāyāma* class that required at least forty-five minutes of daily practice. This practice featured holds of the alternate nostril breathing mentioned earlier, with a special focus on retention of the exhalation.

According to Yoga Sūtra II:49–53, this practice is key to the success of Yoga and the gateway to effective concentration.

> 49. Control of breath cuts off the motion of the inbreath and outbreath.
> 50. Its fluctuations are external, internal, and suppressed. It is observed according to time, place, and number, and becomes long and subtle.
> 51. The fourth is withdrawal from external and internal conditions.
> 52. Thus, the covering of light is dissolved.
> 53. And there is fitness of the mind for concentrations.[21]

These verses describe the process of breath. The inbreath draws external air into the body, where it can be held. The outbreath returns the air to the outside world. The exhaled breath can also be held. Instruction for holding the breath comes in many variations: a slow inhale for a count of eight; holding for a count of sixteen; exhale for a count of sixteen; holding for a count of thirty-two would be one example. As one repeats such an exercise for several minutes, the lengthened breath becomes quite subtle. Purification takes place through the holding of the exhaled breath and, according to Patañjali, can lead to a sense of lightness and readiness for concentration.

Srivatsa Ramaswami, at this printing the only surviving direct disciple of the "father of modern Yoga," Krishnamacharya, teaches a *prāṇāyāma* that requires three hours to fully complete. Students report deep experiences of purification and exhilaration through this practice, which includes alternate nostril breathing, diaphragmatic breathing, rapid breathing, and slow breathing.

Returning to the *Gheraṇḍa Saṃhitā*, we find affirmation of the benefits of concentration on the air:

> 78. Now the fruits of air concentration will be told.
> This highest mudrā destroys old age and death.
> One is not killed by the wind
> and is able to move through space.
> 79. This practice should not be taught
> to anyone who is wicked or bereft of devotion.
> And, if it were given to them, it would be lost.
> I speak the truth to you, Canda!

Gheraṇḍa ends his description of Vāyu Dhāraṇā by emphasizing the benefits and cautioning about the importance of assessing the state of mind of aspiring students.

We have examined the concentration on the wind from various perspectives and have seen commonality among different practices from Hinduism, Buddhism, and Jainism. In the next chapter, we will diverge from the sequence of elemental meditations to explore human and animal narratives that arise from recognition of the interwoven world generated by connections of earth, water, fire, and air.

LH.

6

Animal Stories from the Upaniṣads, the Jātaka Tales, the Pañcatantra, Jaina Narratives, and the *Yogavāsiṣṭha*

Landscape includes the great elements of earth, water, fire, and air contained within space. Landscapes are populated not only with the energetic presence of the elements but also carry the life stories of countless beings: microbes, insects, plants, reptiles, birds, fish, and all manner of mammals. In this chapter we will explore narratives that link animals, including humans, to the landscape, and techniques by which connections can be made with the more-than-human world.

Yoga Training and Animals

During one memorable week in Yoga training, Gurāṇi Añjali asked her Thursday night students to enter into a different style of concentration. Rather than focusing on an element, we were asked to keenly observe an animal at least once each day. It did not matter if the animal were wild or domesticated; it could have been a cat or a dog or a bird or a rabbit. We were also encouraged to recollect past experiences with animals.

During my childhood we reared many litters of Labrador Retrievers, walking long distances through the fields behind our house, training them to fetch. Sadly, the Lab called Jeff, my steady companion on the long afternoons while my older siblings were in school, ran afoul of the local game warden. The warden shot and killed him in the dead of night under the light of the moon. Several months later, Mike, a thick coated Black Lab joined us, as well as a cat from the Adirondacks named Kenmore, for the hotel where my sister had worked in the summer. Our family avidly followed birds, prowling the marshes and woods and country roads in search of geese, pheasants, robins, scarlet tanagers, woodpeckers, warblers, wrens, sparrows, vireos, and so many more. During my teen years, my father and mother began to train standardbred horses, the ones that pull chariots at the races, and a stray dog joined our household, a Cockapoo we named Rover. Animals were an integral part of our childhood and have become the mainstay in the primatology career of my oldest sister, who has studied owl monkeys and lemurs for decades.[1]

Observing animals expands one's sense of self. The empathy felt in the company of a beloved dog, the calm experienced while petting a purring cat, the wonder stirred up by seeing the strength and speed of a mountain lion all call us to something larger. David Abram, who trained with a shaman in Nepal, describes connecting with a crow at the deepest of levels. Sonam, his teacher, trained Abram over the course of several weeks to practice *trāṭakaṃ,* the yogic fixed gaze technique, honing his vision on the chest of a raven.

> "Move into the bird," he said. . . . "Keep your eyes open. Eyes open. Watch." The bird is now hopping, not walking, toward the edge of the gorge, and I feel each hop as a slight jolt. Its shoulders expand as wings spread and lift, and then with a lunge we are aloft . . . the whole canyon opens beneath us. . . . Now we're following the blue ribbon of water as it gets bigger and wider and *louder,* its many voices swelling as a freshness fills the whooshing air. . . . Then cliffs are slanting past and the river is falling away, and the cliffs [are] close by again, then the river, then the cliffs, then that abyss and I finally realize we're spiraling up the side of the canyon, riding one of the warm updrafts like I've seen ravens do so many times. . . . And I'm balancing, floating, utterly at ease in the blue air. . . . Falling, yet perfectly safe. Floating. . . . Among the rocks scattered near the chasm's edge there's a rectangular boulder we're falling toward. . . . And there, off past the other rocks toward the edge of the precipice is an odd creature—no, two creatures, two clothed people crouched together on the ground. Their faces are upturned, staring steadily at us even as we glide downward, their heads turning together as they track us perfectly with their gaze. The eyes of one are especially compelling, achingly so, staring straight toward, straight up into . . . me.[2]

This moment of yogic connection alters Abram's grasp of the world and the grasp of the living world upon Abram. Abram gained an intimacy with and sensitivity to the nonhuman realm that proved instructive for his sense of philosophical emplacement within the natural world.

Nepal and India abound with animals in many forms. I have encountered jackals and gaurs in Lumbini, Nepal; otters and elephants in the Periyar Preserve in Kerala; rhesus and langur monkeys along the roads and in the temples in Orissa and Uttarkhand; cows and pigs in the alleys and byways of Delhi and Jaipur; goats and blackbucks in Rajasthan; thirteen different species of birds on the roadway from Varanasi to Bodh Gaya, and more. Animals can speak to us in many ways, regardless of our locale. To land on the Indian subcontinent places one in the company of abundant life. As D. H. Lawrence states, each place has its own chemistry: "Every continent has its own great spirit of place. . . . Different places on the face of the earth have different vital effluence, different vibration."[3] In the literature that follows, we will explore India's distinct relationship with animals, a relationship that has produced hundreds of millions of vegetarians, a sophisticated philosophy of birth, death, and rebirth, and many fables wherein animals serve as the primary teachers.

Landscape and all that it contains and implies, including the animals and humans that populate it, provides a frame through which to view Brahmanical and Śrāmaṇical traditions of India. By examining five stories from five different landscapes, a sense of intimacy with the elements and other-than-human animals can be gleaned that remains instructive beyond their historical and geographic and religious origins. The story of Satyakāma Jābāla takes place first in a village and then in the countryside. The Blue Bear tale starts in the deeply forested mountains, proceeds to the city, and then returns to the mountains again. The Rishi's tale starts on the banks of a river and includes an encounter with a talking mountain. The Meghakumar narrative takes place in a "contemporary" capital city, a forest, and a constructed meadow created by ingenious elephants, concluding in a heavenly abode. The story of Puṇya and Pāvana takes place on the banks of the Ganges in the Himalayas. In each story, place plays an important role, whether forest, village, mountain, meadow, or riverbank.

Forests still blanketed India during the period of the composition of the Vedas, Upaniṣads, and the early texts of Buddhism and Jainism. Lewis Lancaster has noted that "India of the time of the Buddha was composed of urban islands in the sea of the forest" and that "the forest was a source of pain, danger, and struggle."[4] In fact, the sage Tuladhara recalls in the Mahābhārata a time when "crops sprouted from the earth without cultivation"; people ate from the bounty of the earth before the advent of settled agriculture.[5] It might be said that the literature of this early period describes a simpler time, a time of attunement with the natural order (*ṛta*). It could also be surmised that some of this literature documents a radical transition from hunter-gatherer lifestyles to settled agricultural communities, and a consequent shift in relationships between humans and animals.

Animals in the *Pṛthivī Sūkta* of the *Atharva Veda*

In its celebration of the elements and the gifts of the earth, the *Pṛthivī Sūkta* makes frequent mention of animals.

> 5. She is the home of cows, horses, and of birds.
> May that Earth protect us, grant us prosperity,
> and bestow upon us vigor.[6]
> 15. O Mother Earth!
> Your progeny consists of not only bipeds but also quadrupeds.
> Among the bipeds, there are the five races of humans
> who are sustained by the Sun through its immortal light and
> rays.

This verse celebrates diversity of life, both human and animal. Even today, one encounters so many four-legged beings on India's streets and roads: camels, elephants, dogs, monkeys, goats, cows, and water buffalo. Additionally, India has been home to persons of African, European, and East Asian origin, as well as home to Caucasian peoples to the north and Dravidians in the south.

> 46. O Mother Earth!
> Keep away from us venomous reptiles
> such as snakes and scorpions which cause thirst when they
> sting;
> keep away those poisonous insects which cause fever,
> and let all those terrible crawling creatures
> which are born in the rainy season keep away from us.
> Be kind to us and grant us that which is beneficial.
> 48. The Earth which bears both the good and the wicked
> permits wild animals such as boar and deer to move freely.

The world of nature includes danger. Even today, thousands each year die from snake bite. Pestilence afflicts all communities, particularly during the monsoon, the season long awaited that also generates fear for one's safety, both for the punishing storms as well as for the abundance of life it unleashes.

> 49. O Mother Earth!
> Although various wild animals
> such as the lion, the tiger, the wolf, the jackal, the deer, and others
> are nurtured in your forests,
> keep all menacing animals away from harming us.

Along with snakes and criminals, predatory animals, even today, threaten the well-being of humans in India. Hundreds lose their lives each year, particularly from tigers and elephants, as well as from rabid dogs.

> 51. The two-winged swans, falcons, eagles,
> and birds of all kinds fly fearlessly above the earth,
> where the wind comes rushing,
> raising dust storms and uprooting trees,
> as well as fanning fires.

To complete this acknowledgment of the range of beings, the text describes the flight of birds, linking their feats and temperaments with wind and fire.

The Education of Satyakāma Jābāla

The story of Satyakāma Jābāla[7] appears in the fourth book of the *Chāndogya*, one of the two oldest Upaniṣads, dating perhaps from 2,800 years ago. During the early period when India was lightly settled, cow herders were sent out into the forests and meadows to tend to flocks in distant quarters. One such young drover, Satyakāma Jābāla, achieved great spiritual insight while in the wild, learning profound truths from the elements of nature and from animals.

The young Satyakāma asked his mother about his father, seeking indirectly to learn of his caste or *varṇa*. She claimed not to know which man caused her pregnancy. Because of his curiosity, she named her son Satyakāma (desirous of truth), and urged him to use her own name, Jābāla, as his surname. His quest for truth brought him to the renowned teacher Haridrumata

Gautama. When the great teacher asked Satyakāma about his family origins, the young man shared guilelessly the story told by his mother. Sayakāma's honesty earned him accolades from Haridrumata Gautama, who proclaimed him to be a Brahmin and agreed to teach him. First, however, work needed to be rendered. The teacher charged the young man with tending a herd of four hundred cattle, sending him away from the village into the wilderness. Accepting the task, Satyakāma vowed not to return until the herd had grown to a thousand head. He retreated into a landscape of forests and meadows for a period of some years where four formative experiences transformed him into a sage, a man of wisdom.

The first encounter began when a bull from the herd notified Satyakāma, "We have reached a thousand." The bull himself proceeded to tell Satyakāma the first of four teachings about the nature of Brahman. The bull taught Satyakāma about the importance of always recognizing the four directions: east, west, south, and north. Satyakāma came to understand all the areas and spaces in which light shines (*prakāśa*). To the east he regarded the rising sun. To the south, he enjoyed the fullness and brightness of the day. He watched the sun set into the west. And in the dark of night, he saw the pole star emerge. Satisfied that Satyakāma had awakened to this teaching, the bull indicated that his next lesson would come from the fire.

That night, the fire instructed Satyakāma about the worlds to be found in the earth, the atmosphere, the sky, and the ocean. This teaching, received from the crackling fire, echoed the oft-repeated invocation of Bhūr, Bhuvaḥ, Svaḥ, the chant found in the Vedas and Upaniṣads that evokes the earth and water below, the heat and breath of the middle zone, and the space above that extends into the heavens. To these three the fire added remembrance of the ocean, the vast waters that surround the land and from which the sun seemingly emerges from the eastern coast and sets in the western coast.

After another day of driving the cattle back toward the home of Haridrumata Gautama, a radiant white swan came in the evening and told him of the fourfold nature of the luminous: fire itself, the sun, the moon, and lightning. Fire can be kindled and controlled; fire can also rage out of control, as we saw in the passage from the *Yogavāsiṣṭha* in chapter 4. In the form of great, constant giver of light and heat, it manifests as the sun. It takes the form of cool and changing light in the phases of the moon. Fire also bursts forth with the thunderbolt and as lightning, stern, loud, capable of death and yet welcomed as the herald of the life-giving monsoon. Satyakāma came to experience these various forms of luminosity with greater intimacy and appreciation.

A diving bird gave Satyakāma the final teaching, a fourfold analysis of vital components of human experience: the breath, the eye, the ear, and the mind. All humans breathe. Through the senses they establish contact with the world. Through the mind, the world takes shape and understanding can arise. Combined with awareness of the four directions, geography, and the power and manifestations of fire, this understanding of the human person completed the education of Satyakāma Jābāla.

Through these four remarkable encounters, Satyakāma learned the importance of locating oneself within the four directions. He also grasped the vast expanse of the earth below, the surrounding air, the largeness of space, and the unfathomable ocean as well. He moved on to understand the many manifestations of fire and light and then discovered the inner working of the human being, living in a body through the senses and the mind. His forest teachers were not human. He received instruction from a bull, a fire, a swan, and a diving bird, creatures of the earth, water, fire, and the air. When he returned to his human teacher, Haridrumata Gautama proclaimed to Satyakāma, "You shine like a knower of Brahman!" Satyakāma became himself a great teacher, sharing wisdom based on his intimacy within a living universe.

Pañcatantra: The Rishi Finds a Suitor for His Daughter

The first story narrated a tale of self-discovery, a coming of age process wherein a young man discovered his place within the world. He learned about the operations of the external energies of fire and the structure of the inner portals to experience. The second story deals with a different phase and aspect of life, the dutiful impulse of parenthood. It comes from the Pañcatantra, a collection of lore that dates from at least 2,500 years ago.[8] One day, a Rishi, presumably a composer of Vedic hymns, performed his ablutions as usual at the nearby river. A falcon flew overhead. It released from its talons some freshly caught prey, a mouse that fell into the river, unharmed. The Rishi cupped the mouse in his hands and placed it safely into leaf on the shore and then, having finished his morning bath, began walking home. Midway, he was struck with a feeling of immense responsibility toward the mouse. It dawned on the Rishi that this encounter was somehow auspicious and that his task was not yet complete. He returned to find the mouse still drying off in the sun. He invoked a special mantra and transformed the mouse into an infant girl. The

Rishi placed her in swaddling and then brought her home to his wife. The couple had been childless; now they devoted their doting attention to rearing this little foundling girl.

In traditional India, the task of the parent includes arranging for the marriage of one's children. The Rishi, who clearly had developed a deep love for his daughter, took this responsibility very seriously as she grew into adulthood. He sought out the most appropriate match for the miracle daughter who had been sent from the heavens. Because of her propitious origins, the Rishi aimed very high, choosing as her first suitor the Sun himself. He approached Surya and explained that his daughter came from the sky itself and therefore was his equal. The sun demurred and remarked, "Yes, I am powerful, but there is one more powerful than I. The clouds, which seem so soft and gentle, nonetheless occlude my rays and mute my power. Rishi, approach the clouds; they will make a better match for your girl."

The Rishi then approached a handsome cloud, made of water vapor. The cloud also rejected the Rishi's offer. "Yes, I can be billowy, light or dark, thin or thick and yes I can overpower the sun. But there is one better than I. The wind slices me into pieces, forces me to give up my form into countless drops of rain, destroys the magnificence of my form. Rishi, approach the wind."

The Rishi called out to the wind. "Come here, O great Vāyu. You will meet your match in this daughter of mine, arisen from the sky and the river, beautiful, and ready for marriage." Vāyu, like the others, explained his own limits. "O Rishi, it is true that I can travel the face of the earth and that my power as *prāṇa* courses through the veins of all that lives. But I also have limits. Whether in the heat of the day or the darkness of night, one great force stops my wanderings: the mountain. The mountain, with its great majesty, is the most powerful and the most worthy suitor for your beloved daughter. Approach the mountain and offer to him the hand of your daughter in marriage."

The Rishi traveled along the base of the mountain and looked up at its immense grandeur, covered with forests, boasting spectacular granite boulders. Certainly, nothing could be grander. However, the mountain too spoke from a place of humility. He grumbled, "You flatter me and, yes it would be nice to think that I am above all other beings. But look closely and you will see that one being always gets the best of me, tunneling into hillocks, lacing passages underneath the roots of my forests and around the boulders that adorn me like massive jewels. The smallest of beings can also be the most powerful. Behold the greatest being of all: the mouse!"

The Rishi approached a hole in the face of the mountain. He called out to the best of mice to step up and meet his future spouse. The best of the mice stepped forward and proclaimed: "Indeed, your daughter is lovely. However, she is too large for my lair. How can she fit inside when it is time to sleep?" With that, the Rishi reversed his original spell. His daughter returned to her original form and then joined the best of mice as his wife and queen.

This story explains interactions between three realms: the elements of fire, water, air, and earth; the human world of the Rishi and his wife; and two animal forms, the falcon, powerful and airbound, and the mouse, humble yet tenacious. The Rishi evokes deep sentiment repeatedly in the story: love for the vulnerable mouse, love for his daughter. He beholds the great elements with awe, holding a sense of reverence for the powers of nature. And just as he himself took on the responsibility of rearing a child, he tenderly attends to her future happiness, arranging for her transfer from childhood to adulthood, knowing that he will lose her constant company in the process. As noted above, this story highlights the emotions of parenthood: care, attention, and eventually dispassionate love and surrender. Interestingly, the story focuses almost exclusively on the emotions of the father. Neither wife nor daughter exerts agency. Nonetheless, the deep feelings of the Rishi speak to the supreme values of responsibility and care that well up from within the heart of an individual and go far beyond external mandates. This might also be seen as a call to compassion for all orphans, for all vulnerable beings, heaven-sent or human.

In terms of landscape, this story is cyclical. It begins at the banks of a river. Its narrative soars with the offending hawk who carried the mouse aloft into the air. It transitions to a human village. Successive encounters with the sun, the clouds, the wind, and the mountain bring the story back to humble origins, within the furrows of the earth. The landscape is not merely background for this story. The landscape in its various forms of sun, clouds, wind, and mountain itself has voice, agency, and wisdom.

The Ruby Eyed, Silver Clawed Blue Bear: A Buddhist Jātaka Tale

The 550 Jātaka tales tell about the past lives of the Buddha. These include 225 stories of his prior animal births.[9] One story in particular takes place deep in the forest and involves a bear of great wisdom. Retold by Rafe Martin, this particular narrative, though illustrated in the caves at Ajanta, is only found in written form in the Khotanese *Jatakastava*, a tenth-century text of Central Asia discovered in only one copy in the Tunhuang Caves and translated by Mark Dresden in 1955.[10]

In this story, the future Buddha lived as a "bear with blue fur, silver claws, and ruby-red eyes" in the Himalayas.[11] His pelt and claws would bring a small fortune and eating his flesh would bestow long life. Legends circulated about this magnificent specimen radiating the color of lapis, the world's most precious gem. No one could ever find where this bear lived.

One day a lost hunter, trapped in a blinding snowstorm, called out for help. The great blue bear rescued him, carried the half-dead man back to his cave, and "revived him with the warmth of its own body and breath." The bear protected the man for the duration of the storm, feeding him roots and dried berries, with the understanding that the man would never reveal the location of the bear's cave.

At the end of the storm, the hunter departed and safely reached an inn where he took shelter. All night long he tossed and turned, fantasizing about the fortune he would amass if he let others know about the whereabouts of this legendary blue bear. Despite his promise to the bear that he would not betray him, he went to the king and told him of the bear's location. The hunter neglected to mention the bear's kindness. The king's huntsmen traveled into the mountains, found the bear's den, and sounded their horns, jolting the bear from his slumber into their nets.

Once delivered to the palace, the bear requested a meeting with the king and told the king how he had been betrayed by the original huntsman whose life he had saved. With great wisdom, the bear addressed the king: "Good actions lead to happiness, selfish ones to disaster. Kindness is greater than cruelty. Do not strike back but develop the fortitude of patience. If you practice these virtues diligently you will find happiness without limit."[12] The original huntsman who betrayed the bear was summoned to the court. The king castigated him for his bad behavior and banished him from the palace. The bear, garlanded by the king, was escorted safely back to the mountains. He took up residence in a new cave, never again to be discovered.

The hunter descended in a life of subsistence, hunting wild game and eating roots and berries. His hair became unruly and his eyes were reddened from campfire smoke. One day, he caught a glimpse of his reflection in a slow-moving stream. He exclaimed that he had taken on the appearance of a bear. From this jolt, he saw his own kinship with the bear that he had betrayed.

From that time forward, he stopped hunting, stopped eating meat, and became a beacon of safety, "lending a helping hand to man or beast."[13]

The Prince Who Was an Elephant: A Jain Animal Allegory

The story of Meghkumar, or the Cloud Prince, is told in the *Gyātasūtra* of the Jain canon, also known as *the Jnātadharmakathaṅga*. This complex narrative weaves past life memories in such a way that not only does a prince gain insight into his current state of affairs, but also in his immediate prior incarnation he recalls a lesson from an incarnation prior to that. The prince benefits from lessons learned in two prior lifetimes. Prince Meghkumar was born after his mother Dharinī recalled two dreams: one of a white elephant who came down from the sky and entered her womb through her mouth, and the second of an insatiable desire to ride through the city on a white elephant on a cloudy day. The king Shrenik and his queen consequently named their beloved son Cloud Prince and provided the happiest life possible for him, including his marriage to eight princesses.

Some years passed. The Tīrthaṅkara Bhagavan Mahāvīra came to the capital of Shrenik's kingdom of Magadha, the city known today as Rajagriha. After hearing the Bhagavan speak, Prince Meghkumar decided to leave behind his wives and princely comforts to take up the life of a Jaina monk. The day before his initiation his father arranged for him to be king for a day, lending even greater weight to the significance of Meghkumar's renunciation. After the ceremony initiating Meghkumar into monkhood was completed, the former prince settled on the floor to sleep. As the most junior monk, he was required to sleep near the door. All night long, the monks came and went in order to relieve themselves in the field, disturbing his sleep. He tossed and turned, receiving no rest. He fell into a deep sadness and yearning for his prior life.

In the morning he approached Bhagavan Mahāvīra and asked to be released from his vows. Using his powers of omniscience, the Bhagavan told two stories of Meghkumar's prior lives when he lived as an elephant. In one story he was an elderly pure white elephant named King Sumeruprabh. A forest fire swept through his domain, forcing all the animals to flee. Because of his advanced age, Sumeruprabh stumbled and fell into a muddy lake bed. A younger elephant took advantage of his plight and gored him to death.

The elephant was reborn again, this time as a bright red elephant named Meruprabh, with four tusks, also king of his clan. While witnessing a fire from afar, he recalled the plight of his prior birth and urged his fellow elephants to clear an eight-mile meadow that would be safe in case of fire. Eventually, fires came to the forest and all the animals, including antelope, deer, lions, jackals, cattle, and rabbits crowded into the meadow. Meruprabh lifted his foot to scratch his itchy stomach. A rabbit scampered into the space underneath his leg. For fear of killing the rabbit, Meruprabh stood on three legs for two and a half days. By this time, the fire had died down, but Meruprabh's leg had stiffened and he tumbled to the ground. He lay prone for three days, unable to move, suffering from pain, hunger, and thirst. However, because of the compassion he had manifested in order to save the rabbit, he felt peace even amid the pain and took rebirth in the womb of Dharinī and was born as Prince Meghkumar. Having been reminded of this act of compassion, Meghkumar renewed his religious zeal and after twelve years of monastic life ascended to Mount Vipulchal where he engaged in a final fast, attaining a heavenly state as an angel in his next life.[14]

This story emphasizes the continuity of life from incarnation to incarnation. Elephants become elephants, and elephants become humans and humans become monks and monks become angels. Along the way, many other animals cross paths: antelope, deer, lions, jackals, cattle, and rabbits. According to Jain cosmology, actions toward other life forms determine one's status in the lives to come. If, even in the midst of a natural calamity such as a forest fire, one can seek to spare the lives of others, a reward will be gained.

The Story of Puṇya and Pāvana from the *Yogavāsiṣṭha*

The *Pṛthivī Sūkta* celebrates the presence of animals on the earth. Satyakāma Jābāla received his education from a bull, a campfire, and two birds while deep in the forest. The Rishi plucked a mouse from a river, sparing her certain death, and then sought to find a mate for her in the sun, the clouds, the air, and the mountain before her eventual marriage to the mouse king. The wise bear with blue fur safely returned to his mountain retreat after misadventures with a duplicitous woodsman and through the blessings of a just king. The prince who had been an elephant endures hardship to achieve an angelic state. Each of these stories evoke a sense of place particular to landscape both human and wild, village, forest, meadow, pond, river, ocean shore, and mountain.

The final story in this chapter takes place on the Ganges River, where two brothers lose their parents. One laments excessively, prompting his older, wiser brother to use narrative to help bring his inconsolable brother back to a state of stability, a narrative that calls attention to the beauties of nature and the many forms of life that thrive upon the earth. This story is translated anew in its entirety.[15]

V.19.1. Vasiṣṭha said: Indeed, now they tell an old story
about two brothers on the banks of the Ganges,
said to be the two sons of a sage.
2. Listen, O Rāma, to this wonderfully good story
remembered as a tale about
who is related and who is not.
3. On the continent of Jambudvīpa,
there is a moist mountain covered with forest.
This highest mountain is called Mahendra.
4. Within its peaks extending into space,
with abundant forests rising up,
peaceful sages and musicians can be found
in the shadows of the wishing tree forest.
5. Having obtained the inner heavenly realm,
these sages hum the songs of the Sāma Veda,
which echo through the peaks and caves.
6. On the peak of the mountain which is covered with vines and flowers,
water from dense, playful clouds shimmers like locks of hair.
7. Rain resounds from thunder clouds and lightning,
like the open mouths of Śarabhas flying straight out from their caves.
8. The roar generated by the torrents of water moving through these caves
is equal to that of the resplendent surf in the ocean's waters.
9. Spread out from that singular place on the beautiful jewel encrusted mountain,
the Ganges descends from the sky, to be used by the sages for bathing and drinking.
10. On the banks of that three path Ganges, radiant trees catch flashes of light

up against the slope of the jeweled mountain, illuminated by golden river fog.

11. A highly intelligent sage lived there, called Dīrghatapā,
endowed with noble vision due to his abundant *tapas*.
In fact, due to his *tapas,* his body was unexcelled.

12. This sage had two sons, Puṇya and Pāvana, handsome as the full moon,
as brilliant as those two sons of the father of speech (Bṛhaspati).

13. He, his wife, and his two sons all lived together as one
on the bank of the river under a fruit tree.

14. In due time, one of the two sons became knowledgeable.
The elder brother named Puṇya had superior qualities, O Rāma.

15. Pāvana was only half awakened, like a lotus at twilight.
Due to his slow-mindedness, he had not attained anything and was stuck in doubt.

16. The inevitable passage of time—100 years, in fact—
caused Dīrgha's vitality to diminish and his body to grow old.

17. Having experienced repeated rounds of wealth and pleasure
as well as difficulty and decline, his life, wracked with senility, drew to an end.

18. The sage Dīrghatapa left his body like a bird flies from the nest.
He died in his house hidden on the mountain, laying down his heavy load.

19. With death, he flew into *samādhi,* free from thought, into the abode of consciousness.
He went to the stage free from passion, like the scent of a flower wafts up into the sky.

20. His wife, having seen the body of the lifeless sage,
fell to the earth, like a lotus without a stalk.

21. Through the discipline of Yoga taught to her by her husband over many years,
she renounced her delicate frame, like a bee flying from a lotus.

22. She followed her husband, departing to the place unseen by people,
the light of her soul fading in the sky like the half moon at sunset.

23. With mother and father gone, Puṇya steadfastly focused
on the funeral ceremonies, while Pāvana descended into grief.

24. His mind afflicted with grief, he wandered the forest paths.
Having lost sight of his brother, Pāvana wailed: "Aaaaah!"

25. Having performed the appropriate funeral rites
for the bodies of his mother and father,
Puṇya ventured into the forest after Pāvana, who was afflicted with great sorrow.[16]
26. "Why, boy, this thick cloud of sorrow? It is making you blind and ignorant.
Your violent cloud of tears is like a monsoon season filled with rain.
27. Your mother and father, of great wisdom, have gone together to heaven,
indeed, to that highest Self, that place called Mokṣa.
28. That place is the goal of all people who have overcome this world of form.
Why mourn your parents? They have attained their true nature.
29. You are really bound to this state that is born of delusion.
You mourn for things in *saṃsāra* that should not be mourned.
30. She is not your only mother nor is he your only father.
Nor are we the only two sons of the many who have been born of those two.
31. Child, our mother and father have passed through thousands of births,
as numerous as the streams running deep in each and every forest.
32. Honored son, we are not the only two sons. Our parents have had countless children.
Multitudes of sons have passed through the generations like rapids in a river.
33. Our parents had innumerable distinguished sons who have passed away long ago,
just as the branches of a creeping vine give forth many flowers and fruits.
34. Just as a great tree gives forth an abundance of fruits with the passage of each season,
So also our many friends and relatives have experienced many births.
35. Son, if parents and children are to be mourned out of affection,
Then why should the thousands who die continually not also be mourned?
36. From your perspective of worldliness,
the affairs of wandering people are deemed important.

But from the highest perspective, knowledge reveals that
there is no lasting friend, no lasting relative.
37. On the other hand, brother, from the perspective of absolute truth,
no destruction is known either.
Everything happens only in the mind and then evaporates like water in the desert.
38. The beautiful things that you see are none other than a dream,
fluttering like feathers on a parasol, lasting three or five days in the great mind.
39. By seeing things from the perspective of the ultimate reality, son,
You must regard this truth: 'There is neither you nor we.'
You must renounce all your confusion.
40. Realize that all your previous negative views are now dead and gone.
Such tortures arise in your own imagination and must not be seen as true.
41. In a death characterized by ignorance,
the rolling waves of pure and impure vibrations
cause past impressions to manifest without interruption
into the realm of name and form, like moonlight on water."
20.1. "Who is the father? The friend? The mother? The relatives?
One's conception of them can be swept away as if they are dust in the wind.
2. Love, aversion, and delusion in regard to our friends, relatives, and offspring
are merely accomplished by the projection of our own conceptions.
3. The quality associated with 'relative' makes a relative.
The quality associated with 'stranger' makes one a stranger,
just as the conditions of poison or nectar
depend upon the appearance of fixity (in the mind).
4. How can this notion arise that 'this one is a friend, that one is a stranger'
when the mind of wisdom sees the oneness of the all-pervading soul?
5. Son, reflect on yourself through your mind.
Ask, 'Who am I? What could I be? Something other than the body?
A bony skeleton? A heap of blood, flesh, and bones?'

6. From the perspective of highest truth, there is no 'you,' there is no 'I.'
Only in delusion and ignorance do Puṇya and Pāvana spring forth.
7. Who is your father, who is your friend?
Who is your mother? Who is your enemy?
In regard to the endless luminosity of space,
What can be proclaimed to be the Self? Or not the Self?
8. You are consciousness in the midst of many other prior births
where you have had friends and properties.
Why do you not grieve for them also?
9. Those many deer in the flowery meadow,
born of their mother does, were your relatives.
Why do you not grieve for them?
10. Regard the swans in the bouquets of lotuses on the riverbank.
Why do you not grieve for those swans who were your relatives?
11. Those fine trees in the splendid beautiful forests were also your relatives.
Why do you not grieve for them?
12. Those lions on the awe-inspiring peaks of those mountains
were also your relatives. Why do you not grieve for them?
13. Those fish among the beautiful lotuses in the clear lakes
were also your relatives. Why do you not grieve for them?
14. You were a monkey in the brown woods of the Ten River Land,
a prince in the land of snow, and a crow in the forest of the Pundras.
15. You were an elephant among the Haihaya people,
a donkey in the company of the Trigartas,
a puppy with the people of Salva, and a bird in that tree.
16. You were a fig tree in the Vindhya range, and an insect in a great tree.
You have been a hen on the Mandara Mountain.
You were born also as a Brahmin in Kandar.
17. You were a Brahmin in Kosala. You were a partridge in Bengal.
You were a horse in the land of snow.
And you were the beast killed at the Brahmana sacrifice.
18. The one who was an insect inside the root of a palm tree,
who was a mosquito on a big ficus tree,
the one who was previously a crane in the forest,
that one is now you, my son, my little brother.

19. That small red ant that lived for six months
in the hollow of the thin knotty birch tree bark
on the cliffs of the Himalayas is now you, my little brother.[17]
20. You were the beetle living for a year and a half
in cow dung at the edge of a frontier village.
O Sadhu, that was you, little brother.[18]
21. The child who sat on the six petalled lotus throne of the Pulinda tribal woman,
hidden in the forest, that one was you, little brother.
22. For thousands of prior births in these many woods
you were born of various wombs, my son,
And now you are born on Jambudvīpa.
23. By the purified clear vision of my subtle intellect,
I see the previous successive lives of your self.
24. I remember today my many past lives, born of many wombs
due to ignorance and indolence. This insight has arisen due to knowledge.
25. Having been a parrot in Trigarta and a frog on a riverbank,
and having been a lumberjack in the woods, now I am born here in this forest.
26. I ravished a royal woman in the Vindhyas.
I have been fashioned as a tree in Bengal as well as a camel in the Vindhya range.
I am now born in this forest.
27. That bird in the Himalayan town, that king in the Paundra region,
that tiger in the Salya region . . . that one is now me, your elder brother.
28. I was that vulture who lived for ten years,
that shark who lived five months, and that lion who lived a full century.
That one indeed is now your older brother.
29. Can you believe it? I lived as a prince of a village in Andhra,
as a sovereign king in the Tuṣāra region, and as the son of the Śailācārya.
30. I remember from long ago all the various incarnations and all the various customs
that have arisen into manifestation due to confusion.

31. There, in that place [of memory], so many thousands of relatives
were born in those worlds that have now gone: fathers, mothers, siblings, and friends.
32. Whom shall we two grieve? Whom shall we not grieve?
We grieve all relatives that die. This is the way of life in the world.
33. Like the endless passing of fathers and mothers in this world of *saṃsāra,*
souls drop like leaves, falling off the trees in the forest.[19]
34. Who can measure the varieties of pleasure and pain, O brother?
Therefore, renounce all of them. Let us take our place in the light.
35. Having renounced all cultivation of outward manifestation in the mind,
abiding in the Self, go happily to that place, that place where the wise ones go.
36. Inactive beings fall away. Active persons rise again.
Those with good thoughts do not grieve. They move gradually toward freedom.
37. Be free of confusion. Be free of [attachment to] existence and nonexistence.
Escape from old age and death. Be cool, always remembering your true Self.
38. You are not your suffering. You are not this birth.
You are indeed the Self, not this intellect.
Indeed, how could you be other than true Self?
39. Sadhu! Ignorant people performing various dramas in this journey of *saṃsāra*
attach themselves to the sentiments of existence.
40. One can attain the goal of being the witness,
Self-possessed in the midst of all that can be seen.
Such persons are established in the dharma of the observer,
being the knower and spectator at all times.
41. Whether engaged in action or inactive,
such persons regard actions as if they were the fading light
at the start of the night. The knower stands unperturbed by the world.

42. Those who have arrived at the illumination of the true Self
no longer see the reflection [as real], just as the jewels reflected in the mirror
are taken to be mere reflections by those with wisdom.
43. Through moving away from all this self-made darkness, dwell in your true Self,
which is like the radiant moon in the middle of your heart.
44. Son, find the Self in the Self. Be a sage like the great sages.
Having renounced all impure perplexity, be content!"

In this geographically detailed narrative, the younger brother Pāvana learns that he had been related to swans, trees, lions, and fish and that he had taken birth as a monkey, a regal prince, a crow, an elephant, a donkey, a puppy, a bird, a fig tree, an insect, a hen, a Brahmin (twice), a partridge, a horse, an insect, a mosquito, a crane, a red ant, a beetle, and a child. The older brother Puṇya had lived as a parrot, a frog, a lumberjack, a tree, a camel, a bird, a king (twice), a tiger, a vulture, a shark, a lion, and as a prince. Each brother experiences far many more births as nonhumans than as humans. Furthermore, in the concluding verses above, Puṇya instructs his brother to rise above the vagaries of each birth, to ascend to the place of yogic equipoise, urging him to "attain the goal of being the witness, self-possessed in the midst of all that can be seen." He goes on to state that "[s]uch persons are established in the dharma of the observer, being the knower and spectator at all times." Puṇya exhorts Pāvana to move "away from all this self-made darkness, dwell in your true Self, which is like the radiant moon in the middle of your heart . . . find the Self in the Self. Be a sage like the great sages. Having renounced all impure perplexity, be content!" Through seeing himself in the context of the larger world order, Puṇya can overcome his grief and arrive at a place of wisdom.

This narrative, told over two chapters of the Upaśama Prakaraṇa of the *Yogavāsiṣṭha*, holds many insights relevant for the topic of this book. Like the Abram narrative of "becoming animal" at the start of this chapter, it reminds the listener that we are not limited beings. We carry unfathomable histories and experiences; according to Hinduism, Buddhism, and Jainism, we have taken birth countless times. By appreciating the landscape perspective suggested by Puṇya, that is, being cognizant of the beauty of the meadow, the river, the mountain and all the many lives contained therein, we can move beyond the petty dramas that trap the mind and emotions in negativity. This does not mean that grief is to be avoided; Puṇya channeled his grief into the performance of the funeral rituals. Vasiṣṭha suggests that we must always take the wider view, surrendering attachments in favor of contentment and peace.

Landscapes

Each of these narratives contains a message akin to that found in the classic tale of the country mouse feeling out of place in the city and the city mouse being unable to survive in the wild. This sense of displacement results in an experience of self-discovery, an expansion of horizons. Satyakāma, having left the village to wander for years in the wilderness, returns with the glow of great wisdom. The unnamed Rishi uproots a mouse from her habitat, teaches her human ways, introduces her to the power of the sun, the dampening abilities of water, the strength of the wind, and the vastness of a mountain before returning her to her original form. The Blue Bear, similar to the bear in the children's book *The Bear Who Wanted to Be a Bear*,[20] wrenched from his happy home, haplessly begs to be returned safely, away from the bustle and danger of the king's palace. The lucky elephant of the Jaina narrative learns one lifetime to the next how to be gentle and earns a reward in heaven. In process of leaving behind his kingship, he enters the wild path of renunciation, filled with discomfort, in a sense leaving the city to retreat into a place over which he has little control, but through which he accumulates great merit. And the final narrative of Puṇya and Pāvana, given in its entirety, shows the healing powers of connecting with animals in order to find solace and healing in a time of grief.

Animals as Animals

Each of these stories highlights the special nature of particular animals. The bull, the swan, and the diving bird of the story of Satyakāma, though sparingly described, all convey a sense of their species' special gifts. The bull would know the range and spread of the directions as delineating space. The swan, with its white radiance, would know the nature of light in its various forms. The diving bird, with its penetrative skills and knowledge of what lies beneath the surfaces of the waters it pierces, would understand the origins of things in their relationship with the body and the senses and the mind. The mouse, though tiny, returns regally to its birthright, having bested the sun, the clouds, the wind, and even the mountain. The blue bear lumbers, moving slowly with righteous indignation, and with gravitas sets things right. The elephant, highly sensitive and intelligent, retains memories over a course of three lifetimes, using profound intelligence to help solve the recurrent problem of how to cope with wildfires and then develops profound emotional intelligence. Pāvana's remembrance of past lives celebrates nature's diverse expressions and brings comfort to his grieving brother. In each instance, the storyteller succinctly and insightfully conveys a sense of these animals in their innate mode of presentation, their *zeitgeist*. Cattle roam and occupy and own the fields they graze, as I learned during afternoon rambles through Mulligan Farm in the Genesee Valley. Swans glimmer in the sunlight, like the white swan already mentioned on Smith's Pond in Lyndonville, New York, and the white swans on the Amityville River. The pelicans at Playa Del Rey thrill this viewer with their dramatic dives under the Pacific surf. Mice thwart even the most vigilant and tidy homeowner. Bears inspire fear and awe and respect, as documented by Werner Herzog in the film *Grizzly Man*.[21] Elephants reach out and touch the hearts of responsive humans. During a Buddhist conclave in India some years ago, field ecologist George Schaller, who brought attention to the plight of the snow leopard and helped protect the Tibetan highlands, leaned over to me in sadness as we passed a "working" elephant on the streets of New Delhi, lamenting the enslavement of these majestic animals.[22]

Animals as Future Humans

Two of these stories, the story of Satyakāma Jābāla and the story of the mouse who became a girl, most likely took shape before the doctrine of reincarnation became commonplace in India. Hence, they are represented as animals, not as humans who were once animals or animals destined to become humans. The Buddhist and Jain stories, however, directly narrate animal lives as precursors to human lives. The compassion manifested by the bear toward the lost hunter presaged the later compassion manifested by the Buddha and the ingenuity and kindness displayed by the elephant similarly prefigured qualities displayed in the prince who became a monk. The transition from elephant to human paralleled the transition from nobleman to renouncer.

Humans as Animals

In the Indian system of reincarnation, all beings are said to be equal. As famously stated in the *Bhagavad Gītā*, "People of learning view with equal eye a Brahmin of knowledge and good learning, a cow, an elephant, and even a dog and an outcaste" (BG V:18). The preparatory lessons from past lives shape and guide an individual into the present and future lives. The regal and just nature of the Blue Bear, the intelligence and love manifested by the elephant king demonstrate the great capacity for animal behavior to be seen in human qualities and the reverse. Recognition of innate animal impulses can work for good and for ill; a good animal might be regarded as superior to a bad human. To have been an animal and to have recalled past animal experiences indicates a sign of greatness, an acknowledgment of one's ongoing connections and kinship with other species.

Implications

The animal stories give voice to the prevailing ethic of nonviolence, the keystone of Jaina and Buddhist and Yogic religious practice. Animals are teachers in our first tale, beloved kin in the second tale, and exemplary moral agents in the third and fourth tales. Satyakāma Jābāla as a human being represents truthfulness and humility. Because of his attunement to the natural world, he is able to receive sixteen truths regarding the four directions, the nature of elements, the specific qualities of light, and the operations of the human body and mind. He receives these teachings not from a human but from elements and animals. Due to his receptivity to these other-than-human entities, he returns to the realm of humans with the glow of deep knowledge, a knowledge of connectivity and emplacement and embodiment, a knowledge that qualifies him to become one of India's most renowned sages.

The story of the Rishi and the mouse daughter demonstrates the power of parental love. The sense of care exhibited by the Rishi and his wife extends from the everyday nurturing of basic needs to planning for the eventual marriage of their adopted daughter. Furthermore, though he had great plans for her future, he also accepted her eventual fate, a return to her original innate state. This story presents both a lesson in *dharma* in that parents must do everything for their children and in *svadharma,* the realization that all individuals must follow their own path.

The Ruby Eyed Silver Clawed Blue Bear carries himself with such dignity and aplomb that even in the worst of circumstances he prevails. One cannot hear this story without feeling embarrassed by the greedy selfish hunter and relieved once the just king sets the bear free again. Comportment wins over conniving. Gravitas trumps duplicity. Just as Carol Gilligan articulated an ethic of care that perhaps could characterize the relationship between the Rishi and the mouse girl, this story calls out for the development of a new ethic, an ethic of gravitas and comportment rooted in a quiet moral outrage that simmers until appropriately expressed and adjudicated.

The story of the prince who, having remembered his past lives as different elephants and then became a monk, demonstrates the layered complexity of ethical decision making in Jaina tradition. Human beings sometimes innately know the correct path to follow. This story conveys the classical Indian perspective that knowledge arises from lessons learned both in this life and in prior lives. Because he had fallen victim to a ferocious fire in a prior birth, the elephant who became a prince created a meadow of protection through which he saved many beings, even at his own peril. Because he had become aware of the sufferings endured by all beings, the prince renounced his worldly life, symbolized by the forest fire, in order to gain a heavenly reward after practicing years of asceticism. Ingenuity and kindness arose from horrific experiences. This created a sensitivity within the prince. This tenderness paved the way for a life dedicated to nonviolence and the protection of life in all forms.

Puṇya's friendly advice to his grieving brother outlines a way of understanding human emplacement within the round of birth, death, and rebirth. Kinship defines this story in a radical way: brothers deal with the passing of their parents each in his unique way, with Puṇya expanding the definition of kinship to include all manner of beings: trees, ants, beetles, bees, mosquitoes, scorpions, frogs, crocodiles, cranes, parrots, hawks, swans, eagles, donkeys, deer, camels, elephants, tigers, and lions. By connecting with the broader web of life, Pāvana moves from despair to calm.

The landscape includes the foundational elements of earth, water, fire, wind, and space taking many diverse forms: plains, fields, mountains, rivers, ponds, lakes, oceans, temperate climates, cold climates, gentle winds, fierce winds, sweeping vistas, dense forests, and intimate glades. Human bodies emplace themselves within each of these environments, adapting and flourishing through ingenuity and industry. Similarly, animals of all species can be found in the landscape. Animals in many ways define landscape and arise in reciprocity with the landscape: raccoons in urban North America, armadillos in the American South, elephants in Africa and India, various forms of mountain lions and gazelles worldwide. Foxes and coyotes communicate wiliness. Dogs evoke loyalty, cats independence, and so forth. To be in relationship with animals gives a sense of sameness and difference, a feeling of connection with something to be loved, to be feared, and to be respected. By telling stories of animals we increase our capacity to understand ourselves.

In the next and final chapter we return to the last of the five elements: space. Concentration on space takes many forms, from setting one's gaze skyward to welcoming an awareness of colors, changing one's baseline for identity, and moving into the realm of embodied ethics, attuned to time and place.

7

The Yoga of Space

Space and place interact. Each human narrative occupies different places. In my case, the story moved from the plains south of Lake Ontario to the Genesee Valley and the Finger Lakes and then to the south and north shores of Long Island, finally settling near the Pacific coast. Each move provoked a change of body-sense. At first a wistfulness for the land lost would emerge, only to be replaced with joy in the land newly discovered. Training in Yoga and as a pūjārī allowed a connection to emerge between the emotions of the body, the thoughts of the mind, and the space of landscape.

Maureen and I would arrive early each Sunday morning, having cleaned the Conscience Bay Quaker Meeting House by 6 a.m. With no traffic, we would glide down the parkways and land in Amityville before 7 a.m. We sat on the floor facing north, toward the two large picture windows that open to the magnificent oak trees and the morning sky. We received no instruction other than to gaze into the expanse of the morning sky, a sky transforming from dark into light in the winter and already bright in the summer, except on cloudy and rainy days. On some spring and fall Sunday mornings, freezing rain would glaze the oaks with ice. In the fall, the articulated oak leaves would turn brilliant shades of crimson and orange. In the winter, we would often see snow falling, blanketing the roof and the trees in white. Were we looking for something in the sky? Would we receive answers?

In the twice-daily home practice of concentration on space (*ākāśa*), orientation in space began with a sense of immediacy and intimacy, a grounding of the body upon floor, eyes gazing toward and above a candle, looking outward into the oak trees that separated each home on Palfrey Street. The space to the window was maybe three feet; the space beyond the window stretched into infinity. Arising from the morning sit and walking to the edge of the field, one got a sense of the space that stretches outward and yet contains such an abundance of specifics: rows of onions that had survived the winter freeze, the forest preserve to the left, the crows taking flight, the robins soon to return from their southerly migration. Boarding the bus and feeling its gentle sway, the pace would increase, the trees in the Schiff Preserve, moving by quickly, some bare, some still holding brown leaves as the oaks do on Long Island in the winter. Arriving at the center of campus and disembarking, the space of the day unfolded, walking from building to building, finding the "head space" to absorb the Tibetan alphabet and grammar, entering the energetic field of Vedic studies and its explication of the emergence of the world from the space of nonexistence and confusion (*asat*), building familiarity with and distance from old inclinations and desires. The space of sophomore year at university was filled with self-discovery, discomfort, and resolve.

One word learned that first year in the Ashram captured the emotional tenor of embarking on the spiritual path: *bhāva*. This simple Sanskrit word defies translation. It refers to a state of being and is in fact cognate with the English verb *to be*. As we came to learn, *bhāva* can take many forms, and *bhāva* can be changed, cultivated, nurtured. One correlate term might be mood. Through Yoga practice and meditation, one can shift the mood or general feeling tone of a situation from agitation and anxiety into a place of understanding and acceptance. This inner space permeates the body and breath. By bringing about a physiological space of calm, a correlative calm arises in the mind. It helps bring reassurance to others. Creating and maintaining auspicious space serves as the hallmark of Yoga practice.

Cidambaram: Temple of Space

We arrived at Cidambaram, the temple for space, Ākāśa, on Wednesday, January 23, 2013. In this temple, Śiva takes not the form of the abstract Liṅgaṃ but the anthropomorphic shape of a dancer, known as Śiva Nataraj, the king of the dance. Dance is about movement through space, filling space, occupying space, defining space. This dancing Śiva image, replicated abundantly in the Thanjavur's Saraswathi Mahal Library and in museums worldwide, inscribes Śiva in a circle of his own creation in the midst of destruction. His matted hair flails freely, his hands held in the perfect mudra of repose, with flames shooting from the outer circumference of the circle. This image evokes the much later sedate circle inscribed by Leonardo daVinci, showing the center point of the human body in the lower abdomen and celebrating a fixed symmetry. In contrast, the Tanjore Śiva images, created at the height of the Chola Dynasty, vibrate with rhythm and balance. The Jesuit philosopher Norris Clarke hailed this image of Śiva as a beacon for understanding the presence of the divine in the world.[1]

The movement of Śiva depicts both creative and destructive power. He dances on a dwarf demonic body, a gesture that represents subjugation of passion. His many arms and his hair spiral outward toward the circle that signals the limits of creativity. Flames radiate beyond the circle, signaling the ultimate demise of all created realities. To the right of the Śiva stands the Pārvatī image, indicating their courtship phase. One presumes that his dance played a central role in their courtship. In the core metaphor of Sāṃkhya, she then takes up the dance, while Śiva retreats to the ubiquitous place of witnessing, meditating, and observing. Śiva represents the silent, inactive witness, the Puruṣa. Pārvatī symbolizes the ever-active Prakṛti. To the left of the Śiva and Pārvatī images one finds an empty space, graced with garlands of fresh flowers. Through this space and in this space, the human reflects on the paired powers of the dance and the witness of the dance, the bird who eats sweet berries and the bird who merely looks on.

We were invited to walk back to the house of the pūjārī, Paṇḍit Vasu. His wife served us South Indian coffee while the Paṇḍit shared with us stories of his family's long service at the Cidambaram Temple. We signed the register recording the many visitors to their home dating back many years and enjoyed the colors and simplicity of Indian décor, replete with colorful calendars and embroidery. A sense of timelessness pervaded our visit to Cidambaram, which held a shimmering beauty like that found in the black and white films of Satyajit Ray.

From Cidambaram we returned to Pondicherry, the former French colony where Sri Aurobindo took refuge. We stepped into the "New India" of global capitalism, receiving hospitality from Rajesh Kumar, manager of Le Pondy Resort. We transitioned from the sacred place of the space-honoring temple to a newly built tourist destination designed for international travelers and India's wealthy. Only two years old at the time, it sprawled over several beachfront acres, surrounded with backwaters. We enjoyed a scrumptious lunch including a nouvelle cuisine cabbage and ginger curry and an amazing fresh coconut dessert. Seeking to provide luxury space for upper-class Indians and global guests, each suite in this all-suite hotel sports its own unique swimming pool.

We then drove to Auroville, the remarkable space created by Mirra Alfassa Richard (1878–1973) as an international community "free from the war, greed, and strife that characterized human history."[2] She joined the spiritual community of Sri Aurobindo in 1920 and in 1926 established Sri Aurobindo Ashram in Pondicherry.[3] We walked through Auroville's lovely gardens to the Matrimandir, the spacecraft-like meditation hall in honor of the Mother. We viewed from afar its entrancing sphere of disks and triangles. The circular shapes evoke totality and the eternal. The upward triangles symbolize the observant male energy; the downward triangles symbolize the creative female energy. Their combination forms the Sri Yantra, a visual presentation of the emergence of the created world.[4]

The transition from the space of the temple to varying spaces of modernity reminded us of the process described by Sri Aurobindo as the "descent of consciousness," the inevitable return to the world and the ways of the world, what Friedrich Nietzsche referred to as the Eternal Return in *Thus Spake Zarathustra*. Our pilgrimage to the five elemental temples drew to an end. We reentered the realm of the profane, but without forgetting our immersion into traditional acknowledgments that all things of the world rely upon and are constructed from Earth, Water, Fire, Air, and Space: Pṛthivī, Jal, Agni, Vāyu, Ākāśa.

The *Pṛthivī Sūkta* and Space

Just as Tamil Nadu's temples seek to demarcate and designate the significance of the elements, so also the elements appear in the Vedas as components of existence that must be recognized with reverence. Space, in both its metaphorical and metonymical senses, can be measured by linear feet as well as the passage of time. Space can be seen as an entity to be entered and protected, and can be equated as a place of psychological refuge.

> 10. The dimensions of Mother Earth were measured by the Aśvins.
> Lord Viṣṇu strode victoriously [on the Earth].
> The Earth was made hospitable by Indra
> who also ensured freedom from enemies.
> Like a mother, may She nourish us all.

The Aśvins measure the start of the day and the close of the day. They are the horsemen that pull the sun over the face of the earth. The first Aśvin awakens with the dawn; the second Aśvin emerges with the sunset. The glory of the horizon, illuminated by these two auspicious moments, finds itself revealed during the course of the day. Particularly in India, which lies close to the Equator, this transition is abrupt, with very little twilight to warn of the change or ease people from darkness into light and from light into darkness. Like an archer with arrow drawn, the Aśvins do their work quickly.

Viṣṇu took three strides in creating the world (*Ṛg Veda* VII:99, VIII:29), though it remains somewhat unclear what these three strides accomplished. Did he fashion the earth below, the atmosphere in the middle, and the heavens above? Did he measure out past, present, and future? Did he lay the foundation for the Sāṃkhya principles of lethargy (*tamas*), activity (*rajas*), and illumination (*sattva*)? From other hymns we know that Indra made the earth hospitable by slaying the dragon of drought, opening the rainclouds, and releasing the life-giving waters.

> 12. My mother is this Earth, and I am her son.
> Our father is the sky who sustains us through the rains.
> May the Earth bring us closer to her through her middle-portion,
> and with the energy which resides throughout her body.
> May She nourish, protect, and maintain us in an appropriate manner.

The notion of family serves as a guiding metaphor in Indic traditions. With father as the sky above, sending life-giving rains, and the mother cuddling her human children in her lap, this verse evokes feelings of comfort and security.

> 13. Events for the welfare of all
> are consecrated by performing sacrifices on this Earth.
> Good and virtuous people assemble here to perform such functions.
> Strong sacrificial posts are erected here for making offerings.
> Here is where spirituality gets imparted.
> May that Earth bless us with fortune and prosperity.

Sacrifice (*yajña*) plays a vital role in the Vedic worldview. Through the sacrifice, a person focuses on intentions and desires and invites powers greater than oneself to provide support. The sacrificial posts serve as an axis mundi, a connection pole between the heavenly realms above and the earth below. By invoking these powers, the human person attains balance and the reassurance needed to persevere.

17. May we live longer in order to serve the Land of our Mother.
She is the mother of all the medicinal plants and vegetation.
She is the one who has given us an immense space;
and it is She who grants us the needed firmness.
May our behavior be in accord with Dharma
for securing stability and happiness.

The concept of Dharma emerged during the post-Vedic period as the thread that holds Indian civilization together. Each individual has a responsibility to self and family to perform works in the world for the sake of the greater good. Whether merchant or tax collector, physician or laborer, all tasks contribute to the "Loka Saṃgraha," holding the world with a sense of integrity and participation.

31. O Mother Earth!
May, all the directions (east, north, south, west),
as well as other various sub-directions (northeast, etc.),
be beneficial to us to tread upon.
And, in whatever country we live,
may we never falter.
32. O Mother Earth!
May harm not follow us to those regions
of the east, north, inside, below, and so forth.
Be gracious to us.
May our enemies not locate us in our travels.
May the one who is stalwart among us go to kill our enemies.

These two verses give honor to the cardinal points of the compass. The four directions find repeated mention in the sacred literature of India. Knowing one's location in both the physical and psychological senses of the word is the gateway to self-understanding and understanding the world. The *Bṛhadāraṇyaka Upaniṣad* and the *Ācārāṅga Sūtra* both begin with invoking one's orientation in space. Without knowing the immediacy of and intimacy with one's place, a person becomes lost and vulnerable.

The call for protection from enemies also speaks to one of the most basic human needs: safety.

34. O Mother Earth!
You provide us all sanctuary.

May we not be injured while lying down,
whether we turn upon our right side or left,
or whether we lie straight.

The skill of proprioception allows one to remain oriented within space. This verse draws attention to the safety one feels while knowing one's body position relative to the earth in the basic positions of repose, whether to one side or the other, or on one's back. Yoga *āsana* classes constantly counsel a person to lie on one side, lie on the other, lie on your back, roll over on your belly. From those basic positions, one moves into the shoulder stand, performs various lifts, tests the body against gravity, and moves into balance poses.

38. Places for offering oblations can be found on that Earth.
Here are poles for the sacrifice.
This is where the sacrificial post is situated.
This is where Brahmans well-versed in the Vedas recite hymns.
This is where Indra is invoked to drink Soma.

Vedic sacrifices, particularly in the heat just prior to the monsoon, synchronize with the return of the yearly rainy season. The climatology of India has been remarkably consistent. For instance, in Delhi, the rains are scheduled to arrive on June 29 each year, and they generally keep to schedule. The Brahmin priests, knowing the imminence of the rains, would stage their elaborate rituals to announce the coming of the greatly anticipated cooling, quenching downpours.

39. It is upon that Earth
where the Seven Sages, the creators of worlds,
performed sacrifices and austerities,
chanted hymns, and carried out sacred rites.

The sacred rituals conducted by the priests signaled the ability of the human community to observe and predict the change of seasons. Knowing when to plant, when to reap, when to work, when to rest, when to celebrate marked the constancy of civilization. In northern India, the rainy season of June, July, and August marks the time of planting rice. The dry season of September through January brings coolness and celebrations such as Durgā Pūjā and Nava Rātri in October-November, honoring the creative and destructive powers of the goddess. The harvest of the rice in December-January ensures the safe passage into the next year, followed with the hot months of February through May.

These verses address the measurement of spaces within the calendar, spaces within the human body, spaces and places of safety etched upon the face of the earth. By invoking Indra and the Aśvins and Viṣṇu within the context of Mother Earth, the text offers a celebration of stability, offering a sense that all things can be made happy.

Buddhism and Space

In the three Buddhist texts that we have consistently taken up, the *Dhātu Vibhaṅga*, the *Mahārāhulovada Sutta*, and the *Visuddhimagga*, the treatment of space or *ākāśa* receives extensive attention. Space appears consistently to provide an apt analogy for the state of perfect freedom. The word *nirvāṇa* denotes extinguishment of desire, a state even higher than the wind that has purified and stilled the troubled mind. *Ākāśa* lies within the Abhidharma category of immutable elements (*asaṃskṛta dharma*), also described as the end of suffering (*duḥkha-nirodha*).[5] The French Indologist Sylvain Lévi likens the ultimate experience of mind to a cloudless sky, open and radiant. Maitreya's *Ratnagotravibhāga*, a fifth-century text of Yogācāra Buddhism, refers to the "sky-like nature of the Buddha's body" (*ākāśasvabhāvata*).[6] Śāntideva, the eighth-century Mahāyāna Buddhist author, links the majesty of sound and wind with the vast expanse of space, emplacing within space the undying expression of highest religious meaning or Dharma:

> From birdsong and the sighing of the trees,
> from shafts of light and from the sky itself,
> may living beings, each and every one,
> perceive the constant sound Dharma.[7]

Through measured reflection on living presences within the world such as birds and trees, one gains elevation into higher states and spaces of edification.

In addition to providing the open-frame thinking about freedom after one experiences a sense of release, Buddhist texts engage space as providing a pathway for moving into fields of color (the next four *kasiṇas* in the *Visuddhimagga*) and to provide a roadmap to the experience of Tantric self-transformation. We begin with an examination of how the Buddha taught space to Pukkusati, how he coached Rāhula to befriend space, and we will conclude with some reflections on how Tantra incorporated the directions, colors, and elements within space into a process of inner transformation through visualization.

Dhātu Vibhaṅga

The Buddha's teachings to Pukkusati culminate with a long discourse on the nature of space. He begins by placing attention on the space within the body, noting that all sensory activity enters through the spaces of the ears, the nostrils, the mouth, and that all material waste exits the body through the orifices of the anus and uretha:

> And what is the space property? The space property may be either internal or external. What is the internal space property? Anything internal, belonging to oneself, is space, spatial, and sustained: the holes of the ears, the nostrils, the mouth, the [passage] whereby what is eaten, drunk, consumed, and tasted gets swallowed, and where it collects, and whereby it is excreted from below, or anything else internal, within oneself, that's space, spatial, and sustained: This is called the internal space property.[8]

Repeating the refrain of erasure, the Buddha admonishes that all clinging to or identification with space, internal or external, must be relinquished:

> Now both the internal space property and the external space property are simply space property. And that should be seen as it actually is present with right discernment: "This is not mine, this is not me, this is not my self." When one sees it thus as it actually is present with right discernment, one becomes disenchanted with the space property and makes the mind dispassionate towards the space element.[9]

This ultimate relinquishment of the most subtle element leaves one in a state of simple, pure awareness that must then be put to good use.

> Then there remains only consciousness, purified and bright. What does one cognize with that consciousness? One cognizes "pleasure." One cognizes "pain." One cognizes neither pleasure nor pain."[10]

The Buddha then delivers to Pukkusati an extended teaching on how the purification that arises in the mind through dissolution of attachment to any and all forms of space allows the application of an ongoing state of discernment. One comes to see the nature of pleasure and pain as not defining oneself:

> In dependence on a sensory contact that is to be felt as neither pleasure nor pain, there arises a feeling of neither pleasure nor pain.[11]

This seemingly elliptical assertion points toward the space of equanimity, the prized destination of all Buddhists.

Further metaphors used by the Buddha educate Pukkusati, including the metaphor of the fire sticks that no longer are used to generate heat and flame, signaling the relinquishment of desire, and the careful work of the goldsmith, which begins with praise of equanimity:

> [E]quanimity [is] purified and bright, malleable, wieldy, and radiant. Suppose a skilled goldsmith or his apprentice were to prepare a furnace, heat up a crucible, take some gold with a pair of tongs, and place it in the crucible: He would blow on it time and again, sprinkle water on it time and again, examine it time and again, so that the gold would become refined, well-refined, thoroughly refined, flawless, free from dross, pliant, malleable, and luminous. Then whatever sort of ornament he wished to make from it, whether a golden chain or earrings or a necklace, or a golden garland, it would serve his purpose. In the same way, there remains only equanimity: purified and bright, pliant, malleable, and luminous.[12]

The translator notes that the Buddha affirms in this passage the attainment of the fourth and highest level of meditation, the fourth Jhāna, characterized by Winston King as "a progressive winding down of emotional fervor and a steady eroding of material, external, and even distinguishable components or contents of consciousness . . . the fourth jhāna involves only consciousness purified by equanimity and mindfulness"[13] This moves the meditator from discursive, judgmental mind-states into the space of equanimity.

This place of equanimity leads to freedom from reliance on anything in the world; one moves into a state of freedom:

> This being the case, one is not sustained by anything in the world (does not cling to anything in the world). Unsustained, one is not agitated. Unagitated, one is totally unbound right within. One discerns that "Birth is ended, the holy life fulfilled, the task done. There is nothing further for this world."[14]

The Buddha continues to describe what it is like to be free from attachment from pleasant or unpleasant feelings, the nobility of being grounded in wisdom, having relinquished all acquisitiveness, ignorance, desire, and lust. The Buddha, referring to each of the five elements and power of the mind, declares to Pukkusati: "The tides of conceiving do not sweep over one who stands on these foundations . . . such a one is called a sage at peace . . . Bhikkhu, bear in mind this exposition of the six elements."[15] Starting with extended reflection on earth, water, fire, and air, the Buddha states that through mastering the inner and outer spaces of attachment, one can understand and control the operations of the mind, and hence reach freedom.

At the conclusion of this encounter, it dawns on Pukkusati that he has been in the presence of the Buddha. He begs forgiveness for any unintended impertinence or disrespect. The Buddha offers to initiate him as a monk. While searching for appropriate robes, Pukkusati, as noted earlier, is killed by a stray cow. The Buddha affirms after his death that Pukkusati, whose name means "one who has been cooked" or purified by the fire, had in fact attained the liberated state of *arhat*.

Mahārāhulovāda Sutta

As with the advice given following the pronouncements on earth, water, fire, and air, the Buddha tells his son Rāhula to "develop meditation that is like space" so that "agreeable and disagreeable contacts will not invade your mind and remain."[16] Building on the foundation of the five elemental meditations, the Buddha completes his meditation instructions to his son. He teaches him about the Brahma Vihāra (*mettā, karuṇā, muditā, upekṣā*). To gain mastery in Buddhism, one must cultivate loving-kindness for the purpose of abandoning ill will; compassion to abandon cruelty; altruistic joy to abandon discontent; and equanimity to abandon aversion.[17] The Buddha instructs Rāhula to meditate on the foul nature of the body, and how to fully discern impermanence. One contemplates the foul nature of the body in order to abandon lust. Meditation on impermanence allow one to abandon attachment to the notion that "I am."[18] He teaches him the skill of mindfulness, and how to observe his breathing:

> Here, Rāhula, a bhikkhu, gone to the forest to the root of a tree or to an empty hut, sits down; having folded his legs cross-wise, set his body erect, and established in mindfulness in front of him, ever mindful he breathes in, mindful he breathes out.[19]

From this state, one brings the body into a state of tranquility and rapture, calms the mind, gladdens the mind, and finally liberates the mind. This liberation entails fully understanding and embodying the truths of impermanence, fading away, cessation, and relinquishment, entering the space of freedom.

Visuddhimagga

The first four *kasiṇas* in the *Visuddhimagga* provide instruction on how to build concentration on earth, water, fire, and air. Before taking up instructions on how to concentrate on light and space, the next sequence of four *kasiṇas* moves beyond the elements to the realm of color. Buddhaghosa first advises the meditator to notice the color blue as it manifests in flowers or textiles and even suggests forming a disk as with the Earth Kasiṇa, coloring it blue. The same instructions are given for cultivating awareness of the colors yellow, red, and white. The ninth *kasiṇa* specifies mindfulness of how light penetrates "a hole in a wall, or in a keyhole, or in a window opening."[20] The tenth *kasiṇa* returns to the elements, with a description of how to contemplate space (*ākāśa*). The text states that one who has had previous life experience reflects on the hole created in instances above rather than on the light that passes through, and that those who are new to the practice "should make a hole a span and four fingers broad in a well thatched hut, or in a piece of leather, or in a rush mat."[21]

This section of the *Visuddhimagga* ends with praise for what is to be accomplished through these practices. Through the Earth Kasiṇa, "Having been one, he becomes many" and acquires the "bases of mastery."[22] The Water Kasiṇa allows one to dive in and out of the waters, as well as to see that water is present in "causing rain storms, creating rivers and seas, making the earth and rocks and palaces quake."[23] The author goes on to state

> The Fire Kasiṇa is the basis for such powers as smoking, flaming, causing showers of sparks, countering fire with fire, ability to burn only what one wants to burn, causing light for the purpose of seeing visible objects with the divine eye, burning up the body by means of the fire element at the time of attaining nibbana.[24]

The description for the Air Kasiṇa, though no less powerful, is brief: "The Air Kasiṇa is the basis for such powers as going with the speed of the wind, causing wind storms."[25] The four colors (blue, yellow, red, white) and light are given correlating abilities, with light enabling one in the arts of "creating luminous forms, dispelling darkness, causing light for the purpose of seeing visible objects with the divine eye." The final element Kasiṇa, Space, "is the basis for such powers as revealing the hidden, maintaining postures inside the earth and rocks by creating spaces inside them, traveling unobstructed through walls, and so forth."[26]

Discussion of the elements recurs as Buddhaghosa describes the fortieth form of concentration. This comprises instruction on how to deepen one's meditation. He advises reflecting on thirteen aspects: meaning of words, groupings, particle nature, characteristics, origin, variety/unity, separability/inseparability, similar/dissimilar, external/internal, inclusivity, condition, equanimity, and conditionality. Without repeating in exhaustive detail how the text deals with the elements in each of these categories, two examples will suffice. Buddhaghosa suggests using the words designating each element to appreciate its extended qualities:

> It is earth because it is spread out; it flows or glides or satisfies thus it is water; it heats, thus it is fire; it blows, thus it is air.[27]

Similarly, he suggests reflecting on the atomistic or particle nature of each element, seeing clusters of each element form into particular manifestations. In a sense, the text gives permission for the mind to wander within the sphere of the intended object of meditation, to use thought in all its variegations as a vehicle for focusing.

The *Visuddhimagga* gives practical instruction that brings one successively into connection with earth, water, fire, air, blue, yellow, red, white, light, and space. By gaining intimacy with each in sequence and in tandem, one comes to a state of increased mindfulness or awareness, focusing the mind, preparing it to move forward into reflection on other Buddhist teachings, eventually returning in the fortieth and final state to renewed presence within the elemental world.

Standing high above and overlooking Shambala Mountain Retreat in Colorado stands a multistory stupa, a magnificent pillar-like temple that communicates the elements, the directions, and the call to a sense of self-transcendence.[28] This temple rests upon a square base with seven levels, representing the three jewels of Buddhism (Buddha, Dharma, Sangha) and the four signs of the enlightened life (*maitri/mettā, karuṇā, muditā, and upekṣā/upekkhā*). This base signifies earth, further marked with the color yellow. Above this rises a vase-like structure signifying water, associated with the circle and the color blue. A triangular red shape formed by thirteen disks emerges at the next level, denoting fire and the color red. A crescent or bowl at the top of this triangle evokes the wind, portrayed here with the color green. At the very top, symbolizing space, one finds three nested signifiers: the crescent moon below, the sun in the middle, topped with the jewel (*maṇi*) of enlightenment. This structure also represents the cosmic person, with the architectural features representing different body parts of the Buddha. As we will see below, temple design connects with the human body in a manner that invites reflective transformation of one's sense of self. The cosmos contains the body. The body contains the cosmos. A temple or stupa makes these connections explicit.

Space Narratives in the *Yogavāsiṣṭha*

Thus far, we have followed Vasiṣṭha's descriptions of the *Pañca Mahā Bhūta Dhāraṇās* in sequential chapters of the final book of the *Yogavāsiṣṭha*, aptly titled the Nirvāṇa Prakaraṇa, the book of freedom. In chapter 2 of this book, just prior to his concentration on earth, the sage Vasiṣṭha narrated the relationship between consciousness and activity, symbolized respectively by the meditating Śiva sitting in the cave and by the power (*śakti*) of the various forms of the goddess. Vasiṣṭha described the world-creating process. The story began with an encounter with a seemingly inert rock. A celestial woman brought Vasiṣṭha into the rock, where she showed him her husband, a sleeping "creator," identified as Rudra or Śiva. In proximity to him, the woman assumed the form of Kālī (or *prakṛti*) and began to dance, emitting from her body the entire world.

In an earlier chapter of the *Yogavāsiṣṭha*, Vasiṣṭha described the formation of the operations of the intellect or will (*buddhi*), the ego (*ahaṃkāra*) and the mind (*manas*). Giving poetic expression to the emergence of the world through the categories set forth by Sāṃkhya, Vasiṣṭha linked desire, the soul, the heart, and the functions of the body:

> Any being, following its desires, becomes the living soul.
> It collects these into the parts of the body,
> With the pulsing heart at its center.
> It creates the "I" from the I-maker (*ahaṃkāra*).
> Through naming things, the mind emerges.
> Its understanding forms the intellect (*buddhi*).
> It perceives sense objects through the sense organs (*indriya*).
> The embodied one thus takes on a body

just as a potter creates a pot.
This arises from self-inclination.
It is known by the people that a person has eight aspects:
[the five organs of sense, thoughts and feelings, and the witness].[29]

However, while describing the emergence of the world as a consciousness cascading forth by its observation of the material world, Vasiṣṭha nonetheless cautions Rāma that through mistaken knowledge (*mithyā jñānena*), one thinks, "I am form, I am body, whether standing or moving."[30] This mistaken notion, forgetting one's origins in consciousness, traps one in the world, resulting in the cycle of birth and death.

There is no freedom whatsoever,
when the consciousness is connected with
perception of externals:
this destroys the possibility of insight (*sambodha*).[31]

Vasiṣṭha affirms the operations of the Sāṃkhya system that generate the world and retains its insistence that the consciousness only appears to take on the form of the senses and sense objects; in reality it remains aloof, only a witness (*sakṣitva*).[32] However, the text also celebrates the physical world, stating that the appearance of the physical world depends upon consciousness as the very foundation and premise for its perception.

Nirvāṇa Prakaraṇa II, chapter 87, states that space (*ākāśa*) differentiates into intellect (*buddhi*) and mind (*manas*) (II:87:11). "Then from its powers of perception and sensation it becomes the five senses, to which are added their fivefold organs, leading from mental perceptions to full manifestation (*sthaula*)."[33] Once embedded in a body, all the troubles of the world follow.[34] However, as long as one keeps sight of the passing nature of all things, there can be the possibility of freedom. All things rely upon the *cidākāśa*. They emerge from the space of consciousness and become reabsorbed into that same consciousness.[35] Vasiṣṭha counsels Rāma that he can live life to the fullest bearing this in mind.

Vasiṣṭha, after his encounter with the inert Śiva in the rock, describes the many qualities associated with the goddess who dances the world into existence. Though mentioned earlier in the second chapter on earth, they merit repeating:

She is called by the names Jayā and Siddhā
because she is accompanied by victory and prosperity at all times.

> She is also designated as *Aparājitā* or the invincible, Viryā the mighty,
> and Durgā the inaccessible, and is likewise renowned as Umā,
> composed of the powers of the three syllable Om.
> She is called the Gāyatrī from being chanted by every body
> and Sāvitrī from being the matrix of all things.
> She is named Sarasvatī for giving us insight
> into what appears before our sight.[36]

The goddess is not portrayed here as unconscious or inert. To the contrary, Vasiṣṭha states that:

> She is the form of the beautiful sky, of space (*ākāśa*) itself.
> She is seen as good fortune (*śrī*), moving all that she holds (*spanda-dharminī*).
> She is the goddess (*devī*) of all these various things
> that she dances into being.
> All cities and continents, mountains and islands,
> hang on her agency as a string of gems around her neck.
> She holds together all parts of the world
> and exerts her force as vibration (*spanda*) in them all, . . .[37]
> She is the one great body of the cosmos:
> Her power supports the earth, with all its seas

Within the darkened cave, Vasiṣṭha watched Kālī generate the world through her body and senses. Vasiṣṭha told Rāma how he first observed Kālī's creation of the world as external to himself. He then told Rāma how he himself manifests in his own body the creative powers he had seen in the goddess. He became the goddess, playing with the creation of the world, as we have seen in prior chapters:

> Thinking myself the master of the earth, I became amalgamated with the earth . . . I thought myself as the sovereign of the whole . . . I became changed into the earth's forests and woods, which grew as hairs on its body . . . I was full of villages and valleys, of hills and dales, and of infernal regions and caverns; I was the great mountain chain and connected the seas and their islands.[38]

Vasiṣṭha's descriptions rejoice in the beauties of nature, which he sees as inseparable from his own body.

On the one hand, Vasiṣṭha repeats again and again that ultimately all things are empty (*śūnya*) and that all things are constructed by the mind. But with wild exuberance and clear, pure enjoyment he revels in describing the results of the creative process. In the earth chapter of this book, we saw him rejoice as he proclaimed:

> My chest became the expansive plains.
> My eyes became pools of lotuses.
> My crown was the light and dark clouds.
> My body contained the ten regions.[39]

In the water chapter, Vasiṣṭha celebrated the rising mist, the drops of dew, and the flowing rivers. He likened fire to "the brilliance in gold and rubies" and, in the air chapter, proclaimed himself "the teacher of dancing leaves on grasses, trees, and tender vines."

Having ascended beyond the airy realm into space, he witnessed a perfect adept, a liberated sage. This Siddha falls to the earth and shares with Vasiṣṭha his own insights into the transitory nature of life. The Siddha, the personification of space, tells Vasiṣṭha:

> I wandered on the tops of hills and roved in the airy regions on the summits of the Meru Mountains, I travelled to the cities of many a ruler of men, and met with nothing of any real good to me anywhere. I saw the woody trees, the same land of earth cities, and the same sort of fleshy animal bodies everywhere; I found them all frail and transitory. I saw that no riches, no friends, no relatives nor enjoyments of life were able to save any one from the clutches of death.[40]

Vasiṣṭha, having traversed both inner and outer space, and all the realms in between, from the earth up to the heavens, announces that even in his apparent form, he sees things as none other than a dream. All things emerge from space and to space they return. He exhorts Rāma to grow into this wisdom so that his delusion might also disappear. Space provides the metaphor for freedom, not from the world but within the world.

The story of the rock in the *Nirvāṇa Prakaraṇa* carries an account of how Sāṃkhya categories came to be employed within the larger stories of the Śaiva tradition. Śiva is depicted as a remote, meditating figure, like a king who has lost interest in his domain. The goddess Kālī, in ghostly form, emits the world from her shadow when she comes close (*saṃyoga*) to her beloved. In poetic detail, Vasiṣṭha articulates the relationship between senses (*buddhīdriyas*) and the subtle elements (*tanmātras*) and the gross elements (*mahābhūtas*) of earth, water, fire, air, and space. He sees the entire manifest world within his own body. He receives wisdom from these experiences and also directly from the sage called Siddha. He then returns to the world, ultimately for the purpose of instructing Rāma.

The stories of the *Yogavāsiṣṭha* serve to instruct Rāma that the world must not be seen as fixed or inert. In the story on reincarnation that we examined in chapter 6, Puṇya instructs his younger brother Pāvana that by reflecting on his past births, he will loosen his lament for those he has lost in this birth. In the story of the rock, Kālī shows the processes through which the world emerges and demonstrates the dynamic, living relationship between the material of the world and the processes of sense perception, all of which are in service of consciousness (*cit*).

In the *Yogavāsiṣṭha*, understanding the creation and dissolution of the manifest world as taking place within the mind becomes the gateway to the ultimate metaphysical experience, referred to by Vasiṣṭha as *nirvāṇa*. Vasiṣṭha spins a cosmological story of creation and dissolution. As the goddess wends her way from the darkness of the rock to display the entire universe, the story itself becomes a creative act. The story serves to help Rāma learn how to restructure the subtle body through imaginative engagement. *Pratiprasava,* the yogic practice of reversing the outward, world-creating flow (*pariṇāma*), allows the subtle body (*sūkṣma-śarīra*) to be restructured through repeated encounters with purified consciousness (*sattva*). *Yoga Sūtra* II:10 states that "The subtle ones are to be avoided by a return to their origins" (*te pratiprasava heyāḥ sūkṣmāḥ*).

In the second pāda of the *Yoga Sūtra*, Patañjali advocates the application of *pratipakṣa bhāvana,* the cultivation of opposites, in order to counter past negative impressions or *saṃskāras.* In the first pāda, Patañjali proclaims that the performance of meditation or samādhi has a salutary effect: The impression born of it obstructs other impressions (*taj-jaḥ saṃskāro'nya-saṃskāra-pratibandhī* I:50). The world itself is inseparable from living processes. Impressions (*saṃskāra*) help to create the world as they find expression through one's thoughts and intentions, words and deeds.[41]

Similarly, the *Yogavāsiṣṭha* emphasizes the role of human agency in creating the spaces within the world for experience and freedom. The story of the rock tells of a repeated return to the world of manifestation and creativity, followed with yet another ascent into a state of abeyance and removal from worldly entanglements. In each instance of creative engagement, the world of the senses and elements is described in loving detail, with a constant reminder of its beautiful yet chimerical and fleeting quality.

Space in the *Gheraṇḍa Saṃhitā*

Haṭha Yoga places the realm of space at the ascendancy of practice. Its object of concentration is the open sky. Its color can be seen in the reflection of the sky in the Sindu River, the great river that flows from the Himalayas into the Arabian Sea. As with the other *Pañca Mahā Bhūta* practices, it also includes recitation of a mantra and control of breath. Its great power lies not in accomplishment or procurement of things, but in total freedom:

> 80. Now we will tell about the space concentration mudra.
> Its color resembles the best pure waters of the Sindu River,
> reflecting the shining sky.
> This element is linked with the god Sadāśiva.
> Its seed syllable is "ha."
> One should hold the breath and mind in abeyance for two hours.
> From the performance of the sky concentration
> one can break open the door of liberation.
> 81. Now the results of the space concentration will be told.
> The one who knows the space concentration mudra
> overcomes old age and death.
> At the time of the cosmic collapse,
> that yogi will not perish.

Through concentration on space (*ākāśa dhāraṇā*) one gains immortality.

In the winter of 2013, Mr. B. K. S. Iyengar sat with me and explained the golden amulet that he wore around his neck. He designed it to be a constant reminder of the integrated worldview presented by his beloved tradition of Yoga. Inscribed with the Śrī Yantra at its center, it evokes the blessed relationship between *puruṣa* and *prakṛti,* symbolized by the upward and downward triangles, respectively, located within the gates of a square maṇḍala. The seed syllables associated with each element surround the perimeter. Mr. Iyengar kept this talisman as a constant reminder of the relationship between the manifest and the unmanifest forms of *prakṛti* and the ever-present silent witness, *puruṣa*. It also includes concentric circles representing the eight limbs of Yoga: ethics/*yama,* observances/*niyama,* postures/*āsana,* control of breath/*prāṇāyāma,* inwardness/*pratyāhāra,* concentration/*dhāraṇā,* meditation/*dhyāna,* and the goal of Yoga, *samādhi.*

Space in Jainism

Jainism delineates space with great specificity. It describes the universe as bounded into the shape of a human person, with infernal regions below, planet Earth in the middle, heavens above the earth, and, at the upper reaches of reality, a realm known as the Siddha Loka, a region wherein dwell all those who have been liberated from the shackles of bondage. Karma suffuses space, as do countless individual souls known as *jīvas.* Through willful ascent, these souls attempt to navigate and purge their psychological spaces and move toward freedom. In order to fully comprehend the Jaina ascent within space, its key principles and practices are outlined below to provide the context for the meditation on space found in the *Jñānārṇava* and the *Yogaśāstra.* This will include a description of Jaina temples, which, as with the Buddhist stupa, provide a visual reminder of one's emplacement within and possible transcendence of the realm of the five elements.

The *Tattvārtha Sūtra* of Umasvati, probably written in approximately 450 CE, posits nine core principles of Jaina philosophy, summarized as follows:

1. Multiple forms of life or souls (*jīva*) have existed since beginningless time. These souls can never be created nor destroyed and will live forever, taking birth after birth.
2. These souls interact with four nonliving forces (*ajīva*): matter/karma, time, space, and movement.
3. Purposeful actions committed by the soul cause an influx of karma (*āsrava*) that adheres to the soul, obscuring its innate energy, consciousness, and bliss.
4. These adhesions of karma result in the bondage (*bandha*) of the soul.
5. Karma may take auspicious (*puṇya*) forms.

6. Karmic particles can also be inauspicious (*pāpa*).

7. Through adherence to vows one can stop (*saṃvara*) the influx of 148 forms of karma.

8. This results in the sloughing off of karma (*nirjarā*).

9. Once freed from all karma, one enters liberation/freedom (*mokṣa/nirvāṇa/kevala*).

In addition to these philosophical principles, the *Tattvārtha Sūtra* provides geographical and biological views of reality, delineating specific continents, multiple parallel universes, and historical epochs and eons. Life may take form in the space of hellish, earthly, or heavenly realms or, in the case of freedom from all karma, in the realm of transcendence. In the earthly realm, life may be elemental, microbial, vegetative, or locomotive. Life dwells in rocks, clods of earth, drops of water, flowing streams, radiant sunbeams, flickering flames, gusts of wind, viruses and bacteria, fungi and plants, as well as all manner of insects, fish, reptiles, birds, and mammals, including humans. The *Tattvārtha Sūtra* places these souls into a hierarchy depending upon the number of senses carried. Elemental, microbial, and vegetative souls possess the sense of touch. Worms add the sense of taste. Crawling insects also possess smell. Flying insects add the ability to see. Higher level organisms as listed above can also hear and think.

Spiritual advancement takes place in Jainism within the space of a fourteen-fold path. Due to the density of past karmas, all individuals, including human beings, arrive in the world cloaked in ignorance, the first of fourteen rungs (*guṇasthāna*) of life's ladder. A moment of spontaneous awareness may occur, jolting an individual up to the fourth step, the state of insight and equanimity, through which one receives a glimpse of freedom. Many people forget about this experience, falling back to the second rung, or remember the experience fondly but neglect to take action and remain at the third level. Those who are moved by the momentary taste of freedom pledge to follow the five purifying vows listed above and advance to the fifth stage of the spiritual path. Following this experience of release, the soul then either falls back down into a deluded view, or takes up the resolve to change, to enter into a path of progressive purification.[42]

The status of the liberated soul remains the object of speculation. Umasvati states that the soul soars to the limits of the universe:

Omniscience arises when deluding karma is eliminated
and as a result, knowledge-covering, intuition-covering
and obstructed karma are eliminated (X:1).
There is no fresh bondage because the causes of bondage
have been eliminated and all destructive karma have worn off (X:2).
The elimination of all types of karma is liberation (X:3).
When all karmic bondage is eliminated, the soul soars upward
to the border of cosmic space (X:5).
. . . . it is like castor seeds released from the pod
and like the flame of fire (X:7).[43]

Padmanabh Jaini notes that "it must be borne in mind that any description of the perfected being, or of the infinite cognition and bliss which characterize him, is purely conventional. In reality such things, lying as they do beyond the space-time limitations of ordinary human consciousness, cannot be described at all."[44] However, Paul Dundas, referring to the *Aupapatika*, an early Jain text, is careful to point out that Jainism does specify that the soul "rises . . . to the realm of the *siddhas,* the liberated *jivas* at the top of the universe where it will exist perpetually without any further rebirth in a disembodied and genderless state of perfect joy, energy, consciousness and knowledge."[45] He also notes that the Jains are scrupulous in specifying that the individuality of the enlightened soul will continue. Jainism does not entail any sort of merging into a universal soul or state of oneness.

The *Ācārāṅga Sūtra* describes the liberated soul as follows:

Not long nor small or round nor triangular
nor quadrangular or circular;
not black nor blue nor red nor green nor white;
neither of good nor bad smell;
not bitter nor pungent nor astringent nor sweet;
neither rough nor soft; neither heavy nor light;
neither cold nor hot; neither harsh nor smooth.
The soul is without body, without rebirth,
without contact (with karma),
not feminine nor masculine nor neuter.
The soul perceives and knows but there is no analogy
(to describe the liberated soul).
Its essence is without form.
There is no condition of the unconditioned.[46]

This ascent results in an eternal state of freedom, an inconceivable yet compelling image. As we will see below, the *Jñānārṇava* and the *Yogaśāstra* state that what one encounters in the Siddha Loka will be none other than the presence of liberated souls identical in shape to those found in the many images of Jinas found in the Jaina temple.

The place of the temple in Jaina religious life cannot be overstated. At the temple, Jainas perform *darśan,* viewing the image in a state of meditation, recognizing that just as the Jinas sit in meditation, one also can sit in imitation of them. The construction of Jaina temples has escalated in the last twenty years, both in India and abroad. A remarkable group of new temples have been built in the rural village of Hastinapur, northeast of Delhi, the site of many tales from the Mahābhārata epic. I have visited these temples nearly every year for several years. Three founding teachers or Tīrthaṅkaras of the Jaina tradition were born in Hastinapur: the sixteenth, Shantinath, the seventeenth, Kunthanath, and the eighteenth, Arahnath.

Sri Pujya Ganini Shri Gyanmati Mataji, a Digambara nun born in 1932, arranged for the construction of a complex of temples in Hastinapur that educates its pilgrims regarding the inner and outer spaces of Jainism.[47] One enters an altered landscape of vertical, circular, and horizontal monumental architecture, stretching over several acres. On the horizontal plane one is reminded of the complex composition of this place we call Earth, Jambudvīpa. Marble houses and flowing streams separated by wrought iron fences evoke the various realms and areas of this middle place in which lives take birth: the elements of earth, water, fire, and air, all considered to possess soul; the microbes; the plants; the animals; and human beings. Round and round, the soul takes birth due to past karma, fulfills the needs of those karmas during life, and moves instantly at death into another life form, experiencing the joys and pains of *saṃsāra.* According to this view, in this present age, the best one can hope for is to attain human birth, the birth that allows for self-improvement and purification. This monument also moves its pilgrim physically and symbolically to another cosmic era, another *Yuga,* where it is possible to ascend to the state of perfect freedom, represented by the pillar of pride, Mt. Meru, the lofty point at the very top of the universe from which the liberated soul can survey the continued rounds of existence while not being tempted to fall from the abode of eternal consciousness, energy, and bliss.

Across the moat and a few yards away, one enters a vertical temple depicting the Jaina cosmos. Towering some ten stories above the earthbound detailed likeness of Jambudvīpa, this glass-clad image of the human body dramatically presents dozens of dioramas. At the base, one finds microbes and dirt. Climbing up seven floors of cramped staircases, one can rise up through the various hells where people suffer due to heinous sins and crimes. At the level of Jambudvīpa, one catches a glimpse of the much larger version outdoors, and again one can gaze upon the rivers, oceans, and continents that comprise Middle Earth. From there, one ascends through the multiple stages of the heavens, seeing the joy and pleasure experienced by myriad gods and goddesses. Finally, one reaches the very top, an observation deck from which, having arrived at the top of this symbolic Mt. Meru, one can survey the vast life-filled plains of India in a moment of exhilaration.

The Aṣṭapad Śvetāmbara Temple in Hastinapur rises several stories above the bustle of the village. One enters through a simple portal. The architecture guides the pilgrim to the left, up a circular ramp, into a tunnel of darkness. Every one hundred feet or so, a small aperture allows light to filter into the passageway, and by peering through the small opening, one can barely discern the central pillar-like altar. Step after step, round after round, not unlike the Guggenheim Museum in New York City, one ascends, the light increasing as one reaches the top after what feels like at least seven circumambulations. Finally, one breaks through into the light and enters the final abode, symbolic of the release upward, onto Mt. Meru. In this rooftop temple reside gleaming images of the Tīrthaṅkaras and Siddhas. The light from this lofty perch filters down over the enclosed central pillar. After rejoicing in silence at the exquisite renderings symbolic of beings that have reached the perfection of total freedom, one then can then walk around the plaza that surrounds the temple, gazing outward rather than inward, feeling the delight of being a watcher rather than a doer.

According to Jainism, the cosmos takes the shape of the human body; the human body takes the shape of the cosmos in an interplay of microphase and macrophase. The lower realms of the body, burdened with karmas, hold the soul tightly within *saṃsāra,* the cycle of birth, life, death, and rebirth. Due to karmas committed in this life and prior lives, the individual soul must return again and again, moving from elemental and animal forms to human, hellish, and heavenly forms, depending on the nature of one's deeds. Birth within the human body is a necessary precondition for undertaking the work of spiritual purification. The middle realms of the human body, a place of will and heat, allow for purification and taking up the vows that dispel karma: nonviolence, truthfulness, not stealing, sexual restraint, and nonpossession. The upper realms of the body provide the clarity of heaven-like experiences. Purified senses and a calm mind can erase lifetimes of stress and karma.

Tantra: Outer and Inner Space

Douglas R. Brooks has described Tantra as polythetic, holding multiple meanings depending upon context and practice.[48] Though associated with violative practices such as eating meat and fish, drinking alcohol, and engaging in sexual intercourse, not all forms of Tantra require such rituals, some choosing instead to emphasize the purification of the elements (*bhūta-śuddhi*) through the practice of the elemental concentrations (*pañca-mahā-bhūta dhāraṇā*) as described in this book, combined with mantra recitation, attunement to color, and visualization. Without the encumbrance of secret practices, many Hindus, Buddhists, and Jainas employ the techniques of Tantra regularly. In the words of Paul Dundas, "The possibility of using sanctified language of a general Tantric idiom . . . has never caused the Jains any difficulty, and in common with the Hindus and Buddhists they cultivated an elaborate science of mantra and yantra."[49] As we have seen in the texts and temples we have surveyed and visited, establishing oneself within the geometry and sound and color of the elements results in states of transcendence and even bliss.

Christopher S. George, who studied for many years with Geshe Wangyal in New Jersey and with Padma Gylatsan and Mana Vajra Vajrācārya for six months in Nepal, notes that the practice of Tantra is not to annihilate the ego, but to transform the ego through overcoming ignorance of the many factors that shape it. This requires "the transformation of the mundane *ahaṃkāra* or 'self-image' of the *sādhaka* or candidate into the transcendent self-image."[50] He goes on to write that "for the candidate who has effected this transformation, all his[/her] actions become . . . pure and blameless acts . . . the world in which he[/she] moves is none other than the Vajra-realm, transcending any notion of being or non-being."[51] This process involves three phases: construction of the *maṇḍala,* the palace wherein one redesigns the personality, the consecration of all actions according to religious precepts, and finally, the "dissolution of his[/her] own self-image to rebirth in the form [of the divine]," at which point the candidate proclaims, "I am the perfected one!"[52]

What does it mean to "construct a *maṇḍala*?" Our earlier translations of the *Jñānārṇava* discussed this practice in the context of the "*maṇḍala* of the four elements," the fire *maṇḍala,* and meditating upon the solar plexus while intoning the sixteen syllable mantra. It might be surmised that any meditation process that seeks to transform one into a more worthy person involves some form of a *maṇḍala* practice.

One of the great ideal figures of Buddhist traditions is Avalokiteśvara, the Buddha who gazes downward with compassion. This form of the Buddha developed popularity during the rise of Mahāyāna Buddhism. Many consider the Dalai Lama to be an incarnation of Avalokiteśvara. This Buddha is also known as the holder of great compassion (Mahākaruṇika) and the one who holds the white lotus (Padmapaṇi). The Tibetan name is Chenrezig. In China the gender of Avalokiteśvara changes to female and she is called Kuan-shih-yin or Kuan-yin. Her name in Japan is Kannon.

Janet Gyatso provides guidance in an introductory booklet on how meditate upon Avalokiteśvara through the process of visualization. She writes:

> The basic point of visualization is to transform one's experienced reality, at least during the period of meditation. The idea is that the more mental time one spends visualizing Buddhas, Bodhisattvas, etc., the more the nature of one's entire mental outlook will be benefitted. In addition, the power to visualize the whole universe as having become enlightened will greatly increase one's power over one's feelings, perceptions, and experiences in life. . . . [I]t is within our own power to become enlightened and thereby live in an enlightened world.[53]

She notes that some teachers advise fixing the gaze on only one part of the image to be visualized, and build out the memory field gradually. Other teachers advise staring at the whole image until the field becomes fixed and familiar and can be seen as if an old friend. She recommends the use of a 108-bead mala, noting that "[e]ach bead may be considered a symbol of the deity upon whom one is meditating, and the string running through them is a symbol of the consciousness of the Bodhisattva."[54]

Practices may also be found in the Tibetan tradition that directly correlate the four elements with forms of the goddess, mantras, and body parts. Nāgabodhi's *Samāja-sādhana-vyavasthāli* states that the goddess "Moharatī Locanā is the earth element, Dveṣaratī Māmakī is water, Rāgaratī Pāṇḍaravāsinī is fire, Vajraratī Tārā is *rlung* (Tibetan for air or breath, *vāyu* and *prāṇa*)." The Tibetan commentator Mkhas Grub then identifies Locanā with the genitalia, Tara with the navel, Māmakī with the heart, and Pāṇḍaravāsinī with the throat, proclaiming them to be the abodes of the earth, air, water, and fire energies, respectively.[55] Though the correlations vary from tradition to tradition, the Tantric method remains clear: linking body to the elements and to the larger cosmos.

In the Śaiva Trika system, one gradually blends visualization with mantra and ritual. Sthaneshwar Timalsina "identifies the body as the key constituent of the transformative practices of Tantric visualization."[56] The process of meditation develops a new source of identity; he notes that "[t]his creation of an alternate paradigm aims to nullify habitually given mental patterns and allow the mind to not just be free from previous conditions but also from the conditions created during the meditative practice."[57] The practice of mantra "elevates language to a higher status than that of a merely descriptive mechanism" and one comes to regard "the body as temple and as the cosmos . . . [leading to] bliss and awareness . . . [allowing one to] alter the preconditioned mind by reprogramming it with new meaning to the body and language."[58] Timalsina summarizes the Tantric process into three major moves, common to all the texts we have studied. First, one employs the purification of the elements (*bhūtaśuddhi*) such as we have seen described in the *Dhātu Vibhaṅga*, the *Visuddhimagga*, the *Yogavāsiṣṭha*, the *Gheraṇḍa Saṃhitā*, and the *Jñānārṇava*. He offers the following chart which more or less applies to the various systems we have explored:

Table 7.1

ha	sky	circle	no color
ya	air	hexagon	smoky
ra	fire	triangle	red
va	water	half circle	white
la	earth	square	yellow

Source: Sthaneshwar Timalsina, *Tantric Visual Culture: A Cognitive Approach* (New York: Routledge, 2015), 40.

Second, he notes the importance of fire as the purifying agent, which we saw most poignantly in the *Jñānārṇava* where all the forms of karma, visualized as petals on a lotus, were mentally incinerated. Third, he emphasizes the physical, corporeal nature of this practice: "The body, in this visualization, transforms into a *maṇḍala,* a geometric design, allowing the subject to identify his[/her] body with what the *maṇḍala* represents."[59] For the Buddhist, one gains freedom through the emptiness (*śūnya*) of vast empty space (*ākāśa*). The Śaiva will encounter one or many of the forms of the goddess, as did Vasiṣṭha when he entered the cave. The practitioner of Sāṃkhya-Yoga will overcome the fetters of afflicted karma, moving into a state of abiding happiness. The Jain, as we will see below in the *Jñānārṇava*, will come face to face with the liberated Jina and see that elevated person as no different from one's own self.

The *Jñānārṇava* and the Culmination of Jaina Tantra

Chapter 37 of the *Jñānārṇava*, which appears in nearly identical form in Hemacandra's *Yogaśāstra*, provides a distinctly Jaina approach to the processes of elemental purification and the transformation of self-identity. Though we have already examined select verses in the preceding chapters, the entire chapter will be revisited here. The standard Buddhist and Hindu construal of the elements follows the order of earth, water, fire, air, and space. The earliest record of this specific order appears in the *Dhātu Vibhaṅga*, a Buddhist text. The *Markaṇḍeya Purāṇa*, as noted in the first chapter of this book, provides the early correlations between elements and the body that later takes full blossom in Tantra. The *Jñānārṇava* follows an atypical ascent through the senses. Rather than proceeding from gross to subtle, with earth at the bottom, topped with water, fire, and air before reaching space, the Jaina rendering moves from earth to fire, from fire to air, and from air to water before reaching space.

One reconfigures the gaze upon the earth to visualize the earth as taking the shape of a lotus. The "stuff" of the earth becomes correlated with mountains seen in the distance at dusk. The meditator then visualizes fires scorching the eight downward petals of the lotus that represent the eight Jaina karmas. The four negative karmas, to be purified and expelled through this practice, obstruct knowledge, intuition, and energy, and cause delusional thinking and action. The four karmas that enable feeling, lifespan, physique, and social status must also go up in imaginal flames. The heat of this fire fans strong winds and effortful breathing that carry away the residues of smoke and ash and generate billowy clouds. Pelting rains wash away all the remnants of the burned karmas, and clear away all obstacles and constraints. The final visualization reveals purified space and the presence of the liberated soul and great teacher Mahāvīra. First, the meditator sees the outward form (*murti*) of the Jina seated on a lion throne. Upon closer inspection, as with the moment of transformation mentioned above by George and Timalsina, one sees that one's own self is not different from this vision of the perfected being. The goal has been achieved.

Jñānārṇava Chapter 37

1. According to the auspicious radiant shining souls,
four concentrations are to be recognized:
firm in substance (*piṇḍastha*), firm in movement (*padastha*),
firm in form (*rūpastham*), and beyond form (*rūpavarjitam*).

2. Those who are well controlled (*samyamis*)
and who are totally conscious overcome the snare of birth
using the five concentrations on substances.
These are to be known as explained below by the heroes.
3. (These substances) would be earth, then fire, breath, and eventually water,
all contained within the form of space. These are then to be understood in steps.
4. The Yogi, with equanimity while in the world, focuses on the milky ocean.
The mist of each silent, peaceful wave resembles a garland of pearls.
5. The Yogi should move his or her well formed focus
toward the middle of the thousand petaled lotus,
bringing to mind its blazing immeasurable splendor,
shining as brilliantly as melted gold.[60]
6. Like filaments rising up in the lotus, and like the brilliant mountains
that surround the earth, (these experiences) delight the bee-like mind.
7. (While gazing at these mountains) one should focus on the crown of the lotus
as the golden heavenly Mount (Meru), emitting a web of yellow light,
tinging the horizon in reddish brown.
8. One should think of oneself seated comfortably and tranquil
(high on a white throne) similar to the autumnal moon.
9. Marked with qualities of abstinence, patience, and discipline,
free from attraction and aversion, one cuts off the flow of karma
at its very origin.
10. Then, using the practice of meditation
on the lotus in the *maṇḍala* of the navel,
one focuses on the beautiful uplifted sixteen petals.
11. One should reflect upon the vibration
of the great mantra at the crown of the lotus,
its petals nested within one another
as a glorious garland of (sixteen) syllables.
[From the commentary: a, ā, i, ī, u, ū, ṛ, ṝ, ḷ, ḹ, e, ai, o, au, aṃ aḥ]
12. Through the murmuring of the sixteen seed mantras
comes a state of abeyance adorned with the emptying of sound.

(This experience is like) the glowing of a pendulous moon at its fullest,
its white face extending beauty (everywhere).
13. From the murmuring (of that mantra *raṃ*) one should then focus afterward
on the emerging gentle result, an uninterrupted succession of endless pulsing fire.
14. By this, the eternal Jina (is visualized) within these flickering flames.
Then, when that fire burns continually, one becomes steady,
situated in the white lotus of the heart.
15. The eight upside down petals, representing the eight kinds of karma,
are to be burnt completely by the fierce fire
that arises with the great mantra and meditation.
16. Then the triangular *maṇḍala* of fire (is visualized) outside of the body.
One should focus on those flickering flames as if they are bioluminescence.
17. Marked by a svastika located at the edge,
the fire seed *bīja* is approached (with the syllable *raṃ*).
It is smokeless and glittering with gold as it ascends in the rising wind.[61]
18. The inner fire of the mantra burns like a brush fire burns city after city,
running and resounding swiftly, spreading radiance from its flames.
19. This state reduces both body and lotus to ash.
Burning itself out, the fire gently, softly goes into a state of peace.
20. With great swiftness and great strength,
the Yogi meditates without interruption on moving through the air
as if having entered the path of a sky chariot (*prāṇāyāma*).
21. Rallying an army of gods by bellowing thirty breaths,
he holds in abeyance dense swarms (of karma)
as if dousing them in the mighty sea.
22. In this state, one finds enjoyment in moving about the world
with one's countenance travelling with the wind,
wandering to the abodes of people, settling down on the face of the earth.

23. With the powerful wind, one can speedily rouse oneself up into passion.
Then, through firm, accomplished practice,
one can calm the breath (the inner wind).
24. That virtuous soul should focus on the spectacle
in the western sky of dense clouds,
filled with moisture, rumbling lightning, and rainbows.
25. Then the ascetic should focus diligently
upon the unrelenting, tremendous rains,
each drop illuminated by lightning,
making them shine like large brilliant pearls.
26. Then the Yogi should meditate
on the beautiful water abode resembling a half moon
that causes the ocean to rise up,
overflowing into the face of the sky.
27. Once this inconceivable, powerful, divine meditation on water has arisen,
the body purified from dust is born.
28. Then the accomplished one focuses on his omniscient soul,
liberated from the seven bodily constituents,
shining like the unblemished full moon.
29. His soul, joined with heavenly eminence,
is worshipped by demons, gods, and serpents alike,
possessing both beauty and power,
seated upon the lion's throne [an allusion to Mahāvīra].
30. The Yogi should meditate on the self in one's own body,
an embryo in the form of a person
whose karmas have been diminished without remainder,
trembling with immeasurable beauty.
31. The Yogi whose practice grows
to uninterrupted steadiness in Piṇḍastha Meditation
soon reaches unparalleled, auspicious bliss,
and is called the Noble One.
32. He meditates on the glistening whiteness
of the new nectar on the full moon,
experiencing a moment of blessed omniscience,
seated on the golden mountain peak, free from all sensory outflows.
He meditates on the self and the universal form,

on the multitudes of teachers in the three realms,
as well as on the inconceivable Lord.
That Piṇḍastha Meditation makes one similar to the Jina
who has crossed the great water to the other shore.

This visualization begins with meditation on a lotus-shaped earth, with a focus on a horizon laced with mountains. In a process akin to such Tibetan shamanic practices as *gcod,* one uses a visualization on fire to burn the karmic body to ash. Then one invokes the wind through the practice of rapid breathing, strong enough to shake Mt. Meru, to disperse the ashes of the body, allowing one to sit still and contemplate the sky, filled with rainbows, lightning, and thunderclouds. Rains then wash the burnt body with sacred water, such that its luster resembles a half moon. Then one contemplates the soul as seated upon a throne, adored by benevolent gods, its eight karmas eradicated. In this state, one emulates the liberated souls, most specifically the great teacher, Tīrthaṅkara Mahāvīra. In this Tantric transformation, one uses visualization and mantra to incinerate impurities, obtaining the diamond-like body beyond the reach of all karmas.

Conclusion

Landscapes define us. We choose where to gaze within our geography, whether internal or external. We have surveyed several texts that can help shape the way we view this landscape. The *Pṛthivī Sūkta* helps us celebrate food, abundance, beauty, and protection. The *Dhātu Vibhaṅga* and the *Mahārāhulovāda* remind us to refrain from developing attachment to any particular element. The *Visuddhimagga*, *Yogavāsiṣṭha,* and the *Gheraṇḍa Saṃhitā* offer techniques for steadying the mind and expanding one's scope to include and embrace all of nature's beauties and colors, the play of light and the possibilities offered by open, unimpeded space. Animal narratives and stories of past lives encourage us to think broadly about our history, to be certain to remember that our individual narrative has taken many forms, and that we can manifest empathy naturally for our animal kin. The *Jñānārṇava* encourages us to recognize and externalize karmas so that they may be quelled. This text also recognizes the purifying powers of fire, wind, and water, which wash away all impediments to soulful and liberating transformation.

We also have walked through ritual spaces, spaces within landscapes purpose-built to create connective experiences: the elemental temples in Tamil

Nadu and Andhra Pradesh, the Dharmakāya Stupa in Colorado, and the cosmological temples in Hastinapur. Through performing *trāṭakam,* gazing at each element and absorbing the ambiance of each sacred site, we can move into the experience of being transformed.

These texts, though separated by several centuries and grounded in different theologies, all include elemental meditations. Structural similarities can be seen in their methodologies. They prescribe very specific meditations that involve fixing the gaze, sitting still, and using words or syllables to focus the mind. Each entails a sustained focus of the mind. Each claims to reduce impurities and attachments.

The internal and external recitation of words supports the meditation on the *kasiṇas* in the *Visuddhimagga.* The text gives several options of variant vocabulary that refer in sequence to earth, water, fire, air, and space. The pastoral images in the *Pṛthivī Sūkta* paint an enticing tableau, encouraging one to take another look at the beauties of the earth and land. The *Yogavāsiṣṭha* similarly bubbles over with details about the solidity of earth, the flow of water, the gift and danger of fire, the energizing power of wind. The poetic descriptions for the elements in the *Jñānarṇava* cause one to remember the mountains illuminated by the sunrise and the ocean's waves presenting themselves as waves of pearls.

These texts agree upon the recitation of the semivowels *laṃ, vaṃ, raṃ, yaṃ,* and *haṃ* to invoke earth, water, fire, air, and sky. These very specific seed mantras establish resonance between the body and the elements.

Correlations between the elements and specific colors differ. The Great Stupa of Dharmakāya at Shambhala Mountain lists, from earth to space, yellow, blue, red, green, and white, while Hindu Tantra practice evokes yellow, white, red, smoky, and clear. The Jaina *Jñānarṇava* associates the ochre, white, blue-black, and yellow with the first four elements, and does not "colorize" space. Additionally, concentration on colors comprises an additional, separate practice in the *Visuddhimagga,* with sequential focus on blue, yellow, red, and white, independent from making elemental or bodily correlations.

In general, these texts and temples agree on their geometrical grammar: the earth finds stability on the four-cornered square, water can be contained in a semicircular vase or bowl, fire rises up into triangular tongues, wind circulates in hexagonal or crescent-shaped swirls, and open space finds representation in a full circle or sphere.

How can one make sense of this cascade of correspondences? The foundational concentrations on earth, water, fire, air, and space deliver differing results. The Buddhist practice serves as a gateway to transcendence of ego. The Jaina practitioner comes face to face with the Jina and sees one's own self as not different from this purified being. The Yogi attains a state of equanimity. The devotee of the goddess gains a vision of her various forms.

While traveling from Puri to Bhubaneshwar early one morning, we rounded the corner near a small temple. As the sun rose, its rays captured water being poured from uplifted hands of an elderly man in a dhoti, absorbed in his morning ablutions. His shimmering garment, spun from cotton of the earth, moistened by the glimmering drops of water, illuminated by the rising sun, wafting slightly in the dawn zephyr, created a moment of suspended animation, a space for reflection and the catching of one's breath. All the elements were present within this rarefied space of silence: earth, water, fire, and air.

At the Vallabh Jain Smarak in Alipur, North Delhi, five temples adorn the twelve-acre complex. One honors the twenty-four Tīrthaṅkaras; another honors the teacher from Lahore who safely brought hundreds of Jainas safely to Delhi during partition; another honors an important woman who taught Jainism earlier last century; an outdoor shrine complex honors the gods and goddesses of the earth, learning, and wealth; and one temple honors the goddess Padmavatī.[62] Full-time *pūjārīs* maintain each sacred site every day, invoking mantras, washing the images, performing blessings for pilgrims and visitors and students, and creating an ambience, a space, a *bhāva* of auspiciousness.

In the early morning at Yoga Anand Ashram, having bathed the bricks of the *havan* with clean water and having placed new cuttings of hydrangea and baby's breath in the freshly polished brass vases, I bowed, head to the earth, hands in Añjali Mudrā. Lighting three sticks of incense, each sunrise and sunset I recited the Gāyatrī Mantra, invoking the earth and water of the Bhūr realm, the heat and air of Bhuvaḥ, and the vast space of Svaḥ. Intoning the mantra at the moment of the rising or setting sun, a moment of connection happened at the *havan,* facing west and then moving to the northwest, the northeast, the southeast, and the southwest, reciting the mantra in the ordinal directions before returning once more to face west and bow to the earth. This rhythm continues, a ritual that allows for a connection into the grammar of elements, sounds, and body that brings a sense of peace and being well.

The elemental concentrations in Hindu, Buddhist, and Jaina religious practice provide a Yoga that integrates and links the physical realities of shape, sound, and color, opening into a space of mental acuity and spiritual purification. This grammar repeats in many ways: through ritual, through architecture, through meditative visualization. In this book we have explored specific Hindu, Buddhist, and Jain texts and practices that allow for a reconfiguration of a sense of self from the small to the large, from the intimate to the cosmic. Such an approach to nature and the exploration of human nature evades ideology, though adherents to one ideology or another might want to subsume this practice into their own worldview.[63] By showing the foundational nature of this experiential practice, and by showing how it has manifested in many forms across many traditions, this book suggests not a commonality of practice across traditions but a simultaneous concern for the particular and the general, for the specific and the larger embrace, for the local and the global. Whether transformed into a Rishi or a Buddha or a Jina, even for an instant, one gets a sense through these Yogas of connecting with something larger than the small ideas one may harbor. The honoring of the five great elements and the discovery of kinship with animals can help cleanse worldly woes and invite one into a sense of freedom.

Appendix

Constructing the Maṇḍala through Yoga Sādhana

The Maṇḍala places the person within the cosmos. The cosmos begins with body and breath. In this book we have explored elements and senses and functions of the mind that can be understood and embodied in a Yoga practice that includes the following steps. This sequence of breathing, movement, and suggestions for meditation developed from my personal practice over the course of several years. Recognition of the many teachers who contributed to this can be found in the acknowledgments.

A) Tribandha Prāṇāyāma

Tribandha begins with a recognition and emplacement of Threeness, a triad of triangles. From the sacrum, one triangle extends outward to each knee, brought close to the earth. The elements of earth and water ground this triangle, with the connection to the earth found beneath and behind the sacrum, the area of the Mūlādhāra, and connection with water in front of the sacrum, the Svādhiṣṭhāna Cakra. This landscape of sensation evokes all that can be found with the earth goddess Bhūr and the earth god of Jainism, Bhuiya.

A second triangle extends from the sacrum to the shoulders, rising above the softness of the belly, the lower abdominal abode of life's organs, including the heart and fire of the belly and the processes of digestion, and into the hardiness of the ribcage which protects the all-important heart and lungs. With the bottom of the sternum as midpoint, this area of Bhūr includes both fire and wind, movement and stirring that pulses with life. Two cakras occupy this space: the Maṇipūra or city of jewels below, also known as Nābhi, and the

Hṛdaya or heart or Anāhata (unstruck sound or silence) above. This landscape of the abdomen and torso carries the name Bhuvaḥ.

A third triangle extends from each shoulder to an invisible point above the head. All the senses abide in this upper realm: the nose and its capacity to smell; the mouth and its capacity to taste; the eyes and their capacity to see; the skin and its capacity to touch (the largest of organs, and like its cousin the wind, it cloaks the body just as the wind energizes the body from within); the ears and their capacity to hear. Vyāsa describes a meditation in his commentary on Patañjali: bring awareness to the tip of the nose to understand smell; to the tip of the tongue to understand taste; to the palate to understand color and form; to the texture of the entire tongue to gain intimacy with touch; to the place where the tongue connects with the throat to understand speech and sound (YS I:35). For Vyāsa, this remembrance brings freedom. In the place of the throat, one finds glands that govern emotions as well as the Viśuddha Cakra. In the space between the eyebrows, one connects with insight and intuition. In the space above the crown of the head, one might on occasion feel a sense of ascent and companionship with allies and guardians. This third triangle is called Svaḥ, the space of perception and connection with all that rises above.

Energization of these three zones daily comprise the foundation for Yoga Sādhana. The process begins with the inhale breath, the holding of the inhaled breath, the exhale breath, and holding the exhale breath. According to Patañjali, in that final fourth moment of the exhaled breath, a space emerges that can reveal and uncover the innate luminosity of being human (YS III:43). In Tribandha, one inhales deeply, lifting the musculature of the pelvic floor while inhaling, applying the first lock, Mūla Bandha, establishing connection with the root of existence as found in earth and water. When fully inhaled, and while maintaining Mūla Bandha, one brings the chin to the chest, performing Jālandhara Bandha, named after a town in what we now call Afghanistan, once populated with Yogis. This lock brings the energies of the head toward the heart, and lifts the energies of the earth upward. After a sustained hold, one then releases the musculature of the groin and pelvis, floats the head upward into a neutral position, and then performs the third lock, the Uḍḍīyāna Bandha (also named after a town in Afghanistan), lifting the abdominal muscles up under the ribcage. The energy that had been lifted and grounded toward the heart can ascend through the throat, face, forehead, and crown, allowing one to dwell within Svaḥ, perhaps even in imitation of a chosen deity, whether the Jina or Buddha or Śiva or Lakṣmī or Sarasvatī.

Tribandha, lauded in the *Gheraṇḍa Saṃhitā* and *Haṭha Yoga Pradīpikā*, should be repeated ten times each morning, before proceeding to other forms of practice.

B) Sūrya Namaskar in the Four Directions

Despite disputes over its relative antiquity, Surya Namaskar remains an important aspect of daily Yoga practice. Like the Tribandha, it evokes all three realms of Bhūr, Bhuvaḥ, and Svaḥ. It serves to awaken and energize the entire body. It quickens and deepens the breath. Through this sequence of moves, one becomes large.

First, face toward the East. Bring the hands to the heart in Añjali Mūdra, palm to palm, thumbs pressed to the sternum. Taḍāsana or Samasthiti.

Second, reach upward, inhale. Stretch the hands up to the sky and bend backward slightly.

Third, bend forward, keeping the back straight if possible. Exhale and bring the head toward the knees. Place your palms on the floor and bend the knees as needed. Uttānāsana.

Fourth, step back with the right foot. Follow with the left.

Fifth, hold the body in plank position for a moment. Breathe lightly.

Sixth, bring the knees and chest to the floor. Lower the entire front of your body to the floor and feel the support of the earth. Exhale.

Seventh, sweep the chest and head forward and inhale up into the Cobra or Nāga pose. Bhujaṅgāsana.

Eighth, curl the toes and exhale the sacrum up toward the sky, forming an inverted V. Spread your fingers and elongate your back and the back of your legs. Adho Mukha Śvānāsana.

Ninth, step your right foot forward and follow with your left. Inhale.

Tenth, extend your head forward and then exhale your head back toward your knees, keeping legs straight. Uttānāsana.

Eleventh, inhale the arms upward, reaching backward. Ūrdhva Hastāsana.

Twelfth, bring the hands back to the chest, exhaling.

Repeat as above, also to the East, leading with the left foot.

Visualize what lies east. Ocean? Prairie? Desert? Mountain? City? Name the towns and features. Reflect on the movement of the sun and moon. Is it near dawn? The time of the new moon?

Turn one quarter to the right and face the South. What lies south? Name the towns and features. Repeat Surya Namaskar twice, leading first with the right, and then with the left.

Reflect on the fullness of the day anticipating the sun at noon.

Turn one quarter and face west. Repeat as above. Think about the setting sun. Is it nearing the time of the full moon? At sunset in the West the full moon will rise in the East.

Turn one quarter and face north. Repeat as above. Visualize the geography and topography to the North. Reflect on the darkness of midnight.

As you face and emplace yourself within the four directions, also mark the passing of the morning into day, afternoon into evening, and evening into night, and night into dawn.

C) Headstand / Śīrṣāsana / Peacock / Mayūrāsana / Lion / Siṃhāsana

The next two moves emphasize verticality and horizontality, followed with harnessing and channeling animality. For those who are able, move into the headstand, perhaps forming a triangle from elbows to clasped hands. Cradle the head and ascend, drawing the legs toward the body and then upward. This reversal, like the shoulder stand to be performed later, inverts the energy of gravity, allowing the feet to rise into the sky, like the upside-down peepal tree revered in the Bhagavad Gītā. This reversal of blood flow and breath energizes the shoulders and throat and head, and relieves the burden carried by the legs and feet. Śīrṣāsana.

After a short period of inversion, if possible, perform the Mayūrāsana. This āsana, according to Mallinson, is the earliest nonseated and nonstanding Yoga pose.[1] Place the palms on the floor, fingers pointing backward. Position your ribs above the elbows and then extend the feet and head upward, forming a horizontal, balanced position, gazing forward.

For the last move, assume the Vajrāsana/Vīrāsana with sit bones resting near the heels, knees on the ground. Like the magnificent lion, inhale deeply. Once inhaled open the mouth and eyes as widely as possible, and unfurl the fingers, reaching to maximum capacity. Feel the fullness of energy in the throat and hands and face, imitating the magnificence of the largest of cats. Repeat three times.

These three moves allow full circulation of the body's energy: feet skyward, then face forward, balancing the torso and extending the legs backward, and finally full expansion of the front of the body and face. This sequence claims bodily space in a way that disorients and reorients reality.

D) Bow / Dhanurāsana / Locust / Śalabhāsana / Full Arm Nāga / Bent Elbow Nāga / Pañca Mahābhūtas, Tanmātras, Buddhīndriyas, Karmendriyas; Cakras

Gravity normally pulls the body downward. Every human movement stands in relation to this force. Surrender fully, belly down, to the earth, head turned to the side. In this sequence, to be repeated three or four times, the body rises up away from gravity. Just as the vertical and horizontal movement of the prior sequence inverted and extended the body, the limbs exert an outward and upward movement with similar results.

First, place the chin on the ground. Lift the feet upward. Reach back and grasp the feet or ankles with the hands and lift the body away from the earth into the Dhānurāsana, the Bow pose. With shallow breath, repeat earth, earth, earth, pṛthivī, pṛthivī, pṛthivī. Return both arms and legs to the ground and turn the head to one side.

Second, place the chin on the floor and the arms under the thighs, forming a fist with the hands. Lift the legs up into the Śalabhāsana, the Locust pose. Hold for a few seconds and with shallow breath, repeat water, water, water, jal, jal, jal. Bring the legs back to the earth and turn the head to the other side.

Third, place the hands, fingers facing forward, palms down on the floor under the shoulders. Lift up into the Nāgāsana, the Cobra pose, with arms extended fully. Hold for a few breaths, repeating fire, fire, fire, agni, agni, agni. Lower the torso to the earth and turn the head to the other side.

Fourth, place the hands once again under the shoulders. Place the toes on the floor, with heels elevated. Lift up into the Ardha Nāgāsana, the Half Cobra pose, with elbows bent. Visualize the body as if it were a cloud being billowed forward by the wind. Hold this posture for a few seconds, repeating air, air, air, vāyu, vāyu, vāyu. Lower to the earth and turn the head to the other side.

Fifth, elevate the front of the body, with elbows on the floor, entering the Sphinx Pose. Gaze forward as if looking into the vast sands of the Sahara. Repeat space, space, space, ākāśa, ākāśa, ākāśa. Lower to the earth and turn the head to the other side.

Repeat the sequence as above, moving backward from the elements in a movement known as *pratiprasava,* this time evoking the subtle elements or *tanmātras* and their connection with the sense organs, the *buddhīndriyas.* While in Dhanurāsana, reflect on the process of smelling with the nose, *gandha* (fragrance) known through *nasa* (the nose). While in Śalabhāsana, reflect on the process of tasting with the mouth, *rasa* (flavor) known through the tongue, lips, and palate (*mukha*). While in Nāgāsana, reflect on the process of seeing with the eyes, apprehending *rūpa* or form with the eyes (*akṣa*), rotating the eyes first in one direction and then the other. While in Ardha Nāgāsana, feet perpendicular to the ground, reflect on feeling or *sparśa* through the largest organ, the skin or *tvak.* While in the Sphinx pose, bring attention to the ears or *karṇa,* the gateway to sound or *śabda.*

In the third repetition, focus in turn on the correlations between the Dhanur pose and the lifting of the anus away from the force of gravity; in

Śalabhāsana, the lifting of the genitals away from the earth; in Nāga, the power of the hands as they push against the earth; in Ardha Nāga, the legs as they push into the earth; in Sphinx, bring attention to the voice, the throat, the larynx. These motor functions allow full engagement with all aspects of the manifest world.

This sequence completes mindfulness of the twenty *tattvas* that connect the body and the world: the five gross elements of earth, water, fire, air and space; the five subtle elements that allow smelling, tasting, seeing, touch, and hearing; the five sense organs of nose, mouth, eyes, skin, and ears; and the five motor capacities of evacuating, allowing passage of water, grasping with the hands, walking with the arms and feet, and speaking with the voice.

An additional repetition may be added to bring focus to the cakras using the same sequence. While in Dhanurāsana, invoke Mūlādhāra; in Śalabha, Svādhiṣṭhāna; in Nāga, Nābhi or Maṇipūra, the city of jewels located in the lower abdomen; in Ardha Nāga, Hṛdaya or Anāhata, in the heart and lungs; in Sphinx, the Viśuddha Cakra. Returning to the earth, clasp the hands behind the back and lift the head and face upward, with focus on the Ājñā Cakra. Return to the earth and for the final and seventh move, shape the body into the form of a crescent, reaching hands forward and upward, and the legs backward and upward, embracing the space of the heavens above.

E) Cat-Horse / Mārjāra / Aśva Āsana

Come into table pose, palms on the floor, fingers extending outward and knees and the tops of the feet on the floor. Loosen the spine by arching the back. Exhale. Then, with a slow gradual inhale, tilt the sacrum upward, bringing thought and attention to the earth and to the Mūlādhāra Cakra. Then tilt the pelvis downward, acknowledging water and the Svādhiṣṭhāna Cakra, Yoni for women and Liṅgaṃ for men. Continue the inhale and let the belly descend downward, focusing on fire and the Nābhi Cakra. Continue the inhale and move the sternum and heart slightly upward, experiencing air with the increasing inhale, and bringing attention to the Hṛdaya Cakra. Extend the throat into awareness of space (*ākāśa*) and the Viśuddha Cakra. Bring the face forward, focusing on the Ājñā Cakra. Then, exhale into silence, arching the back toward the sky, entering silence and the Uḍḍīyana Bandha. Repeat thrice.

This may also be performed in rhythm with the mantra *Namaḥ Śivāyaḥ Om* as follows: Sacrum up: *Na*; Pelvis down: *Ma*; Stomach toward the floor: *Śi*;

Chest forward and upward: *Vā*; Throat elevated: *Ya*; Head stretching upward, eyes wide open: *Om*.

F) Side Child Pose, Left and Right / Balāsana / Puruṣa / Prakṛti

Returning to table pose, place the right hand in front of the left hand, fingers pointing forward. Rock back into child's pose, feeling the stretch under the right shoulder. "Puruṣa, bound from within, without looking on"—Gurāṇi Añjali. Return to table pose. Place the left hand in front of the right hand. Rock back into the child's pose. "So I dance, yes I dance, yes I dance, yes I dance, for you alone"—Gurāṇi Añjali. This sequence evokes the symmetry between Puruṣa, the silent witness, and Prakṛti, the realm of action.

G) Pigeon Pose: Buddhi / Eka Pāda Rājakapotāsana

Having returned to the table pose, spread the knees apart and slowly lower the shoulders to the earth in a full pigeon pose, eventually bringing the length of the back and the buttocks to the floor. This restorative pose might require some bolster support under the back. Stretch the arms to either side. Feel the emotions and *saṃskāras* that dwell within the Buddhi, the repository for emotions.

H) Marīci Āsana / Three Guṇas / Ahaṃkāra

Hug the knees to the chest. Extend the left foot forward, continuing to hug the right knee. Crook the right hand over the right knee and reach through, grabbing the left hand. Turn to the left, feeling the awkward density of the body. Speak "*tamas*." Clasp both hands together and raise them over the torso, keeping the right knee bent and the left leg straight. As you lift up into the sky, speak the word "*rajas*." Bend forward, with the intention of bringing the energy and spaciousness of the sky downward and outward toward the extended left leg, grasping the left foot if possible. Speak the word "*sattva*." Release and repeat on the other side, in acknowledgment of the three *guṇas* and the creative process of Prakṛti.

I) Straight Forward Bend / Paścimatānāsana / to the Left / Right / Jānu Śīrṣāsana / Butterfly / Baddha Koṇāsana / Eight Bhāvas

Sit up straight extending both legs to the front. Bring the right foot inside the left thigh. Reach up toward the sky and extend outward, bringing the head toward the knee and grasping the big toe or foot if possible. Speak the positive quality (*bhāva*) that indicates empowerment, *aiśvarya*. Release both feet forward. Bring the left foot inside the right thigh. Reach upward and then bring the head toward the right knee, grasping the big toe or foot. Speak the positive quality for nonattachment, *virāga*. Bring both feet forward. Stretch upward and outward, bringing the head toward the knees, grasping the big toes or feet if possible. Speak the word for liberative knowledge, *jñāna*. Release and bring the feet out in front once more. Bring sole to sole, moving the heels toward the perineum. Speak the word *dharma*. These four terms indicate the positive attitudes and states of being (*bhāva*) that can be cultivated through yogic intention: *aiśvarya*, *virāga*, *jñāna*, and *dharma*. Repeat twice more, utilizing your own phrases for each positivity.

J) Forward Bend in four variations / Brahma Vihāra

Sit up straight, with legs in front. Spread the legs as far as possible. Reach your left hand to the left big toe. Bring the right hand to the forearm. Speak and think about their first of the Brahma Vihāras, *maitrī,* lovingkindness and friendliness. Direct this thought to someone you admire. Repeat on the other side.

Sit up straight, legs remaining extended and away from each other. Lift your right arm and place it behind your back. Stretch the left hand out to the left foot. Think of some person or some situation in distress. Speak the word for compassion, *karuṇā*. Repeat on the other side.

Sit up straight. Reach both hands out to the left and reach for the toes or the heel of the left food. Speak the word for sympathetic joy, *muditā,* expressing happiness for all those who excel.

Sit up straight. Lift the hands above the head and bend the torso forward between the outstretched feet. Speak the word for equanimity, *upekṣā,* to be cultivated in the company of unsavory people or situations.

K) Butterfly and Five Yamas and Five Niyamas

Bring the extended feet, sole to sole, toward the perineum. Articulate each of the ten fingers around the ten toes. Speak in sequence the *Yamas*: *ahiṃsā,* nonviolence, *satya,* truthfulness, *asteya,* not stealing, *brahmacarya,* sexual restraint, and *aparigraha,* nonpossession, activating each of the five fingers and toes in succession. Repeat with the *Niyamas*: *śauca,* purity, *santoṣa,* contentment, *tapaḥ,* austerity, *svādhyāya,* self-study, and *īśvara-praṇidhāna,* devotion.

L) Shoulder Stand / Sarvāṅgāsana / Plow / Halāsana / Bhūr / Pada / Pāyu-Mūla

Lie down on the back. Lift the feet and legs into the air above your head, supporting your lower back with your hands as needed. Gaze up to the feet, recalling the following verses from the *Bhagavad Gītā*:

> The Blessed One said:
> They speak of the changeless peepal tree,
> its roots above, its branches below.
> Its leaves are the Vedic hymns.
> The one who knows it knows the Vedas.
> Its branches stretch below and above, nourished by the *guṇas.*
> Its sprouts are the sense objects.
> In the world of people,
> it spreads out the roots that result in action (BG 15:1–2).

Speak the word for feet, *pada,* and the word for sky, *svaḥ.*

Lower the feet behind the head into *halāsana,* the plow. With purpose, elevate the anus toward the sky, speaking the words *mūla* (root) and *pāyu* (anus) followed with *svaḥ.*

M) Half Cakra / Liṅgaṃ / Yoni

Lower both legs back to the ground. Place the feet on the floor, knees in the air. Lift the pelvis upward into the bridge, *ardha-seṭu.* Direct the sacrum away from the shoulders, as if they are stretching into a space between the legs. Reflect on bringing the front of the pelvis toward the sky. Men can speak *liṅgaṃ svaḥ.* Women can speak *yoni svaḥ.*

N) Full Cakra / Nābhi

Return both legs to the ground. Bring the hands under the shoulders, fingers pointing toward the buttocks. Bring the knees into the air, feet planted on the floor. If possible, push up into the full wheel (*cakrāsana*). Speak the words *nābhi svaḥ,* indicating a connection that lifts the navel to the sky. All the lower extremities have been lifted toward a place of lightness and *sattva.*

O) Leg Lifts / Ūrdhva Prasarita Pādāsana

Lift the legs, one at a time and then in tandem, stretching the heels outward.

P) Windmill / Jaṭhara Parivartanāsana

Remaining on the back, stretch both arms directly out from the shoulders, palms on the floor. Bend the knees to the chest and then bring them to the right, toward the arms. Bring the left arm to meet the right arm, and return. Repeat three times. Rejoin the left hand to the right hand. Leaving the right arm on the ground, rotate the left arm in a large circle, first in one direction and then the other, three times. Repeat on the other side.

Q) Extended leg, grasped at big toe / Utthita Supta Pādāṅguṣṭhāsana

Stand with hands at the side. Extend the right foot into the air. Grab the big toe with the right hand as possible. Stretch. Return to the floor and repeat on the other side.

R) Ek Pada

Stand with weight distributed evenly on each foot. Lift the right knee. Reach forward with the arms, gazing at a single point. Extend the right leg in back until the leg and arms are equally horizontal to the earth. Repeat on the other side.

S) Śiva Naṭarājāsana

Stand on both feet equally. Lift the right leg toward the buttocks. Grab with your right hand. Extend the right hand into the sky and arch the back, lifting the leg. Repeat on the other side.

T) Side reach / Warrior / Vīrabhadrāsana

Turn to the side. Extend both arms parallel to the earth. Turn the right foot outward, and let the left foot follow slightly. As if a sheet of paper, extend the left hand out and over the head, letting the right arm slide down the right leg. Hold only briefly to avoid stress on the hips. Repeat on the other side.

U) Tree / Vṛkṣāsana

Stand on both feet equally. Bring the right foot to the inner left thigh. Lift the arms and raise over the head. Alternate bringing them palm to palm and letting them stretch upward and away from another. Balance by focusing on a single point. Repeat on the other side.

V) Arms toward heart

Stand on both feet. Stretch the arms outward. Gather the hands toward the heart, bringing the good work of the world to the heart. Repeat three times.

W) Arms away from heart

Stand with both hands palm to palm at the level of the heart. Reach outward, bringing the intent of the good heart out to the world. Repeat three times.

X) Hand to shoulder and reverse

Stand on both feet equally. Hold the arms outstretched, parallel to the earth, palms up. Reach the right hand to the left shoulder, behind the head. Switch, bringing the left hand to the right shoulder. Repeat three times.

Y) Japa and meditation

Sit in a meditative pose. Perform 108 rounds of a chant or phrase or mantra of your choosing. Sit in silence. Choose a reading to revisit daily.

Z) Devi Mantra:

Yā Devī
Sarva Bhūteṣu
Śakti Rūpeṇa
Saṃsthitā
Namastasyai
Namastasyai
Namastasyai
Namo Namaḥ
She, the goddess, through the power of her form, stands in all beings. Amazing!

Notes

Foreword

1. K. L. Seshagiri Rao, "The Five Great Elements (*Pañcamahābhûta*): An Ecological Perspective," in *Hinduism and Ecology: The Intersection of Earth, Sky, and Water*, ed. Christopher Key Chapple and Mary Evelyn Tucker (Cambridge: Harvard Press for the Center for the Study of World Religions, 2000).

2. Thomas Berry, "The Great Work," in *The Great Work: Our Way into the Future* (New York: Bell Tower, 1999), 7.

Introduction

1. https://www.yogajournal.com/page/yogainamericastudy.

2. Christopher Key Chapple, "Four Recent Books on Yoga," review essay in *Religious Studies Review* 27, No. 3 (July 2001): 239–42.

3. Christopher Key Chapple, *Yoga and the Luminous: Patanjali's Spiritual Path to Freedom* (Albany: State University of New York Press, 2008), 252–53.

4. Ibid., 250–51.

5. Elizabeth De Michelis, *A History of Modern Yoga: Patanjali and Western Esotericism* (London and New York: Continuum, 2004), 228.

6. Christopher Key Chapple, ed., *Yoga and Ecology: Dharma for the Earth* (Hampton, VA: Deepak Heritage Books, 2009).

7. David Gordon White, ed., *Yoga in Practice* (Princeton: Princeton University Press, 2012); Geoffrey Samuel, *Origins of Yoga and Tantra: Indic Religious Religions in the Thirteenth Century* (Cambridge: Cambridge University Press, 2009); James Mallinson and Mark Singleton, *Roots of Yoga* (London: Penguin Books, 2017).

8. Andrea Jain, *Selling Yoga: From Counterculture to Pop Culture* (New York: Oxford University Press, 2015).

9. Farah Godrej, "The Neoliberal Yogi and the Politics of Yoga," *Political Theory* (2016): 1–29.

10. Christopher Miller, "Yoga Bodies and Bodies of Water: Solutions for Climate Change in India?" in *Flourishing: Comparative Religious Environmental Ethics*, ed. Laura Hartman (Oxford: Oxford University Press, 2018).

11. Richard Louv, *Last Child in the Woods: Saving Our Children from Nature-Deficit Disorder* (New York: Workman Publishing, 2005).

12. George James, "Ethical and Religious Dimensions of Chipko Resistance," in *Hinduism and Ecology: The Intersection of Earth, Sky, and Water*, ed. Christopher Key Chapple and Mary Evelyn Tucker (Cambridge: Harvard University Center for the Study of World Religions, 2000), 526.

13. George James, *Ecology Is Permanent Economy: The Activism and Environmental Philosophy of Sunderlal Bahuguna* (Albany: State University of New York Press, 2015).

14. See Amitav Ghosh, *The Great Derangement: Climate Change and the Unthinkable* (Chicago: University of Chicago Press, 2017).

15. See description of British law defining the Hindu religion in David L. Haberman, *River of Live in an Age of Pollution: The Yamuna River of Northern India* (Berkeley: University of California Press, 2006), 28. See also how Haberman has "demonstrated how Orientalist representations of Hinduism were used to undermine established religious authority in Indian societies," in "On Trial: The Love of the Sixteen Thousand Gopees," *History of Religions* 33 (Aug. 1993): 44–70.

Chapter 1. The Inner World as Precondition for Experience

1. *The Bṛhadāraṇyaka Upaniṣad* dates from 850 BCE. The *Ācārāṅga Sūtra* dates from 350 BCE, making these two of the earliest representative texts of Hinduism and Jainism, respectively.

2. John Gatta, *Making Nature Sacred: Literature, Religion, and Environment in American from the Puritans to the Present* (New York: Oxford University Press, 2004).

3. T. R. Ayyaṇgār Śrīnivāsa, trans., *The Yoga Upaniṣads* (Madras: Adyar Library, 1938).

4. Joel Brereton, "The Upanishads," in *Approaches to the Asian Classics*, ed. Wm. Theodore de Bary and Irene Bloom (New York: Columbia University Press, 1990), 115–35.

5. *Ṛg Veda* V:84. Translated by Stephanie W. Jamison and Joel P. Brereton, *The Rigveda: The Earliest Religious Poetry of India* (New York: Oxford University Press, 2014), 767.

6. Hermann Jacobi, *Jaina Sutras, Part I*, Sacred Books of the East, Volume 22 (Oxford: Oxford University Press, 1884), I.1.4, 6.

7. For recent studies of the elements in cross-cultural comparative perspective, see Marzenna Jakubczak, Zdenka Salnicka, Maria Popcyzyk, and Malgorzata Sacha-Pieklo, *Aesthetics of the Four Elements: Earth, Water, Fire, Air* (Warsaw: University of Ostrava Tilia Publishers, 2001); Swami Nityananda / Christa-Maria Herrmann, *The Five Great*

Elements: A Comprehensive Guide to the Expression of Life in Earth, Water, Fire, Air, and Space (Lonavla: Kaivalyadhama, 2005); Adrián Villaseñor-Galarza, "The Transparency of the Earth-Human Cosmos: Intimacy, Healing, and Wholeness Based on an Integral Typology of Ecopsychic Ailments" (Ph.D. dissertation, California Institute for Integral Studies, 2012); and Emmanuelle Patrice, "The Alchemic Mythos of the Elements in Psyche and Nature: A Philosophical and Depth Psychological Evaluation of Interconnectedness" (Ph.D. dissertation, Pacifica Graduate Institute, 2015). See also Kapila Vatsyayan, ed., *Concepts of Space: Ancient and Modern* (New Delhi: Indira Gandhi National Centre for the Arts and Abhinav Publishers, 1991) and *Prakṛti the Integral Vision: Man in Nature* (New Delhi: D. K. Publications, 1995).

8. Ludwig Wittgenstein, *Philosophical Investigations*, trans. G. E. M. Anscombe (Oxford: Basil Blackwell, 1960), 390.

9. Ibid., 283.

10. Ibid., 284.

11. Ed Casey, *The Fate of Place: A Philosophical History* (Berkeley: University of California Press), 1997.

12. Robin George Collingwood, *The Idea of Nature* (New York: Oxford University Press, 1960), 112.

13. Joel Brereton, "The Upanishads." In *Approaches to the Asian Classics*, ed. Wm. Theodore de Bary and Irene Bloom (New York: Columbia University Press, 1990), 115–35.

14. Brian K. Smith, *Classifying the Universe: The Ancient Indian Varṇa System and the Origins of Caste* (New York: Oxford University Press, 1994), 323.

15. Mokṣadharmaparvan—Mahābhārata 182:14–19, adapted from O. P. Dwivedi and B. N. Tiwari, *Environmental Crisis and Hindu Religion* (New Delhi: Gitanjali Publishing House, 1987), 126.

16. Carol Lee Flinders, *At the Root of This Longing: Reconciling a Spiritual Hunger and a Feminist Thirst* (San Francisco: Harper San Francisco, 1998), 260.

17. Ralph Waldo Emerson, "Nature," as quoted in Gatta, op. cit.

18. "They say the senses are high; the mind is higher than the senses; the intellect (*buddhi*) is higher than the mind; yet there is something even beyond (*paratas*) that."

19. This translation by Christopher Key Chapple was completed in collaboration with Jodi Shaw, Christopher Miller, Griffin Guez, Amparo Denney, and Wijnanda Jacobi.

20. For detailed explanations of several variant *cakra* systems, see André Padoux, trans., *The Heart of the Yogini: The Yoginīhṛdaya, A Sanskrit Tantric Treatise*, with Roger-Orphé Jeanty (Oxford: Oxford University Press, 2013), 24–57.

21. Christopher Key Chapple and Yogi Anand Viraj (Eugene P. Kelly Jr.), *The Yoga Sūtras of Patanjali: An Analysis of the Sanskrit with English Translation* (Delhi: Satguru Publications, 1990), 99.

22. David Abram, *The Spell of the Sensuous: Perception and Language in a More-Than-Human World* (New York: Pantheon Books, 1996), 65.

23. James J. Preston, *Cult of the Goddess: Social and Religious Change in a Hindu Temple* (Prospect Heights, IL: Waveland Press, 1985), 52, 53.

24. Vijaya Rettakudi Nagarajan, "The Earth as Goddess Bhu Devi: Toward a Theory of 'Embedded Ecologies' in Folk Hinduism," in *Purifying the Earthly Body of God: Religion and Ecology in Hindu India*, ed. Lance Nelson (Albany: State University of New York Press, 1998), 269–96.

25. Madhu Khanna, "The Ritual Capsule of Durga Pūjā: An Ecological Perspective," in *Hinduism and Ecology: The Intersection of Earth, Sky, and Water*, ed. Christopher Key Chapple (Cambridge: Harvard University Center for the Study of World Religions, 2000).

26. Eliza F. Kent, *Sacred Groves and Local Gods: Religion and Environmentalism in South India* (New York: Oxford University Press, 2013), 23.

27. Jaideva Singh, trans., *The Yoga of Delight, Wonder, and Astonishment* (Albany: State University of New York Press, 1991).

28. Collette Caillat and Ravi Kuman, English rendering by R. Norman, *The Jain Cosmology* (New York: Harmony Books, 1981), 20, 21, 54.

29. Theodore Stcherbatsky, *The Central Conception of Buddhism and the Meaning of the Word "Dharma"* (Delhi: Motilal Banarsidass, 1974), 7–14, 96–97. First published by the Royal Asiatic Society, London, 1923.

30. Taittirīya Upaniṣad II, Robert Ernest Hume, *The Thirteen Principal Upanisads* (New York: Oxford University Press, 1979), 283–86.

31. See *Sāṃkhya Kārikā* 39–41.

32. Helmuth von Glasenapp, *The Doctrine of Karman in Jain Philosophy* (Bombay: Bai Vijibai Jivanlal Panalal Charity Fund, 1942), 11–18.

33. See *Sāṃkhya Kārikā* 43–52.

34. Bhadantācariya Buddhaghosa, *The Path of Purification (Visuddhimagga)*, translated from the Pali by Bhikkhu Nyanamoli (Boulder: Shambhala, 1976), VI:1, 185.

35. Ibid., VI:88, 201.

36. Artemus Engle, manuscript translation of *Abhidharmakosa* (Carmel, NY: The Institute for Advanced Studies of World Religions Microfiche Edition, 1980), VI, 36–37; Prahlad Pradhan, ed., *Abhidharmakosabhasyam of Vasubandhu* (Patna: K. P. Jayasawal Research Institute, 1975), 337.

37. *Lalita-vistara* 208; 328.20; *Sikāsamuccaya* 229, 77, 81; *Sata-sāhasrikā Prajñāpāramitā*, 1430; *Bodhisattvavadanakalpata*, ii, 578; *Divyavadana*, 39, 11, as given in Har Dayal, *The Bodhisattva Doctrine in Buddhist Sanskrit Literature* (New York: Samuel Weiser, 1978), 92.

38. W. Y. Evans-Wentz, compiler and ed., *The Tibetan Book of the Dead or the After-Death Experiences on the Bardo Plane, according to Lama Kazi Dawa-Samdup's English Rendering* (New York: Oxford University Press, 1960).

39. Śāntideva, *Bodhicaryāvatāra* III:12, as translated in Har Dayal, op. cit., 58.

40. von Glasenapp, op. cit., 48.

41. Ibid., 52–61.

42. See my comparison between Jainism and Gaia theory in *Nonviolence to Animals, Earth, and Self in Asian Traditions* (Albany: State University of New York Press, 1993).

43. By imitating animals in such poses as the cobra (*nāgāsana*), the lion (*simhāsana*), etc., one acknowledges and expresses kinship with the wider network of bodily forms, which, as we have seen, one presumably assumed in earlier lives. For a full description of Hatha Yoga, see Pancham Sinh, trans., *The Hatha Yoga Pradipika* (New Delhi: Oriental Reprint, 1980) and Rai Bahadur Srisa Chandra Vasu, trans., *The Gheranda Samhita* (Delhi: Sri Satguru Publications, 1979).

44. Chapple. *Yoga and the Luminous*, 192.

45. Evans-Wentz, op. cit., 216; Mircea Eliade, *Yoga: Immortality and Freedom* (Princeton: Princeton University Press, 1958), 241–44.

46. Eliade, *Yoga: Immortality and Freedom*, 244.

47. Sanjukta Gupta, Dirk Jan Hoens, and Teun Goudriaan, *Hindu Tantrism* (Leiden: E. J. Brill, 1971), as noted in Katherine Anne Harper, *The Iconography of the Saptamatrikas: Seven Hindu Goddesses of Spiritual Transformation* (Lewiston, NY: Edwin Mellen Press, 1989).

48. Ibid., 161.

Chapter 2. Earth

1. Diana Eck, *India: A Sacred Geography* (New York: Harmony Books, 2012), 447.

2. Ibid., 450. Eck quotes Simon Schama, *Landscape and Memory* (New York: Randon House, 1995), 6–7.

3. David Abram, *Becoming Animal: An Earthly Cosmology* (New York: Vintage, 2010), 14–15.

4. James McHugh, *Sandalwood and Carrion: Smell in Indian Religion and Culture* (New York: Oxford University Press, 2012), 35.

5. Thomas Berry, *The Great Work: Our Way into the Future* (New York: Bell Tower, 1999), 12.

6. Ibid., 20.

7. *Śvetaśvatāra Upaniṣad* II:17, as translated by Thomas Berry, *Religions of India: Hinduism, Yoga, Buddhism* (Chambersburg, PA: Anima Publications, 1992; first edition 1970), 29.

8. Douglas E. Christie, *The Blue Sapphire of the Mind: Notes for a Contemplative Ecology* (New York: Oxford University Press, 2013), 337.

9. For fuller accounts of Yoga training at Yoga Anand Ashram and education at Stony Brook, see "Raja Yoga and the Guru: Gurāṇi Añjali of Yoga Anand Ashram, Amityville, New York," in Thomas A. Forsthoefel and Cynthia Humes, *Gurus in America* (Albany: State University of New York Press, 2005), 15–35; and "Guru Centered Edu-

cation: Gurāṇi Añjali," in *Antonio T. deNicolas: Poet of Eternal Return*, ed. Christopher Key Chapple (Los Angeles and Ahmedabad: Sri Yogi Publications, 2014), 273–98.

10. See Katherine Harper, *The Iconography of the Saptamātrikās: Seven Hindu Goddesses of Spiritual Transformation* (Lewiston, NY: Edwin Mellen Press, 1989.

11. For a remarkable study of the contemporary training of Brahmin priests in the oral tradition, see Joël André-Michel Dubois, *The Hidden Lives of Brahman: Śaṅkara's Vedānta through His Upaniṣad Commentaries, in Light of Contemporary Practice* (Albany: State University of New York Press, 2013).

12. *Prthivi Sukta,* verses 4, 5, 11, 16, *In Praise of Mother Earth: The Pṛthivī Sūkta*, trans. O. P. Dwivedi and Christopher Key Chapple (Los Angeles: Marymount Press, 2013).

13. Ibid.

14. Antonio T. deNicolas, trans., *Meditations through the Ṛg Veda* (New York: Nicolas-Hayes, 1976), ch. 4–7.

15. Anthony Cerulli, *Somatic Lessons: Narrating Patienthood and Illness in Indian Medical Literature* (Albany: State University of New York Press, 2012), 139.

16. Eck, op. cit., 43–44.

17. B. L. Atreya, *The Philosophy of the Yoga-Vāsiṣṭha*, 2nd ed. (Moradabad: Darshana, 1981, originally published 1935), 52.

18. "Dhatu-vibhanga Sutta: An Analysis of the Properties" (MN 140), translated from the Pali by Thanissaro Bhikkhu, *Access to Insight (Legacy Edition*; http://www.accesstoinsight.org/tipitaka/mn/mn.140.than.html); Nov. 30, 2013. *The Middle Length Discourses of the Buddha. A Translation of the Majjhima Nikāya*, trans. Bhikkhu Nāṇamoli and Bhikkhu Bodhi, 2nd ed. (Boston: Wisdom Publications, 2001), 1087–96.

19. "Mahārāhulovāda Sutta: The Greater Discourse of Advice to Rāhula," in *The Middle Length Discourses of the Buddha. A Translation of the Majjhima Nikāya*, trans. Bhikkhu Nāṇamoli and Bhikkhu Bodhi, 2nd ed. (Boston: Wisdom Publications, 2001), 529.

20. Bhadantācariya Buddhaghosa, *The Path of Purification (Visuddhimagga)*, xv–xxvii.

21. Ibid., III:57, 98.

22. Ibid., III:72, 104.

23. Ibid., III:97, 109.

24. Ibid., III:104, 112.

25. Ibid., III:121, 117.

26. Ibid., IV: 24–26, 127–29.

27. Ibid., IV:29, 129–30.

28. *Yoga Sūtra* I:50. See Christopher Key Chapple, *Yoga and the Luminous*, 121.

29. Ibid., IV:22, 127.

30. Ibid., IV:24, 127.

31. Ibid., IV:25, 128.

32. Ibid., IV:28, 129.
33. Ibid., IV:29, 130.
34. Ibid., IV:30, 130.
35. Ibid., IV:31, 130.
36. Ibid., IV:150, 164.
37. Ibid., IV:195, 175.
38. Ibid., IV:31, 130.
39. F. C. Woodward, trans., *Manual of Mystic, Being a Translation from the Pali and Sinhalese Work Entitled the Yogāvachara's Manual* (London: Pali Text Society, 1916), 72–79.
40. Ibid., xii.
41. Ibid., xii–xiii.
42. Ibid., xiv.
43. Ibid.
44. Bodhipaksa, *Living as a River: Finding Fearlessness in the Face of Change* (Boulder: Sounds True, 2010).
45. Hermann Jacobi, trans., *Jaina Sutras, Part I: The Ācārāṅga Sūtra, The Kalpa Sūtra* (Oxford: Clarendon Press, 1884), I:1:4:6, 8.
46. Ibid., II:4:2:12, 154–55.
47. Ibid., II:4:2:16, 155.
48. Ibid., II:4:2:6, 153.
49. The translations that follow are by the author, in consultation with Sanskrit seminar students. These students include Griffin Guez, Jodi Shaw, Wijnanda Jacobi, Natale Ferreira, and Amparo Denney. Griffin Guez rendered preferable translations for the following verses, which have been used here and in subsequent chapters: 37: 6, 25, 26, 28, 29, 31. Jodi Shaw's translation has been used for 37:17.
50. See Gerald J. Larson, *Classical Samkhya: An Interpretation of Its History and Meaning* (New Delhi: Motilal Banarsidass, 1969); and Frank R. Podgoski, *Ego, Revealer-Concealer: A Key to Yoga* (Lanham, MD: University Press of America, 1984); and recent studies by Knut Jacobsen.
51. See Rita DasGupta Sherma, "Sacred Immanence: Reflections of Ecofeminism in Hindu Tantra," in *Purifying the Earthly Body of God: Religion and Ecology in Hindu India*, ed. Lance Nelson (Albany: State University of New York Press, 1998), 102–103.
52. See my articles "India's Earth Consciousness," in *The Soul of Nature: Celebrating the Spirit of the Earth* ed. Michael Tobias and Georgianne Cowan (New York: Plume, 1994), 145–50); and "Hinduism and Deep Ecology," in *Deep Ecology and World Religions: New Essays on Sacred Grounds*, ed. David Landis Barnhill and Roger S. Gottlieb (Albany: State University of New York Press, 2001), 60–75.
53. See Paul E. Murphy, *Triadic Mysticism: The Mystical Theology of the Saivism of Kashmir* (Delhi: Motilal Banarsidass, 1986); John Hughes, *Self Realization in Kashmir Shaivism: The Oral Teachings of Swami Lakshmanjoo* (Albany: State University of New York Press, 1994); and Paul Mueller-Ortega, *The Triadic Heart of Siva: Kaula*

Tantricism of Abhinavagupta in the Non-Dual Shaivism of Kashmir (Albany: State University of New York Press, 1989).

54. Grace E. Cairns, *Man as Microcosm in Tantric Hinduism* (New Delhi: Manohar, 1992), 45.

55. Ibid.

56. For more on the history and development of the *Yogavāsiṣṭha*, see *Engaged Emancipation: Mind, Morals, and Make-Believe in the Mokṣopāya/Yogavāsiṣṭha*, ed. Christopher Key Chapple and Arindam Chakrabarti (Albany: State University of New York Press, 2015), and the many works of Walter Slaje.

57. Sam Mickey, "Contributions to Anthropocosmic Environmental Ethics," *Worldviews: Global Religions, Culture, and Ecology* XI, no. 2 (2007).

58. Karen Pechilis, ed., *The Graceful Guru: Hindu Female Gurus in India and the United States* (New York: Oxford University Press, 2004), 16–17, 19, 26–27.

59. Another tale that highlights the elevated status of womanhood is the story of Līlā, who through worship of the goddess Sarasvatī attains *samādhi* and releases her husband, King Padma, from the clutches of death. See "The Story of Līlā," in *Vasiṣṭha's Yoga*, trans. Swami Venkatesananda (Albany: State University of New York Press, 1993), 55–91.

60. Translations by the author accompanied by the team of Jodi Shaw, Amparo Denny, Wijnanda Jacobi, Ben Zenk, Daniel Levine, and other students. These verses are from the Nirvāṇa Prakaraṇa part two, chapter 84. See *The Yoga-Vāsiṣṭha of Vālmīki, Sanskrit Text and English Translation, Vol. IV: Nirvāṇa-prakaraṇa*, trans. Vihari Lal Mitra, ed. and rev. Ravi Prakash Arya (Delhi: Parimal Publications, 1998), 283.

61. Ibid., NPII:87:2.

62. NPII:87:9.

63. NPII:87:12.

64. NPII:87:44.

65. NPII:87:45–47.

66. This is the title of the story given in the translation by Swami Venkatesananda. This segment is referred to with various chapter titles in Ravi Prakash Arya's editing of Vihari Lal Mitra's 1890s translation, starting with "Description of the Last Night of Death or General Doom" [VII:81] and ending with "Description of the Current Air, as the Universal Spirit" [VII:92].

67. Venkatesananda, *Vasistha's Yoga*, 588, VII:96.

68. Gurāṇi Añjali, *Yoga Anand Ashram Devotional Songs* (Amityville, NY: Yoga Anand Ashram, 1981), 25.

69. Pratapaditya Pal, *The Peaceful Liberators: Jain Art from India* (Los Angeles: Los Angeles County Museum of Art, 1995), 220–21.

70. Vandana Shiva, "Women in the Forest," in *Ethical Perspectives on Environmental Issues in India*, ed. George A. James (New Delhi: A. P. H., 1999), 84.

71. Vijaya Nagarajan, "Rituals of Embedded Ecologies: Drawing Kolams, Marrying Trees, and Generating Auspiciousness," in *Hinduism and Ecology: The*

Intersection of Earth, Sky, and Water, ed. Christopher Key Chapple and Mary Evelyn Tucker (Cambridge, MA: Center for the Study of World Religions, Harvard Divinity School), 453–54.

72. Vijaya Nagarajan, "The Earth as Goddess Bhu Devi: Toward a Theory of 'Embedded Ecologies' in Folk Hinduism," in *Purifying the Earthly Body of God: Religion and Ecology in Hindu India* ed. Lance Nelson (Albany: State University of New York Press, 1998), 272–73.

73. Madhu Khanna, "The Ritual Capsule of Durga Puja: An Ecological Perspective," in *Hinduism and Ecology: The Intersection of Earth, Sky, and Water*, ed. Christopher Key Chapple and Mary Evelyn Tucker (Cambridge, MA: Center for the Study of World Religions, Harvard Divinity School), 491.

74. Vasudha Narayanan, "Water, Wood and Wisdom: Ecological Perspectives from the Hindu Traditions" in *Worldviews, Religion, and the Environment*, ed. Richard C. Foltz (Belmont, CA: Wadsworth Press, 2003), 137.

Chapter 3. Water

1. See Deepak Shimkhada and Michael Reading, "Return to the Womb: Feminine Creative Imagery of *arghya* in a Tantric Ritual," *International Journal of Hindu Studies* 3, no. 12 (2015): 1–19.

2. Shivaji Sawant, *Mrityunjaya the Death Conqueror: The Story of Karna*, English version by P. Lal and Nandini Nopany (Calcutta: Writers Workshop, 1989), 179.

3. This web translation differs slightly from the version given in the second edition of *The Teachings of the Buddha: The Middle Length Discourses of the Buddha, A Translation of the Majjhima Nikāya*, trans. Bhikkhu Ñāṇamoli and Bhikkhu Bodhi, op. cit., 1090, which states "When one sees it thus as it actually is with proper wisdom, one becomes disenchanted with the water element and makes the mind dispassionate toward the water element."

4. Ibid., 530.

5. Bhadantācariya Buddhaghosa, *The Path of Purification. A Classic Textbook of Buddhist Psychology*, 177.

6. Ibid.

7. Hermann Jacobi, trans., *Jaina Sutras, Part I: The Ākārāṅga Sūtra, The Kalpa Sūtra* (Oxford: Clarendon Press, 1884), 6.

8. Ibid.

9. Ibid., 170.

10. Umasvati, *That Which Is: The Tattvārthasūtra*, trans. Nathmal Tatia (San Francisco: HarperCollins, 1994), 41.

11. Śāntisūri, *Jīva Vicāra Prakaraṇam with Pāthaka Ratnākara's Commentary*, trans. Jayant P. Thaker (Ahmedabad: Sri Jaina Siddhanta Society, 1950), 143.

12. Ibid., 75–80.

13. Ibid., 99.

14. Ibid., 102.

15. Monier Monier-Williams, *A Sanskrit-English Dictionary* (Oxford: Oxford University Press, 1899; Delhi: Motilal Banarsidass, 1970), 409.

16. Robert Ernest Hume, *The Thirteen Principal Upaniṣads* (Oxford: Oxford University Press, 1921, reprinted 1971), 427.

Chapter 4. Fire

1. Antonio T. deNicolas, Ibid.

2. Ibid., *Ṛg Veda* I:1.

3. *mātrāsparśās tu kauteya, śītoṣṇasukhaduḥkhadāḥ, āgamāpāyibi'nityās, tāṃstitikṣava bhārata* (*BG*, II:14): "Indeed, material sensations, O Son of Kuntī, generate pleasure and pain in the midst of heat and cold. They come and go incessantly. Strive to endure them, O Descendant of Bharata."

4. *paramātmā samāhitaḥ, śītoṣṇasukhaduḥkheṣu* (BG VI:7).

5. John Seed, "Spirit of the Earth: A Battle-Weary Rainforest Activist Journeys to India to Renew His Soul," *Yoga Journal* 138 (Jan./Feb. 1998): 135.

6. Ibid., 136.

7. *The Middle Length Discourses of the Buddha*, trans.: *A Translation of the Majjjima Nikaya*, trans. Bhikkhu Nāṇamoli and Bhikkhu Bodhi, 1090.

8. Ibid., 530.

9. Bhadantācariya Buddhaghosa, *Visuddhi Magga: The Path of Purification,* Vol. I, 178.

10. Ibid.

11. Ibid.

12. Ibid.

13. Hermann Jacobi, trans., op. cit., 7.

14. Ibid., 8.

15. Ibid., adapted.

16. See *Yoga Sūtra* I:31, I:34, and II:49–53.

17. See Umasvati, op. cit., 33–63.

18. Brian Dana Akers, trans., *The Haṭha Yoga Pradīpikā of Svātmarāma* (Woodstock, NY: YogaVidya.com, 2002), I:28–31, 12–14.

19. Ibid., I:7–12, 34–36.

Chapter 5. Air

1. *Ṛg Veda* I:134 as translated by Stephanie Jamison and Joel Brereton, *The Rigveda: The Earliest Religious Poetry of India* (New York: Oxford University Press, 2014), 304.

2. Ibid., 305.
3. *Ṛg Veda* VIII:7, Ibid., 1042.
4. *Ṛg Veda* X:168, Ibid., 1648–49.
5. Ibid., 1658.
6. *In Praise of Mother Earth: The Pṛthivī Sūkta*, trans. O. P. Dwivedi and Christopher Key Chapple (Los Angeles: Marymount Institute Press, 2001), 51.
7. Ibid., 59.
8. Bhikkhu Nāṇamoli and Bhikkhu Bodhi, trans., op. cit., 1090.
9. Ibid.
10. Ibid., 529.
11. Bhadantācariya Buddhaghosa, op. cit., 179.
12. Ibid.
13. Ibid.
14. Hermann Jacobi, trans., op. cit., 11.
15. Ibid., 12.
16. Ibid., 13.
17. Śāntisūrīśvaraji, *Jīva Vicāra Prakaraṇam with Pāṭhaka Ratnākara's Commentary*, ed. Muni Ratna-Prabha Vijaya, trans. Jayant P. Thakar (Madras: Jain Mission Society, 1950), 33–34.
18. Ibid., 142.
19. Ibid., 144.
20. Vihari Lal Mitra, trans., revised by Ravi Prakash Arya, *The Yoga-Vāsiṣṭha, Sanskrit Text and English Translation*, Vol. IV (Delhi: Parimal Publications, 1998), 315.
21. Chapple. *Yoga and the Luminous*, 179–80.

Chapter 6. Animal Stories

1. See Patricia Chapple Wright, *High Moon Over the Amazon: My Quest to Understand the Monkeys of the Night* (New York: Lantern Books, 2013); and *For the Love of Lemurs: My Life in the Wilds of Madagascar* (New York: Lantern Books, 2014).
2. David Abram, *Becoming Animal: An Earthly Cosmology* (New York: Vintage Books, 2011), 256–58.
3. D. H. Lawrence, *Studies in Classic American Literature* (1923), as quoted in David Mazel, ed., *A Century of Early Ecocriticism* (Athens: University of Georgia Press, 2001), 238.
4. Lewis Lancaster, "Buddhism and Ecology: Collective Cultural Perceptions," in *Buddhism and Ecology: The Interconnection of Dharma and Deeds*, ed. Mary Evelyn Tucker and Duncan Ryuken Williams (Cambridge, MA: Harvard University Center for the Study of World Religions, 1997), 12.
5. *MB* 9:262 as translated in Christopher Key Chapple, "Ahimsa in the Mahābhārata: A Story, A Philosophical Perspective, and an Admonishment," *Journal of Vaisnava Studies* 4, no. 3 (1996): 110.

6. From *In Praise of Mother Earth: The Pṛthivī Sūkta*, trans. O. P. Dwivedi and Christopher Key Chapple (Los Angeles: Marymount Institute Press, 2011).

7. Retold from various translations, most notably Robert Ernest Hume, trans., *The Thirteen Principal Upanishads* (Oxford: Oxford University Press, 1921), 218–22.

8. The following sources were consulted for the retelling of this story: Patrick Olivelle, trans., *Pañcatantra: The Book of India's Folk Wisdom* (New York: Oxford University Press, 1997); McComas Taylor, *The Fall of the Indigo Jackal: The Discourse of Division and Pūrṇabhadra's Pañcatantra* (Albany: State University of New York Press, 2007); and Franklin Edgerton, trans., *The Panchatantra Reconstructed: Volume 2: Introduction and Translation* (New Haven, CT: American Oriental Society, 1924).

9. For my earlier publications on the Jātaka tales, see "Noninjury to Animals: Jaina and Buddhist Perspectives," in *Animal Sacrifices: Religious Perspectives on the Use of Animals in Science*, ed. Tom Regan (Philadelphia: Temple University Press, 1986), 213–36; *Nonviolence to Animals, Earth, and Self in Asian Traditions* (Albany: State University of New York Press, 1993); and "Animals and Environment in the Buddhist Birth Stories," in *Buddhism and Ecology: The Interconnection of Dharma and Deeds*, ed. Mary Evelyn Tucker and Duncan Ryuken Williams (Cambridge, MA: Harvard University Center for the Study of World Religions, 1997).

10. Mark D. Dresden, "The Jātakastava or Praise of the Buddha's Former Births: Indo-Scythian (Khotanese) Text, English Translation, Grammatical Notes, and Glossaries," *Transactions of the American Philosophical Society, New Series* 45, part 5 (1955).

11. Rafe Martin, *Endless Path: Awakening within the Buddhist Imagination: Jataka Tales, Zen Practice, and Daily Life* (Berkeley: North Atlantic Books, 2010), 57.

12. Ibid., 60.

13. Ibid., 62.

14. Muni Shri Purnachandra Vijayji, *Inspiring Story of Meghkumar* (Mumbay: Mahavir Seval Trust, n.d.); *Jnatadharmakathanga (Nyayadhammakaao)*, ed. Pupphabhikkhu. The story is also in *Suttagame*, Part 9 (Gudgaon: Sutragamaprakashaka Samiti, 1952). It is also retold in Padmanabh S. Jaini, *Collected Papers on Jaina Studies* (Delhi: Motilal Banarsidass, 2000), 261–261.

15. This translation unfolded over the course of many months as a project of the Tuesday afternoon Sanskrit seminar at Loyola Marymount University. The translations are by Christopher Key Chapple unless otherwise noted and are based on the Sanskrit edition found in Vihari Lal Mitra, *The Yoga-Vāsiṣṭha of Vālmīki Sanskrit Text and English Translation, Vol. II, Sthiti Prakaraṇa, Upaśama Prakaraṇa*, ed. and rev. Ravi Prakash Arya (Delhi: Parimal Publications, 1998), 254–60.

16. Translation by Griffin Guez.

17. Translation by Kija Manhare.

18. Translation by Erika Burkhalter.

19. Translation by Natalé Ferreira.

20. Jorg Steiner and Jorg Muller, *The Bear Who Wanted to Be a Bear* (New York: Atheneum, 1976).

21. Werner Herzog, *Grizzly Man*, Lionsgate Films, 2005. Timothy Treadwell regularly visited my wife's first grade classroom at Chadwick School before his untimely death.

22. See George Schaller, *Tibet Wild: A Naturalist's Journey on the Roof of the World* (New York: Island Press, 2012). Also, this review: http://www.nytimes.com/2012/10/21/books/review/tibet-wild-by-george-b-schaller.html.

Chapter 7. The Yoga of Space

1. Norris Clarke, S.J., shared these observations at the Lenten Luncheon Lecture, Loyola Marymount University, in the spring of 1986: "[W]hen I was travelling in India and was studying a splendid bronze sculpture of Shiva, the dancing God, with eight arms, I came rather suddenly to the realization of the metaphysical and epistemological structures latent in religious art. . . . It is the reaching out of the finite toward the Infinite, expressed through finite sensible symbols . . . [an] unfinished effort to express in form what is beyond all form and expression." Published: "The Metaphysics of Religious Art: Reflections on Text of St. Thomas Aquinas," in *Graceful Reason: Essays in Ancient and Medieval Philosophy Presented to Joseph Owens*, ed. Lloyd P. Gerson (Toronto: Pontifical Institute of Mediaeval Studies, 1983), 301–14.

2. Kent, *Sacred Groves and Local Gods*, 119.

3. http://www.auroville.org/contents/533; accessed March 5, 2017.

4. We next traveled a few blocks south to Ananda Ashram, also known as the International Centre for Yoga Education and Research, founded by Swami Gitananda. Born of a Sindhi father and an Irish mother, Gitananda practiced medicine for many years in Vancouver before settling with his South Dakota–born wife in Pondicherry. Their son, Ananda Balayogi Bhavanani, did his medical degree at Wardha University near Gandhi's ashram and in addition to conducting six-month trainings for yoga teachers, also maintains a medical practice. Their facility was originally four blocks from the ocean, but the Tsunami rendered their property waterfront. His mother, Yogcharini Meenakshi Devi Bhavanani, lamented to her son, "be careful what you wish for," as in years past she had expressed longing for a seaside retreat.

5. Stcherbatsky, *The Central Conception of Buddhism and the Meaning of the Word "Dharma,"* 75, 106.

6. Jikido Takasaki, *A Study on the Ratnagotravibhāga (Uttaratantra) Being a Treatise on the Tathāgatagarbha Theory of Mahāyāna Buddhism* (Roma: Istituto Italiano per il medio ed estremo oriente, 1964), 193.

7. Verse X:37, Shantideva, *The Way of the Bodhisattva: A Translation of the Bodhicharyāvatāra*, trans. Wulstan Fletcher and the Padmakara Translation Group (Boston: Shambhala, 2006), 168.

8. Bhikkhu Ñāṇamoli and Bhikkhu Bodhi, op. cit., 1091.

9. Ibid.

10. Ibid.
11. Ibid.
12. Ibid., 1092.
13. Winston L. King, *Theravāda Meditation: The Buddhist Transformation of Yoga* (University Park: Pennsylvania State University Press, 1980), 42.
14. Bhikkhu Ñāṇamoli and Bhikkhu Bodhi, op. cit., 1092–93.
15. Ibid., 1095.
16. Ibid., 530.
17. Ibid., 530–31.
18. Ibid., 531.
19. Ibid.
20. Bhadantācariya Buddhaghosa, op. cit., 181.
21. Ibid.
22. Ibid., 182.
23. Ibid.
24. Ibid.
25. Ibid., 183.
26. Ibid.
27. Ibid., 397.
28. https://www.shambhalamountain.org/great-stupa/great-stupa-symbolism/.
29. *Yogavāsiṣṭha Nirvāṇa Prakaraṇa* I, 50:51–53.
30. Ibid., 50:21.
31. Ibid., 50:28.
32. Ibid., 50:18.
33. *Yogavāsiṣṭha Nirvāṇa Prakaraṇa* II, 87:11–12.
34. Ibid., 87:13.
35. See the threefold explanation of space as given in the *Concise Yogavāsiṣṭha*, translated by Swami Venkatesananda: "Space is threefold: the infinite space of undivided consciousness, the finite space of divided consciousness, and the physical space in which the material world exists" (Swami Venkatesananda, trans., *Concise Yogavāsiṣṭha* (Albany: State University of New York Press, 1984), 97. See also the discussion of space by Garth Bregman, "The Existence of an Endless Number of Worlds," 97–118, esp. 102–105; and Bruno Lo Turco, "Ākāśa and Jīva in the Story of Līlā," 23–52, esp. 30, in Christopher Key Chapple and Arindam Chakrabarti, *Engaged Emancipation: Mind, Morals, and Make-Believe in the Mokṣopāya (Yogavāsiṣṭha)* (Albany: State University of New York Press, 2015).
36. *Yogavāsiṣṭha Nirvāṇa Prakaraṇa* II, 84:10–12.
37. Ibid., 84:19–21.
38. Ibid., 87:58–61.
39. Ibid., 87:68.
40. Ibid., 93:56–58.

41. David Carpenter, "Practice Makes Perfect: The Role of *Abhyāsa* in Pātañjala Yoga," in *Yoga: The Indian Tradition*, ed. Ian Whicher and David Carpenter (London: Routledge, 2003), 25–50.

42. For a full discussion of the Jaina spiritual path, see Padmanabh S. Jaini, *The Jaina Path of Purification* (Berkeley: University of California Press, 1979).

43. Umasvati, op. cit., 253–55.

44. Jaini, op. cit., 271.

45. Paul Dundas, *The Jains*, 2nd ed. (London and New York: Routledge, 2002), 104–105.

46. Jacobi, op. cit. I:V:6, 52.

47. N. Shāntā, *The Unknown Pilgrims: The Voice of the Sādhvīs, The History, Spirituality, and Life of the Jaina Women Ascetics,* trans. Mary Rogers (Delhi: Sri Satguru Publications, 1997), 673–83.

48. Douglas Renfrew Brooks, *The Secret of the Three Cities: An Introduction to Hindu Śākta Tantra* (Chicago: University of Chicago Press, 1990), 52–54, 72, 106, 227. See also his *Auspicious Wisdom: The Texts and Traditions of Śrīvidyā Śākta Tantrism in South India* (Albany: State University of New York Press, 1992).

49. Paul Dundas, "The Jain Monk Jinapati Sūri Gets the Better of a Nāth Yogī," in *Tantra in Practice*, ed. David Gordon White (Princeton: Princeton University Press, 2000), 232.

50. Christopher S. George, "The Dynamics of the *Ahaṃkāra* in Vajrayāna Buddhism with Special Regard to the *Caṇḍamahāroṣaṇa Tantra*," presented at the Columbia University Seminar on Oriental Thought and Religion, 1973, 5.

51. Ibid.

52. Ibid., 5–6.

53. Janet Gyatso, *A Technique for Developing Enlightened Consciousness: A Traditional Buddhist Meditation on Avalokiteshvara by the Tibet Saint Tangtong Gylabo* (Fort Lee, NJ: The Institute for Advanced Studies of World Religions, 1980), 9.

54. Ibid., 12.

55. Rae Dachille, "Piercing to the Pith of the Body: The Evolution of Body Mandala and Tantric Corporeality in Tibet," presented at the Society for Tantric Studies Conference, Flagstaff, Arizona, 2016.

56. Sthaneshwar Timalsina, *Language of Images: Visualization and Meaning in Tantras* (New York: Peter Lang, 2015), 48.

57. Ibid., 49.

58. Ibid.

59. Ibid., 71. Timalsina also notes the correlation between the visualized body of Tantra and the habitual body of Merleau-Ponty (70).

60. This seems to refer to the sunrise. This verse was translated by Griffin Guez, as were verses 25, 26, 28, 29, and 31.

61. This verse is translated by Jodi Shaw.

62. Padmāvatī helped rescue the twenty-third Tīrthaṅkara Pārśvanāth from drowning. Pārśvanāth had bested a Yogi called Kamath in debate. Kamath's fiery austerities had resulted in the near-death of the cobras Padmāvatī and her husband Dhararendra who were concealed in a log being burned by Kamath. Kamath ascended after death into the clouds in his next birth as the god Indra. He sent torrential storms that threatened to drown Pārśvanāth as he meditated. Padmāvatī and Dharanendra lifted Pārśvanāth's body above the rising water and sheltered him under an umbrella formed by their cobra hoods.

63. Nicholson has written in this regard: "The dynamic tension between unity and difference has existed since the beginning of philosophical speculation in India." See Andrew J. Nicholson, *Unifying Hinduism: Philosophy and Identity in Indian Intellectual History* (New York: Columbia University Press, 2010), 205.

Appendix

1. "The *c.* tenth-century *Vimānārcanākalpa* ('Ritual for Palace Worship'), a text of the Vaikhānasa Vaiṣṇava tradition, includes *mayūrāsana* (the peacock posture) among the nine *āsanas* it teaches and is the earliest text so far identified to include a non-seated posture among the *āsanas* of yoga." James Mallinson and Mark Singleton, *Roots of Yoga* (London: Penguin Books, 2017), 87.

Bibliography

Abram, David. *Becoming Animal: An Earthly Cosmology*. New York: Vintage, 2010.

———. *The Spell of the Sensuous: Perception and Language in a More-Than-Human World*. New York: Pantheon Books, 1996.

Akers, Brian Dana. trans. *The Haṭha Yoga Pradīpikā of Svātmarāma*. Woodstock, NY: YogaVidya.com, 2002.

Añjali, Gurāṇi. *Yoga Anand Ashram Devotional Songs*. Amityville, NY: Yoga Anand Ashram, 1981.

Atreya, B. L. *The Philosophy of the Yoga-Vāsiṣṭha*. 2nd ed. Moradabad: Darshana, 1981; originally published 1935.

Barnhill, David L., and Roger S. Gottlieb, eds. *Deep Ecology and World Religions: New Essays on Sacred Grounds*. Albany: State University of New York Press, 2001.

Berry, Thomas. *Religions of India: Hinduism, Yoga, Buddhism*. Chambersburg, PA: Anima Publications, 1992; first edition 1970.

———. *The Great Work: Our Way into the Future*. New York: Bell Tower, 1999.

Bodhipaksa. *Living as a River: Finding Fearlessness in the Face of Change*. Boulder: Sounds True, 2010.

Brooks, Douglas Renfrew. *The Secret of the Three Cities: An Introduction to Hindu Śākta Tantra*. Chicago: University of Chicago Press, 1990.

Buddhaghosa, Bhadantācariya. *The Path of Purification. A Classic Textbook of Buddhist Psychology*, Vol. 1. Translated by Bhikkhu Nyāṇamoli. Boulder and London: Shambhala, 1976.

Caillat, Collette, and Ravi Kuman, English rendering by R. Norman. *The Jain Cosmology*. New York: Harmony Books, 1981.

Cairns, Grace E. *Man as Microcosm in Tantric Hinduism*. New Delhi: Manohar, 1992.

Carpenter, David. *Yoga: The Indian Tradition*. London: Routledge, 2003.

Casey, Ed. *The Fate of Place: A Philosophical History*. Berkeley: University of California Press, 1997.

Cerulli, Anthony. *Somatic Lessons: Narrating Patienthood and Illness in Indian Medical Literature*. Albany: State University of New York Press, 2012.

Chapple, Christopher Key. "Ahimsa in the Mahābhārata: A Story, A Philosophical Perspective, and an Admonishment." *Journal of Vaisnava Studies* 4, no. 3 (1996).

———. *Nonviolence to Animals, Earth, and Self in Asian Traditions*. Albany: State University of New York Press, 1993.

———. *Yoga and the Luminous: Patanjali's Spiritual Path to Freedom*. Albany: State University of New York Press, 2008.

———, ed. *Antonio T. deNicolas: Poet of Eternal Return*. Los Angeles and Ahmedabad: Sri Yogi Publications, 2014.

———, ed. *Yoga and Ecology: Dharma for the Earth*. Hampton, VA: Deepak Heritage Books, 2009.

Chapple, Christopher Key, and Arindam Chakrabarti. *Engaged Emancipation: Mind, Morals, and Make-Believe in the Mokṣopāya/Yogavāsiṣṭha*. Albany: State University of New York Press, 2015.

Chapple, Christopher Key, and Mary Evelyn Tucker, eds. *Hinduism and Ecology: The Intersection of Earth, Sky, and Water*. Cambridge, MA: Harvard University Center for the Study of World Religions, 2000.

Chapple, Christopher Key, and O. P. Dwivedi. *In Praise of Mother Earth: The Pṛthivī Sūkta*. Los Angeles: Marymount Press, 2013.

Chapple, Christopher Key, and Yogi Anand Viraj (Eugene P. Kelly Jr.). *The Yoga Sūtras of Patanjali: An Analysis of the Sanskrit with English Translation*. Delhi: Satguru Publications, 1990.

Christie, Douglas E. *The Blue Sapphire of the Mind: Notes for a Contemplative Ecology*. New York: Oxford University Press, 2013.

Collingwood, Robin George. *The Idea of Nature*. New York: Oxford University Press, 1960.

Dachille, Rae. "Piercing to the pith of the Body: The Evolution of Body Mandala and Tantric Corporeality in Tibet." Presented at the Society for Tantric Studies Conference, Flagstaff, Arizona, 2016.

Dayal, Har. *The Bodhisattva Doctrine in Buddhist Sanskrit Literature*. New York: Samuel Weiser, 1978.

De Bary, Wm. Theodore, and Irene Bloom, eds. *Approaches to the Asian Classics*. New York: Columbia University Press, 1990.

DeMichelis, Elizabeth. *A History of Modern Yoga: Patanjali and Western Esotericism*. London and New York: Continuum, 2004.

DeNicolas, Antonio T. trans. *Meditations through the Ṛg Veda*. New York: Nicolas-Hayes, 1976.

Dresden, Mark D. "The Jātakastava or Praise of the Buddha's Former Births: Indo-Scythian (Khotanese) Text, English Translation, Grammatical Notes, and Glossaries." *Transactions of the American Philosophical Society, New Series* 45, part 5 (1955).

Dubois, Joël André-Michel. *The Hidden Lives of Brahman: Śaṅkara's Vedānta through His Upaniṣad Commentaries, in Light of Contemporary Practice*. Albany: State University of New York Press, 2013.

Dundas, Paul. *The Jains.* 2nd ed. London and New York: Routledge, 2002.

Dwivedi, O. P., and B. N. Tiwari. *Environmental Crisis and Hindu Religion.* New Delhi: Gitanjali, 1987.

Eck, Diana. *India: A Sacred Geography.* New York: Harmony Books, 2012.

Edgerton, Franklin. trans. *The Panchatantra Reconstructed: Volume 2: Introduction and Translation.* New Haven: American Oriental Society, 1924.

Eliade, Mircea. *Yoga: Immortality and Freedom.* Princeton: Princeton University Press, 1958.

Engle, Artemus, trans. *Abhidharmakosa.* Carmel, NY: The Institute for Advanced Studies of World Religions Microfiche Edition, 1980.

Evans-Wentz, W. Y., compiler and ed. *The Tibetan Book of the Dead or the After-Death Experiences on the Bardo Plane, according to Lama Kazi Dawa-Samdup's English Rendering.* New York: Oxford University Press, 1960.

Flinders, Carol Lee. *At the Root of This Longing: Reconciling a Spiritual Hunger and a Feminist Thirst.* San Francisco: Harper San Francisco, 1998.

Foltz, Richard C., ed. *Worldviews, Religion and the Environment.* Belmont, CA: Wadsworth Press, 2003.

Forsthoefel, Thomas A., and Cynthia Humes, *Gurus in America.* Albany: State University of New York Press, 2005.

Gatta, John. *Making Nature Sacred: Literature, Religion, and Environment in America from the Puritans to the Present.* New York: Oxford University Press, 2004.

George, Christopher S. "The Dynamics of the *Ahaṃkāra* in Vajrayāna Buddhism with Special Regard to the *Caṇḍamahāroṣaṇa Tantra.*" Presented at the Columbia University Seminar on Oriental Thought and Religion, 1973.

Gerson, Lloyd P., ed. *Graceful Reason: Essays in Ancient and Medieval Philosophy Presented to Joseph Owens.* Toronto: Pontifical Institute of Mediaeval Studies, 1983.

Ghosh, Amitav. *The Great Derangement: Climate Change and the Unthinkable.* Chicago: University of Chicago Press, 2017.

Glasenapp, Helmuth. *The Doctrine of Karman in Jain Philosophy.* Bombay: Bai Vijibai Jivanlal Panalal Charity Fund, 1942.

Godrej, Farah. "The Neoliberal Yogi and the Politics of Yoga." *Political Theory* (2016).

Gupta, Sanjukta, Dirk Jan Hoens, and Teun Goudriaan. *Hindu Tantrism.* Leiden: E. J. Brill, 1971.

Gyatso, Janet. *A Technique for Developing Enlightened Consciousness: A Traditional Buddhist Meditation on Avalokiteshvara by the Tibet Saint Tangtong Gylabo.* Fort Lee, NJ: The Institute for Advanced Studies of World Religions, 1980.

Haberman, David L. "On Trial: The Love of the Sixteen Thousand Gopees." *History of Religions* 33 (August 1993).

———. *River of Love in an Age of Pollution: The Yamuna River of Northern India.* Berkeley: University of California Press, 2006.

Harper, Katherine. *The Iconography of the Saptamātrikās: Seven Hindu Goddesses of Spiritual Transformation.* Lewiston, NY: Edwin Mellen Press, 1989.

Hartman, Laura, ed. *Flourishing: Comparative Religious Environmental Ethics.* Oxford: Oxford University Press, 2018.

Herzog, Werner. *Grizzly Man*, Lionsgate Films, 2005.

Hughes, John. *Self Realization in Kashmir Shaivism: The Oral Teachings of Swami Lakshmanjoo.* Albany: State University of New York Press, 1994.

Hume, Robert Ernest. *The Thirteen Principal Upanisads.* New York: Oxford University Press, 1979.

Jacobi, Hermann, trans. *Jaina Sutras, Part I: The Ācārāṅga Sūtra, The Kalpa Sūtra.* Oxford: Clarendon Press, 1884.

Jain, Andrea. *Selling Yoga: From Counterculture to Pop Culture.* New York: Oxford University Press, 2015.

Jaini, Padmanabh S. *The Jaina Path of Purification.* Berkeley: University of California Press, 1979.

Jakubczak, Marzenna, Zdenka Salnicka, Maria Popcyzyk, and Malgorzata Sacha-Pieklo. *Aesthetics of the Four Elements: Earth, Water, Fire, Air.* Warsaw: University of Ostrava Tilia Publishers, 2001.

James, George A., ed. In *Ethical Perspectives on Environmental Issues in India.* New Delhi: A. P. H. Publishing, 1999.

James, George. *Ecology Is Permanent Economy: The Activism and Environmental Philosophy of Sunderlal Bahuguna.* Albany: State University of New York Press, 2015.

Jamison, Stephanie W., and Joel Brereton. *The Rigveda: The Earliest Religious Poetry of India.* New York: Oxford University Press, 2014.

Kent, Eliza. *Sacred Groves and Local Gods: Religion and Environmentalism in South India.* New York: Oxford University Press, 2013.

King, Winston L. *Theravāda Meditation: The Buddhist Transformation of Yoga.* University Park: Pennsylvania State University Press, 1980.

Larson, Gerald J. *Classical Samkhya: An Interpretation of Its History and Meaning.* New Delhi: Motilal Banarsidass, 1969.

Lawrence, D. H. *Studies in Classic American Literature* (1923); quoted in David Mazel, ed., *A Century of Early Ecocriticism.* Athens: University of Georgia Press, 2001.

Louv, Richard. *Last Child in the Woods: Saving Our Children from Nature-Deficit Disorder.* New York: Workman, 2005.

Mallinson, James, and Mark Singleton. *Roots of Yoga.* London: Penguin Books, 2017.

Martin, Rafe. *Endless Path: Awakening within the Buddhist Imagination: Jataka Tales, Zen Practice, and Daily Life.* Berkeley: North Atlantic Books, 2010.

McHugh, James. *Sandalwood and Carrion: Smell in Indian Religion and Culture.* New York: Oxford University Press, 2012.

Mickey, Sam. "Contributions to Anthropocosmic Environmental Ethics." *Worldviews: Global Religions, Culture, and Ecology* (2007).

Mitra Vihari Lal, trans. *The Yoga-Vāsiṣṭha of Vālmīki, Sanskrit Text and English Translation, Vol. IV: Nirvāṇa-prakaraṇa.* Edited and revised by Ravi Prakash Arya. Delhi: Parimal Publications, 1998.

Monier-Williams, Monier. *A Sanskrit-English Dictionary*. Oxford: Oxford University Press, 1899; Delhi: Motilal Banarsidass, 1970.

Mueller-Ortega, Paul. *The Triadic Heart of Siva: Kaula Tantricism of Abhinavagupta in the Non-Dual Shaivism of Kashmir*. Albany: State University of New York Press, 1989.

Murphy, Paul E. *Triadic Mysticism: The Mystical Theology of the Saivism of Kashmir.* Delhi: Motilal Banarsidass, 1986.

Ñāṇamoli, Bhikkhu, and Bhikkhu Bodhi, trans. "*Dhātuvibhanga Sutta*: The Exposition of the Elements." In *The Teachings of the Buddha: The Middle Length Discourses of the Buddha. A Translation of the Majjhima Nikāya*. 2nd ed. Boston: Wisdom Publications, 2001.

Nelson, Lance, ed. *Purifying the Earthly Body of God: Religion and Ecology in Hindu India*. Albany: State University of New York Press, 1998.

Nicholson, Andrew J. *Unifying Hinduism: Philosophy and Identity in Indian Intellectual History*. New York: Columbia University Press, 2010.

Nityananda, Swami, and Christa-Maria Herrmann. *The Five Great Elements: A Comprehensive Guide to the Expression of Life in Earth, Water, Fire, Air and Space.* Lonavla: Kaivalyadhama, 2005.

Olivelle, Patrick. trans. *Pañcatantra: The Book of India's Folk Wisdom*. New York: Oxford University Press, 1997.

Padoux, André trans. *The Heart of the Yogini: The Yoginīhṛdaya, A Sanskrit Tantric Treatise*, with Roger-Orphé Jeanty. Oxford: Oxford University Press, 2013.

Pal, Pratapaditya *The Peaceful Liberators: Jain Art from India*. Los Angeles: Los Angeles County Museum of Art, 1995.

Patrice, Emmanuelle. "*The Alchemic Mythos of the Elements in Psyche and Nature: A Philosophical and Depth Psychological Evaluation of Interconnectedness*." PhD dissertation, Pacifica Graduate Institute, 2015.

Pechilis, Karen ed. *The Graceful Guru: Hindu Female Gurus in India and the United States*. New York: Oxford University Press, 2004.

Podgoski, Frank R. *Ego, Revealer-Concealer: A Key to Yoga*. Lanham, MD: University Press of America, 1984.

Pradhan, Prahlad. ed. *Abhidharmakosabhasyam of Vasubandhu*. Patna: K. P. Jayasawal Research Institute, 1975.

Preston, James J. *Cult of the Goddess: Social and Religious Change in a Hindu Temple.* Prospect Heights, IL: Waveland Press, 1985.

Regan, Tom, ed. *Animal Sacrifices: Religious Perspectives on the Use of Animals in Science.* Philadelphia: Temple University Press, 1986.

Samuel, Geoffrey. *Origins of Yoga and Tantra: Indic Religious Religions in the Thirteenth Century*. Cambridge: Cambridge University Press, 2009.

Śāntisūri. *Jīva Vicāra Prakaraṇam with Pāthaka Ratnākara's Commentary*. Translated by Jayant P. Thaker. Ahmedabad: Sri Jaina Siddhanta Society, 1950.

Sawant, Shivaji. *Mrityunjaya the Death Conqueror: The Story of Karna*. English version by P. Lal and Nandini Nopany. Calcutta: Writers Workshop, 1989.

Schaller, George. *Tibet Wild: A Naturalist's Journey on the Roof of the World*. New York: Island Press, 2012.

Seed, John. "Spirit of the Earth: A Battle-Weary Rainforest Activist Journeys to India to Renew His Soul." *Yoga Journal* 138 (January/February 1998).

Shāntā, N. *The Unknown Pilgrims: The Voice of the Sādhvīs, The History, Spirituality, and Life of the Jaina Women Ascetics*. Translated by Mary Rogers. Delhi: Sri Satguru Publications, 1997.

Shantideva, *The Way of the Bodhisattva: A Translation of the Bodhicharyāvatāra*. Translated by Wulstan Fletcher and the Padmakara Translation Group. Boston: Shambhala, 2006.

Shimkhada, Deepak, and Michael Reading. "Return to the Womb: Feminine Creative Imagery of *arghya* in a Tantric Ritual." *International Journal of Hindu Studies* (2015).

Singh, Jaideva, trans. *The Yoga of Delight, Wonder, and Astonishment*. Albany: State University of New York Press, 199.

Singh, Pancham, trans. *The Hatha Yoga Pradipika*. New Delhi: Oriental Reprint, 1980.

Smith, Brian K. *Classifying the Universe: The Ancient Indian Varṇa System and the Origins of Caste*. New York: Oxford University Press, 1994.

Śrīnivāsa, T. R. Ayyaṇgār, trans. *The Yoga Upaniṣads*. Madras: Adyar Library, 1938.

Stcherbatsky, Theodore. *The Central Conception of Buddhism and the Meaning of the Word "Dharma."* Delhi: Motilal Banarsidass, 1974.

———. *The Central Conception of Buddhism and the Meaning of the Word "Dharma."* London: Royal Asiatic Society, 1923.

Steiner, Jorg, and Jorg Muller, *The Bear Who Wanted to Be a Bear.* New York: Atheneum, 1976.

Takasaki, Jikido. *A Study on the Ratnagotravibhāga (Uttaratantra) Being a Treatise on the Tathāgatagarbha Theory of Mahāyāna Buddhism*. Roma: Istituto Italiano per il medio ed estremo oriente, 1964.

Taylor, McComas. *The Fall of the Indigo Jackal: The Discourse of Division and Pūrṇabhadra's Pañcatantra*. Albany: State University of New York Press, 2007.

Timalsina, Sthaneshwar. *Language of Images: Visualization and Meaning in Tantras*. New York: Peter Lang, 2015.

———. *Tantric Visual Culture: A Cognitive Approach*. New York: Routledge, 2015.

Tobias, Michael, and Georgianne Cowan. *The Soul of Nature: Celebrating the Spirit of the Earth*. New York: Plume, 1994.

Tucker, Mary Evelyn, and Duncan Ryuken Williams, eds. *Buddhism and Ecology: The Interconnection of Dharma and Deeds*. Cambridge, MA: Harvard University Center for the Study of World Religions, 1997.

Umasvati. *That Which Is: The Tattvārthasūtra*. Translated by Nathmal Tatia. San Francisco: HarperCollins, 1994.

Vasu, Rai Bahadur Srisa Chandra, trans. *The Gheranda Samhita*. Delhi: Sri Satguru Publications, 1979.

Vatsyayan, Kapila, ed. *Concepts of Space: Ancient and Modern.* New Delhi: Indira Gandhi National Centre for the Arts and Abhinav Publishers, 1991.

———. *Prakṛti the Integral Vision: Man in Nature.* New Delhi: D. K. Publications, 1995.

Venkatesananda, Swami, trans. *Vasiṣṭha's Yoga.* Albany: State University of New York Press, 1993.

Villaseñor-Galarza, Adrián. "*The Transparency of the Earth-Human Cosmos: Intimacy, Healing, and Wholeness Based on an Integral Typology of Ecopsychic Ailments.*" PhD dissertation, California Institute for Integral Studies, 2012.

Whicher, Ian, and David Carpenter, eds. *Yoga: The Indian Tradition.* London: Routledge, 2003.

White, David Gordon ed. *Tantra in Practice.* Princeton: Princeton University Press, 2000.

———. *Yoga in Practice.* Princeton: Princeton University Press, 2012.

Wittgenstein, Ludwig. *Philosophical Investigations.* Translated by G. E. M. Anscombe. Oxford: Basil Blackwell, 1960.

Woodward, F. C., trans. *Manual of Mystic, Being a Translation from the Pali and Sinhalese Work Entitled the Yogāvachara's Manual.* London: Pali Text Society, 1916.

Wright, Patricia Chapple. *For the Love of Lemurs: My Life in the Wilds of Madagascar.* New York: Lantern Books, 2014.

———. *High Moon over the Amazon: My Quest to Understand the Monkeys of the Night.* New York: Lantern Books, 2013.

Index

Abhidharma, 15–17, 42, 158
Abhidharmakośa, 15, 202n36, 217, 219
Abhinavagupta, 57–58, 206n53, 219
Abram, David, 12, 23, 126–27, 144, 201n22, 203n3, 209n2, 215
Ācārāṅga Sūtra, 1, 4, 24, 49, 64, 78, 96, 114–15, 156, 172, 200n1, 205n45, 218
activity, 4, 9, 54–55, 100–101, 143, 153, 155, 159, 164
Advaita Vedānta, 50, 58, 82, 116, 204n11, 216
Agni, 2, 4, 5, 7, 26, 29, 35, 39, 49, 56, 87–89, 91–93, 99, 104–107, 117, 132, 134, 151, 154, 163, 190–91. See also *tejas*
agriculture, 23, 34, 74, 128
ahaṃkāra, 4, 55–56, 60, 164, 175, 213n50, 217
ahiṃsā, 32, 194, 209n5, 216. *See also* nonviolence
Ajanta (caves), 134
ākāśa, 4–5, 12, 25, 60, 62, 130, 151–52, 154, 158, 162, 165–66, 169, 177, 191, 192, 212n35, 220
Akers, Brian Dana, 208n18, 215
alternate nostril breathing, 106, 110, 121–22
Amityville, 26, 71, 146 151, 203n9
Amrita Devi, 67
Andhra Pradesh, 24, 110, 142, 183
Añjali, Gurāṇi, xii, 66, 69, 72, 88, 125, 203n9, 206n68, 215
Annamalai Reforestation Society, 91
Anscombe, G. E. M., 201n8, 221
anthropocosmic, the, 7, 58, 62, 64, 206n57, 218
āsana, xii, xxi, 11, 20, 26, 96, 106, 157, 170, 189–97, 203n43, 214n1
asat, 33, 93, 155
Aśvins, 154–55, 158
Atharva Veda, 4, 24, 28–29, 41, 64, 67, 69, 91, 94, 110, 112, 128
Atreya, B. L., 204n17, 215
attachment(s), 10–12, 16, 20, 43–46, 56, 58, 69, 113, 143, 145, 159, 161, 182–83
Auroville, 153–54, 211n3
austerities, 157, 195, 214n62
axis mundi, 156

Barnhill, David L., 205n52, 215
Berry, Thomas, xii–iii, xvi, 23–24, 69, 199n2, 203n5, 203n7, 215
Bhagavad Gīta, xvi, xx, 9, 14, 62, 146, 190, 195
Bhagavatī, 59, 68
Bharata Natyam, 68

bhāva, 2, 4, 16, 56, 152, 168, 184, 194
Bhūmi Devī (Bhū Devī), 13, 28, 34, 46–47, 67–68, 187
bhūr, 85, 130, 184, 187, 189, 195
bhūta śuddhi, xix, 1, 3, 175, 177
Bhūvaḥ, 130, 184, 188, 189
bīja, 97–98, 180. See also *mantra*
Bishnoi movement, 67
Bloom, Irene, 200n4, 201n13, 216
Bloomfield, Maurice, 29
Bodh Gaya, 44, 127
Bodhi, Bhikkhu, 204n18, 207n3, 208n7, 209n8, 211n8, 212n14, 219
Bodhipaksa, 48, 205n44, 215
Boehme, Jakob, 48
Bose, Abinash Chandra, 29
Brahmā, 35, 41, 74
Brahman, 7, 8, 10, 36, 42, 82, 130–31, 204n11, 216
Brahma Vihāra, 44–45, 161, 194
Brahmin (caste), 6, 28, 42, 44, 130, 144, 157, 204n11
breath, 5–7, 15, 33, 44–45, 48, 52, 55, 57, 65, 69, 74, 83, 89, 97, 106, 109–13, 117–22, 130–31, 134, 152, 161, 169, 176, 179–82, 187–91
breathing exercises, xx, 20, 45, 51, 57, 65, 69, 83, 106, 110, 121–22, 161, 169–70, 178, 180–82, 187–90. See also *prāṇāyāma*
Brereton, Joel, 3, 6, 112, 200, 201, 208n1 chap. 5, 218
Bṛhadāraṇyaka Upaniṣad, 1, 3, 7, 12, 14, 64, 156, 200n1
Bṛhaspati, 138
Brooks, Douglas Renfrew, 175, 213n48, 215
Brown, W. Norman, 33, 202n28, 215
Buddha, the, xix, 1, 14, 18, 34, 42–46, 49, 54, 60, 69, 76–77, 94–96, 107, 113–14, 127, 133–34, 146, 158–64, 176, 185, 188, 204n19, 207n3, 208n7, 210n10, 216, 219
Buddhaghosa, Bhadantācariya, 16–17, 44–45, 69, 77, 96, 107, 114, 162–63, 202n34, 204n20, 207n5, 208n9, 209n11, 212n20, 215. See also *Visuddhimagga*
buddhi, 4, 9–10, 55, 60, 81, 164–65, 201n18
buddhīndriya, 5, 15, 55–56, 60, 81, 168, 190–91
Buddhism, xi, xvi, xix–xxii, xxiv, 2–3, 11, 14–18, 20, 24, 34, 44–48, 50, 58, 60, 68, 76–77, 94, 105, 113, 116–17, 123, 127, 133, 144, 146–47, 158, 160–61, 163, 170, 175–78, 183–84, 202n29, 202n37, 203n7, 207n5, 209n4, 210n9, 210n11, 211n5, 212, 212n13, 213n50, 213n53, 215, 216, 217, 218, 220

Caillat, Collette, 202n28, 215
Cairns, Grace E., 206n54, 215
cakra, 8, 10, 11, 14, 20–21, 187–88, 190, 192, 195, 196, 201n20
Carpenter, David, 213n41, 215, 221
Casey, Ed, 6, 201n11, 215
Cassian, John, 176
caste (*varṇa*), 3, 129–30, 147, 201n14, 220
Cerulli, Anthony, 38, 204n15, 215
Chakrabarti, Arindam, xi, 206n56, 212n35, 216
Chāndogya Upaniṣad, 27, 129
chants, 28, 59, 73, 110, 130, 157, 166, 197
Chennai, 27, 68, 110
Chipko Movement, xxiii, 35, 67–68, 200n12

Chittoor (district), 110
Christianity, 48, 69, 76
Christie, Douglas E., 24, 203n8, 216
Cidambaram, 152–53
Clarke, Norris, 153, 211n1
Clooney, Frank, xi, 26
Collingwood, Robin George, 201n12, 216
color(s), 2, 19–20, 24, 45–46, 50–52, 56–57, 65, 80, 83, 97, 100, 106, 116, 121, 149, 158, 162–64, 169, 175, 177, 183–84, 188
compassion, 19, 49, 133, 136, 146, 161, 176, 194
concentration(s), xi, xix, xxiii, 1, 5, 8–10, 12, 16, 20–21, 44, 46–48, 51–52, 59, 61–63, 65, 72, 77, 80–81, 83–84, 87–88, 95–96, 99, 106–107, 109, 116–17, 121–23, 125, 149, 151, 162–64, 169–71, 175, 178–79, 183–84. See also *dharāṇā*
confusion, 140, 142–43, 152
consciousness, xx, xxi, 1, 3–5, 14–16, 20, 24, 43, 45, 49, 50, 54–56, 58–59, 61–62, 67, 72, 81–82, 101, 138, 141, 159–60, 164–65, 168, 170, 172–73, 176, 205n52, 212n35, 213n53, 217
contentment, 69, 144–45, 195. *See also* peace
continents, 59, 63–64, 120, 127, 137, 166, 171, 174
correlationism, 3
cosmicization, xv, 3, 14, 21
cow, xx, 29, 32, 38, 40, 96, 111, 127–28
Cowan, Georgianne, 205n52, 220
creativity, xx, 4, 24, 30, 33, 36, 55–61, 67, 69, 87, 89, 153–54, 157, 166–69, 193, 207n1, 220
creation, 37, 40, 60, 87, 112, 154–55, 166, 168, 177
Cūḍālā, 58

Dachille, Rae, 213n55, 216
dance, 4, 27, 55, 56, 59, 60, 61, 62, 67, 105, 152, 153, 164, 165, 166, 182, 193
danger in nature, 39–40, 82, 92, 127, 129, 183
darśanas, 2, 55
Dattatreya, 74
DaVinci, Leonardo, 152
Dayal, Har, 202n37, 202n39, 216
DeBary, Wm. Theodore, xiii, 200n4, 201n13, 216
DeMichelis, Elizabeth, xii, 199n5, 216
DeNicolas, Antonio T., 33, 204n9, 208n1 chap. 4, 216
desire(s), 4, 10, 16, 17, 18, 20, 33–34, 37, 45, 77, 87, 89, 91, 103–104, 107, 117, 119, 152, 155, 158, 160, 161, 164
detachment, 61, 143
Dhandapani, Karthik, xi, 26, 73, 90, 110
dharāṇā, xix, 1, 5, 25, 50, 59, 61–62, 65, 72, 80, 83, 88, 99, 106–107, 109, 117, 123, 164, 169–70, 175. *See also* concentration(s)
Dharinī, 135–36
dharma, 15, 29, 44–45, 48, 119, 143–44, 147, 156, 199n6, 209n4, 210n9, 216
dharma-kāya, xvi, 21
dharmas, 17, 18, 158, 163, 202n29, 211n5, 220
Dhātu Vibhaṅga, 42, 48, 94, 113, 158–59, 177–78, 182
Dhṛtarāṣṭra, 34
Digambara, 50, 173
digestion, 11, 113, 187

directions (geographical), 1, 5, 7, 27, 31, 39, 56, 89, 130–31, 145, 147, 156, 158, 163, 184, 189–90
discernment, 11, 43, 76, 94, 113, 159
dissolution, 105, 159, 168, 175
dream, 135, 140, 167
Dresden, Mark D., 134, 210n10, 216
Dundas, Paul, 172, 175, 213n45, 213n49, 217
Durgā, 13, 59, 68, 157, 166, 202n25, 207n73
Dwivedi, O. P., 201n15, 204n12, 209n6, 210n6, 216–17

Eck, Diana, 23, 38, 203n1, 217
Edgerton, Franklin, 210n8, 217
ego, xvi, 2, 4, 8, 15, 55, 113, 164, 175, 183, 205n50, 219
elemental beings, 4, 49, 114–15, 171, 174
elephant, xx, 2, 135–36, 145–47
Eliade, Mircea, xv, xxi, 3, 21, 58, 203n45, 217
embodiment, 21, 147
Emerson, 7–8, 201n17
emotion(s), 2, 4–5, 24–25, 29, 42, 55, 64, 80, 84, 89, 133, 144, 146, 151–52, 160, 188, 193. *See also* feelings
emplacement, 42, 121, 127, 147–48, 157, 170, 187
Engle, Artemus, 202n36, 217
enlightenment, 1, 18, 58, 93, 163–64, 172, 176, 213n53, 217. *See also* liberation
equanimity, 17, 47, 79, 95, 113–14, 160–61, 171, 179, 184
equipoise, 53, 77, 144
Eternal Return, 154, 204n9, 216
ethics, xxiv, 29, 65, 116, 148–49, 170, 200n10, 206n57, 218
Evans-Wentz, W. Y., 90, 202n38, 203n45, 217
family, 19, 90, 112, 130, 155–56
fasting, 88, 136
feeling(s), 18, 24, 32, 35, 48–49, 51, 98–99, 110, 131, 133, 145, 147–48, 152, 155, 160–61, 165, 174, 176, 178, 191. *See also* emotion(s)
feeling tone. See *bhāva*
female xxi, 58, 133, 154, 176, 206n58, 219
fixed gaze technique. See *trāṭakaṃ*
Fletcher, Wulstan, 211n7, 220
Flinders, Carol Lee, 7, 201n16, 217
Foltz, Richard C., 207n74, 217
Forsthoefel, Thomas A., 203n9, 217
Free, Katharine, 73

Gandharvas (Gandharvis), 34, 104
Gandhi, 28, 32, 34, 66
Ganeśa, 28, 33, 34, 89, 90, 110
Ganges (Ganga), 31, 46, 59, 63, 72–74, 92, 119, 127, 137
Gatta, John, 2, 200n2, 201n17, 217
Gāyatrī, 41, 88, 184
Genesee Valley, 25, 31, 71, 82, 146 151
geometry, 24, 50, 51, 80, 83, 97, 116, 175, 177, 154, 183. See also *maṇḍala*
George, Christopher S., 175, 178, 213n50, 217
Gerson, Lloyd P., 211n1, 217
Gheraṇḍa Saṃhitā, 2, 25, 48, 64–66, 83, 106–107, 121–22, 169, 177, 182, 188
Ghosh, Amitav, 200n14, 217
Gilligan, Carol, 147
Glasenapp, Helmuth, 202n32, 217
goddess, ix, x, 2, 4, 12–13, 19, 21, 27–29, 33–34, 38–39, 41, 46, 59–61, 66–68, 157, 164–68, 174, 176–77, 184, 187, 198, 202n23, 202n24, 203n47, 204n10, 206n59, 207n72, 217, 219

Godrej, Farah, xxii, 199n9, 217
Goodman, Trudy, xi, 48
Gopuram, 27, 89, 90
Gottlieb, Roger S., 205n52, 215
Goudriaan, Teun, 203n47, 205n51, 217
Great South Bay, 71, 109
Green Yoga, xi, 66
grief, 47, 138, 144–46
Griffith, Ralph T., 29
Grim, John, xiii, xv, xvii
guṇas, 55, 100, 193, 195
Gupta, Sanjukta, 21, 203n47, 217
Gurāṇi Añjali, xii, 66, 69, 72, 88, 125, 203n9, 206n68, 215
Gyātasūtra, 135
Gyatso, Janet, 176, 213n53, 217

Haberman, David L., 200n15, 217
Hanuman, 31
Haridrumata Gautama, 129–30
Harper, Katherine A., 21, 203n47, 204n10, 207n10, 217
Hartman, Laura, 200n10, 218
harvest, 13, 25, 32, 157
Haṭha Yoga, xx, 65, 69, 106–107, 121, 169
Haṭha Yoga Pradīpikā, 81, 188
havan, 88, 93, 184
healing, 24, 31, 112, 145, 201n7, 221
Hemacandra, 24, 50, 116, 178. See also *Yogaśāstra* (Hemacandra)
Herzog, Werner, 146, 211n21, 218
Hill Street Center (Santa Monica), xi, 109
Himalayas, 7, 23, 31, 63, 67–68, 79, 89, 92, 127, 134, 142, 169
Hinduism, xvi, xix–xxii, xxiv, 2, 3, 7, 11, 12–16, 21, 23–25, 27, 28, 32, 34, 35, 42, 50, 54, 58, 74, 77, 81, 96, 116–17, 123, 144, 175, 178, 183–84, 199–207, 213–17, 219–20
Hoens, Dirk Jan, 203n47, 217
Hughes, John, xi, 205, 218
humans, xv, xx, 6, 19, 32–23, 39, 57, 75, 92, 98, 114, 125, 127–31, 136, 144, 146, 147, 155, 171
Hume, Robert Ernest, 202n30, 208n16 chap. 3, 210n7, 218
Humes, Cynthia, 203n9, 217
humility, 36, 132, 147
hunter-gatherer lifestyles, 128
Hymn of Creation (*Ṛg Veda*), 87, 112

identity, 15, 18, 42, 52, 56, 149, 177–78, 214n63, 219
ignorance, 2, 16–17, 100, 105, 139–43, 161, 171, 175
impressions, mental, 4, 56, 140, 168
incarnation. *See* past lives; reincarnation
incense, xx, 88, 109, 184
India, xi, xii, xv–xvi, xix–xxiv, 1–7, 13–15, 23–24, 26–38, 41–42, 55–56, 66–69, 72, 74–75, 78, 82, 90–92, 113, 127–29, 132, 146–48, 153, 155–57, 173–74, 200n10, 200n15, 200n5, 201n14, 202n24, 202n26, 203n1, 203n4, 203n7, 204n15, 205n 51, 205n52, 206n58, 205n69, 205n70, 207n72, 208n5, 210n8, 211n1, 213n41, 213n48, 214n63, 215, 217–21
Indira Gandhi National Centre for the Arts, 68
Indra, 29, 32–33, 36–37, 92, 111, 120, 154–55, 157–58, 214n62
initiation, 43, 96, 135, 161
interiorization, xix, 1, 54
introspection, 140–41
Īśvarakṛṣṇa, 4

Jacobi, Hermann, 200n6, 205n45, 207n7, 208n13 chap. 4, 209n14, 213n46, 218
Jain, Andrea, xxii–xxiii, 199, 218

Jaini, Padmanabh S., 172, 210n14, 213n42, 218
Jainism, xvi, xix–xxii, xxiv, 2–4, 6, 11, 14–15, 18–21, 24, 32, 34, 42, 49–52, 67, 69, 77–79, 80–81, 83, 96–97, 107, 114–17, 123, 125, 127, 135–36, 144–48, 170–75, 177, 178, 183–84, 187, 200n1, 200n6, 202n28, 202n32, 203n42, 205n45, 206n69, 207n7, 210n9, 210n14, 213n42, 213n47, 213n49, 215, 217, 218, 219, 220
Jaipur, 127
Jakubczak, Marzenna, 200n7, 218
jal, 4, 5, 56, 72–73, 83, 154, 191
Jambudvīpa, 67, 137, 142, 173–74
James, George A., xiii, 200n12, 200n13, 206n70, 218
James, William, 90
Jamison, Stephanie W., 3, 6, 112, 200n5, 201, 208n1 chap. 5, 218
Jātakastava, 134, 210n10, 216
Jātaka Tales, 125, 133–34, 210n9, 216, 218
Jhāna, 47, 95, 160
jīva, 3, 4, 20, 49–50, 52, 78, 114–16, 170–74, 172, 178, 181–82. *See also* soul
Jīva Vicāra Prakaraṇam, 114–15, 207, 209, 219n17, 219
Jñānārṇava, 5, 24, 49–51, 65, 79, 83, 96–97, 114, 116, 170, 173, 175, 177–78, 182–83
Jnātadharmakathaṅga, 135, 210n14

Kalahasti, 110
Kālarātrī, 59
Kālī, 59–61, 67–68, 105, 164, 166–68
Kāma Sūtra, 15
Karkaṭī, 41
karma, xxiv, 3, 11, 12, 15, 16, 18–19, 49–51, 53, 79, 96–98, 115–16, 134, 136, 170–74, 177–82, 202n32
Karmendriyas, 55, 190
Kashmir Śaivaite, 57, 61, 205n53, 206n53, 217–19
kasiṇa, 45–48, 77, 96, 107, 114, 158, 162–63, 183
kāya, xvi, 14, 21
Kelly, Eugene P. (Yogi Anand Virāj), 201n21, 216
Kent, Eliza, 13, 202n26, 211n2, 218
Kerala, 84, 127
Khanna, Madhu, 13, 68, 202n25, 207n73
kindness, 41, 44, 134, 146, 148, 161, 194
King Sumeruprabh, 135
King Shrenik, 135
King, Winston L., 160, 212n13, 218
kinship with animals, xxv, 134, 147–48, 185, 203
knowledge, 16, 18, 20, 51, 58, 69, 83, 98, 104, 138, 140, 138, 140, 142, 145, 147–48, 165, 172, 178, 194. *See also* wisdom
Kolam, 13, 67, 68, 206n71
Kornfield, Jack, xi, 48
Krishnamacharya, xxi, 122
kuṇḍalinī, 21

Lake Ontario, 151
Lakṣmī, 33, 188
Lancaster, Lewis, 127, 209n4
landscape, xv, xix–xx, xxv, 1–2, 10, 13, 23, 26, 30, 32, 34, 53, 62, 64, 125, 127, 133, 136, 144–45, 148, 151, 173, 182, 187–88, 203n2
Larson, Gerald J., 205n50, 218
Lawrence, D. H., 127, 209n3, 218
lemurs, 126, 209n1, 221
liberation, xvi, 12, 16, 21, 56, 58, 78, 115–16, 169, 171–72. *See also* enlightenment
lightning, 4, 13, 51, 54, 82, 92, 99, 102, 104, 119, 130, 137, 181–82

Liṅgaṃ, 11, 27, 67, 73, 152, 192, 195
Long Island, 25–26, 71, 109, 151–52
Louv, Richard, xxiii, 200n11, 218
love, 7, 11, 79, 102–103, 118, 132–33, 140, 147–48, 200n15, 209n1, 217, 221
Lumbini, 127

Magadha, kingdom of, 135
Mahābhārata, xx, 7, 127, 173, 201, 209, 216
mahābhūta, xix, 1, 2–3, 5, 15, 25, 50, 56, 60–61, 69, 168, 190
Mahārāhulovāda Sutta, 42, 44, 76, 94, 113, 158, 161, 182, 204n19
Mahāvīra, 4, 42, 49, 54, 135
Mahāyāna (Buddhism), xx, 14, 17, 18, 158, 176, 211n6, 220
Maitri Upaniṣad, 2, 85
male, 56, 154
Mallinson, James, xxii, 190, 199n7, 214n1, 218
manas, 4, 10, 55–56, 60, 164–65
maṇḍala, 50–51, 53, 97–98, 111, 116, 169, 175, 177, 179–80, 187. *See also* geometry
mantra, 24, 41, 50, 54, 59, 77–78, 88, 131, 169, 175–77, 179, 182–84, 192, 197–98
  laṃ, 51, 65, 116
  ram, 97–98, 106, 116, 180
  vaṃ, 80, 83, 116
  yaṃ, 116, 121
Markaṇḍeya Purāṇa, 8, 11, 51, 178
marriage, 104, 132, 135–36
Martin, Rafe, 133, 210n11, 218
Maruts, 111
Mataji, Sri Pujya Ganini Sri Gyanamati, 97, 173
Matrimandir, 154
McHugh, James, 23, 203n4, 218
medicinal plants, 29–30, 93, 113, 117, 156
Meghkumar, story of, 135–36, 145
Mehta, M. C., 30, 74, 92
Mickey, Sam, 206n57, 218
Miller, Christopher Patrick, xi, xii, xxii, xxiii, 26
Mīmāṃsā, 55
mindfulness, 44–45, 47–48, 114, 160–63, 192
Mitra, Vihari Lal, 206n60, 206n66, 209n20, 210n15, 218
mokṣa, 12, 16, 21, 55–56, 139, 171
Mokṣadharmaparvan, 7
Mokṣopāya, 58
Monier-Williams, Monier, 208n15, 219
monk(s)
  in Jainism, 4, 49, 135, 78, 96, 115, 135–36, 148
  in Buddhism, 16–17, 43–44, 46–47, 76–77, 146, 161
monsoon, 12, 29, 31, 33, 36–37, 39–40, 82, 92, 111, 129, 130, 139, 157
Mother Earth, xii, 29, 32, 34–36, 38–41, 48, 67–68, 128–29, 154, 158
mourning, 137, 139–46
mudrā, 84, 106, 121–22, 152, 169, 184
Mueller-Ortega, Paul, 205n53, 219
Murphy, Paul E, 205n53, 219

Nagarajan, Vijaya, 7, 13, 67
Narayanan, Vasudha, 68, 207n74
Nava Rātri, 157
Nelson, Lance, 202n24, 205n51, 207n72, 219
Nepal, 126–27, 175
negative karmas, 51, 98, 178
Nicholson, Andrew J., 214n63, 219
Nietzsche, Friedrich, 154
Nirvāṇa Prakaraṇa, 58, 80, 164–65, 167
Nityananda, Swami, 200n7, 219
nonhuman teachers, 127, 131, 147
nonviolence, 4, 17, 20, 32, 115, 147–48, 174. See also *ahiṃsā*

Nyāṇamoli/Nāṇamoli, Bhikkhu, 204n18, 204n19, 205n34, 207n3, 208n7, 209n8, 211n8, 212n14, 219
Nyāya, 55

observance, 6, 26, 45, 49, 60–61, 81, 84, 105, 109–10, 115, 122, 125–26, 143–44, 153–54, 157, 161, 165–66, 170
observer. *See* witness
Olivelle, Patrick, 210n8, 219
oneness, 55, 110, 119–20, 140, 172
orientation. *See* emplacement
Orissa, 127

Padoux, André, 201n20, 219
Pal, Pratapaditya, 206n69, 219
Pāli Canon, 42
pañca mahābhūta. See *mahābhūta*
Pañcatantra, 127, 131–33, 145–47
Panda, Kumar, 13
parenthood, 131–33
Pārvatī, 27, 28, 73, 110, 153
passion(s), 19, 116, 138, 181
past lives, 2, 77, 95, 133–36, 139, 142, 144, 146–48, 182. *See also* reincarnation
Patañjali, xxiv, 12, 20, 44, 46, 122, 168, 188
Patrice, Emmanuelle, 201n7, 219
Pāvana. *See* Puṇya and Pāvana
peace, 32, 40, 45, 99, 112, 136, 145, 161, 180, 184. *See also* contentment
Pechilis, Karen, 58, 206n58, 219
Periyar Preserve (Kerala), 127
pilgrimage, 23–24, 26, 92, 110, 154
pleasure and pain, 18, 47, 89, 143, 159–60
Podgoski, Frank R., 205n50, 219
Pondicherry, 26, 110, 153–54
prakṛti, 4, 12, 15, 18, 55–57, 67, 100, 153, 164, 169–70, 193
prāṇa, 113, 120, 132, 176
prāṇāyāma, xii, 20, 26, 106, 110, 121, 122, 170, 180, 187. *See also* breathing exercises
pratipakṣa bhāvanaṃ, 2, 168
Preston, James J., 13, 202n23, 219
prince, 99, 105, 135–36, 141–42, 144, 146, 148
proprioception, 156
Pṛthivī, 2, 12, 29, 46, 80, 136, 191, 204
pṛthivī dhāraṇā, 5, 25, 62, 65
Pṛthivī Sūkta (of the *Atharva Veda*), 4, 29, 33, 42, 69, 74, 76, 107, 111–12, 128, 154, 182–83, 204n12, 209n6, 210n6, 216
Pukkusati, 42–43, 69, 76, 94, 113, 158–61. See also *Dhātu Vibhaṅga*
pūjā, 2, 93, 96, 110, 157, 184
pūjārī, 88, 151, 153, 184
Puṇya and Pāvana, 127, 136–45, 148, 168
Purāṇas, xix, 67, 74
purification, 1, 3, 11–12, 36, 42, 44, 47, 49, 51, 61–63, 71, 73–74, 80, 87–88, 95–98, 106–107, 122, 142, 158–61, 168, 171–84
puruṣa, 4, 16, 55, 57, 62, 67, 153, 169–70, 193
Puruṣa Sūkta, 3, 5, 7, 14, 94

Rāhula, 42, 44, 77, 95–96, 113–14, 158, 161. See also *Mahārāhulovāda Sutta*
Rajagriha, 135
rajas, 55, 68, 100, 155, 193
Rajasthan, 127
Rāma, 31, 58, 60–62, 83, 137–38, 165–68. See also *Yogavāsiṣṭha*
Ramana Maharshi, 90–91
Rāvaṇa, 31
Reading, Michael, 207n1, 220

realms, xx, xxv, 4, 11, 14, 19, 56, 67, 79, 98, 133, 155, 167, 171, 173–74, 182, 189
reflection, xvi, xix, xxiv, 2, 13, 16, 24–25, 48, 52, 55, 65, 69, 84, 134, 144, 158, 161, 163, 169, 184
Regan, Tom, 210n9, 219
reincarnation, 16, 18, 48, 73, 98, 127, 136–44, 146–48, 168, 172, 174–75. *See also* past lives
renunciation, 9–10, 34, 76, 135, 138, 140, 143, 144–46, 148. *See also* monk(s)
respiration, 113. *See also* breath
responsibility, 30, 67, 131–33, 156
Ṛg Veda, 2–5, 7, 14, 24, 28–29, 33, 55, 87, 91, 93–94, 111–12, 155
Rhys Davids, Caroline Augusta Foley, 47–48
Rhys Davids, T. W., 47
Richard, Mirra Alfassa, 153
Rishi, 127, 131–33, 136, 145, 147, 185
ritual, xv, xix–xx, xxiv, 1–3, 13, 21, 23, 28, 42, 50, 55, 68, 72–73, 76, 88, 93, 96, 157, 175, 177, 182, 184, 202n25, 206n71, 207n73, 214n1
ṛta, 33, 87, 128

sacrifice, 3, 18, 29–30, 33–34, 50, 67, 87, 93, 96, 141, 155, 157, 210n9, 219
sādhana, xii, 11–12, 21, 88, 176, 187–88
safety, 99, 107, 129, 135, 156–58
sage, xvii, 41, 60, 62, 74, 90, 97, 130, 137–38, 144, 147, 157, 161, 167–68. *See also* Vasiṣṭha
Śakti, 13, 21, 61, 110, 164, 198
Śakyamuni, 18
Sāma Veda, 28, 137
samādhi, 3, 52, 80, 138, 168, 170
Sāṃkhya, xiii, 2, 4–5, 15–17, 20, 25, 42, 55–58, 60–61, 67, 94, 153, 155, 164–65, 167, 177
Sāṃkhya Kārikā, 4, 15, 43, 69
saṃsāra, 15, 139, 143, 173–74
saṃskāra, 4, 11, 16, 17, 46, 56, 168, 193
Samuel, Geoffrey, xxii, 199n7, 219
Sangha, 45–46, 163
Śāntideva, 18, 158
Śāntisūrīśvara, 219. See also *Jīva Vicāra Prakaraṇam*
Santosha Vegetarian Dining, 89
Sarabhai, Mallika, 68
Śarabhas, 137
Sarasvatī, 33, 188
sat, 33
Satipatthāna, 44, 48
sattva, 9, 12, 55, 100, 121, 155, 168, 193, 196
Satyakāma Jābāla (story), 27, 127, 129–31, 136, 145–47
Sawant, Shivaji, 72, 207n2, 219
Schaller, George, 146, 211n22, 220
Schama, Simon, 23, 203n2
Schiff Preserve, 152
Seed, John, 90–91, 208n5, 220
self, 2–3, 9, 12, 15, 18, 20–21, 24, 28, 43, 53, 60, 69, 76, 83, 89, 94, 96, 113, 120, 126, 131, 139, 140–45, 152, 156, 158–59, 163–65, 175, 177, 178, 181, 183–84, 195
self-realization, 83, 205n53, 218
senses, xix–xx, 2–3, 8, 9, 10, 12–13, 15, 19–20, 46, 48, 52, 55–56, 59–61, 69, 115, 131, 145, 165–66, 168–69, 171, 174, 178, 187–88, 201n18
shaman, 126, 182
Shāntā, N., 213n47, 220
Shantideva, 211n7, 220
Shimkhada, Deepak, 207n1, 220
Shiva, Vandana, 7, 37, 67

Shrenik (King), 135
Siddha Loka, 52, 79, 99, 170, 173
Singh, Jaideva, 202n27, 220
Singh, Pancham, 203n43, 220
Singleton, Mark, xxii, 199n7, 214n1, 218
Śiva, 27–28, 35, 59–61, 68, 73–74, 89–90, 105, 110, 152–53, 164–65, 167, 188, 193, 196
Smith, Brian K, 6, 201n14, 220
soil, 6, 23, 26, 32, 36, 57, 62, 66–67, 74, 77, 115
soma (drink), 7, 29, 111, 157
soul, 6, 8, 15, 82, 101, 105, 138, 140, 143, 164. See also *jīva*
spanda, 59, 60–61, 118, 166
Sri Aurobindo, 153–54
Sri Lanka, 31, 44, 48
Śrīnivāsa, T. R. Ayyaṇgār, 200n3, 220
Srivatsa Ramaswami, 122
Stcherbatsky, Theodore, 202n29, 211n5, 220
Stephen, Graeme, 48
Stony Brook University, 25–26, 31, 109
storms, 37, 82, 102, 110–12, 129, 162
story
  of Meghkumar, 127, 135–36, 145
  of Puṇya and Pāvana, 127, 136–45
  of Satyakāma Jābāla, 127, 129–31, 145–47
  of the Blue Bear, 127, 133–35, 145–46
  of the Rishi and the mouse, 127, 131–33, 145–46
Sumeruprabh, 135
śūnya, 60, 167, 177
surrender, 133, 145, 190
Surya, 93, 132, 189
Svaḥ, 130, 184, 188–89, 195–96
Śvetāmbāra, 50, 174
swan, ix, 81, 112, 121, 129–31, 141, 144–46, 148
syllable. See *mantra*

Takasaki, Jikido, 211n6, 220
tamas, 55, 100, 155, 193
Tamil Nadu, 154
tanmātras, 5, 55, 56, 60, 168, 190–91
Tantra, xvi, xxii, 3, 5, 8, 11, 14, 15, 20, 21, 24, 54, 56, 57, 58, 67, 116, 158, 175, 178, 183
tapas, 87–88, 96, 107, 138
Tatia, Nathmal, 207n10, 220
tattva, 4, 55, 61, 65, 121, 192
Tattvārtha Sūtra, 24, 78, 170, 171
Taylor, Bron, xiii
Taylor, McComas, 210n8, 220
teacher(s), xi–xxiv, 4, 48–49, 52, 58, 88, 117, 126–27, 129, 130–31, 147, 167, 173, 176, 178, 182, 184, 187
tejas, 5, 12, 56, 87. *See also* Agni
temples, elemental, xi, 24, 26–27, 34, 41, 44, 73–74, 89–90, 107, 110, 152–54, 175, 182–83
Thanissaro, Bhikkhu, 43, 204n18
Theravāda Buddhism, 3
Thoreau, 8
thought(s), 2, 5, 8, 16, 23, 47–48, 53, 55, 57, 65–66, 69, 83–84, 88, 96, 101, 117–19, 138, 143, 151, 163, 165, 168, 192, 194
thunderbolt, 37, 92, 111, 119, 130
Thus Spake Zarathustra, 154
Timalsina, Sthaneshwar, 177–78, 213n56, 213n59, 220
Tīrthaṅkara, 4, 49, 97, 135, 173–74, 184, 214
Tiwari, B. N., 201n15, 217
Tobias, Michael, 205n52, 220
trāṭakaṃ, 46–48, 51, 53, 65–66, 69, 72, 81, 88, 95, 121, 126, 149, 151, 174, 176, 178–79, 183, 191, 196
truthfulness, 147, 174, 195

Tucker, Mary Evelyn, xiii, xv, xviii, 199n1, 216, 200n12, 207n71, 207n73, 209n4 chap. 6, 210n9, 216, 220
Tunhuang Caves, 134

Umasvati, 170, 207n10, 208n17, 213n43, 220
University of Florida, xiii, 68
Upaniṣads, xix, xx, 1–3, 7, 12, 14–15, 24, 27, 36, 39, 54, 64, 85, 125, 127, 129–30, 156
Upaśama Prakaraṇa. See *Yogavāsiṣṭha*
Uttarkhand, 127

Vaiśeṣika, 55
Varanasi, 127
varṇa, 129–30
Vasiṣṭha, 58–65, 67–69, 78, 80–83, 99–103, 105, 107, 117–18, 120–21, 137, 145, 164–68, 177. See also *Yogavāsiṣṭha*
Vasu, Rai Bahadur Srisa Chandra, 203n43, 220
Vasubandhu, 17, 202n36, 219
Vatsyayan, Kapila, 201n7, 221
Vāyu, 2, 4–5, 12, 56, 109–12, 116–18, 123, 132, 154, 176, 191
Vedānta, 15–16, 55–56
Vedas, xix, 2, 28, 29, 33, 54, 67, 74, 75, 87, 110–12, 127, 130, 154–55, 157, 195
Vedic, xx, 2, 3, 24, 33, 41, 42, 44, 83, 92, 96, 112, 131, 152, 155, 156, 157, 195
vegetarianism, 127
Venkatesananda, Swami, 206n59, 206n66, 206n67, 212n35, 221
Villaseñor-Galarza, Adrián, 201n7, 221
Vilpulchal (Mount), 136
Virāj, Yogi Anand (Eugene P. Kelly), 201n21, 216
Viṣṇu, 35, 74, 83, 154–55, 158
Viṣucikā, 41
Visuddhimagga, 5, 16, 24, 42, 44, 48, 51, 76, 94–95, 113–14, 158, 162, 163, 177, 182, 183
Vivekananda, xx, 31

Whicher, Ian, 213n41, 221
White, David Gordon, xxii, 199n7, 213n49, 221
Whitney, Josiah, 35
Whitney, William Dwight, 29
Williams, Duncan Ryuken, 209n4, 210n9, 220
wisdom, 9, 33, 39, 41, 58, 60, 69, 89–90, 115, 130–31, 133–34, 139–40, 144–45, 167–68, 207n74, 207n3, 210n8, 213n48. *See also* knowledge
witness, 4, 16, 27, 34, 136, 143–44, 153, 165, 167, 170, 193
Wittgenstein, Ludwig, 5–6, 201n8, 221
Woodward, F. C., 47–48, 205n39, 221
Wright, Patricia Chapple, 209n1, 221

yajña, 33, 93, 155
Yajur Veda, 28, 110
yantra, 67, 154, 169, 175
Yoga Anand Ashram, 25, 65, 72, 81, 84, 88, 107, 109–10, 121, 125–26, 151–52, 184
Yoga Sūtra, xxii, 11, 12, 20, 52, 61, 65, 80, 122, 168
Yogaśāstra (Hemacandra), 24, 50, 79, 116, 170, 173, 178
Yogatattva Upaniṣad, 2
Yogāvacara, 47–48
Yogavāsiṣṭha, xi, 5, 25, 41, 57, 58, 61, 65, 67, 78, 80, 94, 99, 117, 120, 125, 127, 130, 136–45, 164, 168, 177, 182, 183
Yoni, 11, 67, 192, 195

www.ingramcontent.com/pod-product-compliance
Lightning Source LLC
Chambersburg PA
CBHW030537230426
43665CB00010B/927
9781438477947